Islam Is Easy

(Volume 1)

PROF. AMINUL ISLAM LASKAR

Contents

Preface

In the name of Allah, the Merciful, the Compassionate
And all praise is due to Allah, the Lord of all creation; O Allah, send your grace, honour and mercy upon Prophet Muhammad and upon the family of Muhammad PBUH.

Allah SWT says in the Qur'an (that means): *Certainly, Allah's only Way is Islam.* (Ch 3:19) Whoever meets Allah following a path other than Islam will not be accepted. But sometimes we make the religion difficult. We should not be extremist nor negligent so that our day to day life becomes impractical. It is important that we learn the religion properly in accordance with the Book and the Sunnah of the Prophet (PBUH) to make the purpose of our life meaningful here and hereafter.

It is my privilege and honour to author '**Islam is Easy**' (Vol 1). Obligatory activities of Islam are presented in a lucid manner on the basis of the Qur'an and authentic Hadiths. The motivation of the attempt to present this book is the Hadith of the Prophet (peace and blessings be upon him) from Sahih al-Bukhari. Abdullah ibn Amr reported: The Prophet, peace and blessings be upon him, said: "Convey from me, even a single verse...". Primary focus of the volume 1 of the book is the pillars of Islam. Significance of each pillar, exploring their importance and relevance in the lives of Muslims have been discussed with references.

I beg Allah SWT to make us learn how to pray with ease. The contents in this book are designed for both males and females, old and young and particularly young generations who are very busy in this competitive world and are in scarcity of time to refer to huge collections of the treasures of the religion.

I understand that there are differences in opinions in relation to certain actions and I respect all, although I tried not to include them in this book in order to simplify the learning process and to make the book acceptable to all.

Knowledge of reading Arabic text is pre-requisite to go through this book. Arabic text from Qur'an and Hadiths along with their English transliterations have been included. However, it is not possible to pronounce the words correctly from transliteration (especially similar sounding alphabets) and the readers are advised to learn those from the Arabic text.

Transliteration of the Verses of the Qur'an are reproduced from online version available at www.quran.com and the Hadiths are reproduced mainly from the website www.sunnah.com. I gratefully acknowledge my sincere gratitude to these websites. Many issues, Hadiths, comments and definitions included in the book have been reproduced from www.islamqa.info/en. I have also incorporated many contents, comments, ideas and Hadiths from research papers, lecture videos and other documents from www.ahlesunnatpak.com to whom I also acknowledge my sincere gratitude. May Allah grant the efforts of these websites towards spreading of Islam.

Suggestion for rectification of mistakes if any will be highly appreciated. May Almighty increase our knowledge of Islam and grant us the best life here and Jannat-ul-Firdous hereafter. Amin

Aminul Islam Laskar

2024

1. Faith or Imaan

Islam

The word *Islam* means "submission" or "surrender". It is faithful surrender to the will of Almighty Allah. Followers of Islam are called *Muslims*. The term 'Muslim' was coined by the Prophet Ibrahim (Peace be upon him). Muslims believe that there is one Allah and prophet Muhammad (Peace be upon him, abbreviated as PBH) is the last messenger of Allah. Allah sent prophets to mankind to teach them how to live according to His law.

Islam is a way of life. Islam is how one spends his/her limited life-time on the earth. Its teachings can be used to provide fair solutions to the problems faced by individual and society. It covers social, economic, political and diplomatic aspects of human life. Everything is covered in Islam, including the rights of the oppressed and weaker people, orphans, widows and minors, and non-Muslims residing in Muslim lands.

Islam is a religion of love and non-violence. It conveys message of peace and brotherhood to all nations and teaches mutual brotherhood, love, respect and mutual justice of all mankind. Islam is peaceful in itself and teaches others' peace, love, affection, and tolerance. In the sight of Almighty, the religion to be followed by mankind is only Islam. In the light of the Quran, Allah Almighty says (that means):

- o *Let there be no compulsion in religion, for the truth stands out clearly from falsehood. So, whoever renounces false gods and believes in Allah has certainly grasped the firmest, unfailing hand-hold. And Allah is All-Hearing, All-Knowing. (Ch 2:256)*
- o *Indeed, the religion in the sight of Allah is Islam. And those who were given the Scripture did not differ except after knowledge had come to them - out of jealous animosity between themselves. And whoever disbelieves in the verses of Allah, then indeed, Allah is swift in [taking] account. (Ch 3:19)*

- o *This day, I have perfected your religion for you, completed My Favour upon you, and have chosen Islam as your religion. (Ch 5:3)*
- o *They consider it a favour to you that they have accepted Islam. Say, "Do not consider your Islam a favour to me. Rather, Allah has conferred favour upon you that He has guided you to the faith, if you should be truthful. (Ch 49:17)*
- o *If anyone desire a Deen/judgment other than Al-Islam, the Peace never will be accepted of him and in the here-after he will be from those who are the losers. (Ch 3:85)*
- o *Ibrahim was not a Jew nor a Christian; but he was true in Faith Muslim/submitter, and he was not one of the polytheists. (Ch 3:67)*
- o *And you strive in Allah as the right of striving in Him. He has chosen you and He has made no difficulty over you in the Din/Judgment. The religion of your Father Ibrahim. And He has named you Muslim/submitters from before and in this, so the messenger be a witness over you and you be a witness over mankind. (Ch 22:78)*

All the prophets starting from Adam (as) preached the same religion: oneness in Allah. The religion which was brought by Muhammad (peace and blessings of Allah be upon him) confirms the message brought by the prophets before him, in its basic principles and advocation of noble characteristics, as Allah says (interpretation of the meaning):

"He (Allah) has ordained for you the same religion (Islamic Monotheism) which He ordained for Nuh, and that which We have revealed to you (O Muhammad), and that which We ordained for Ibrahim, Musa and 'Isa saying you should establish religion (i.e. to do what it orders you to do practically) and make no divisions] in it (religion) (i.e. various sects in religion)." [al-Shura, Ch 42:13]

"And verily, We have sent among every Ummah (community, nation) a messenger (proclaiming): "Worship Allah (Alone), and avoid (or keep away from) Taghut (all false deities, i.e. do not worship Taghut besides Allah)." [al-Nahl, Ch 16:36]

Following Hadiths may be referred in this regard.

Hadith: Narrated Abu Huraira (raḍiyallahu anh, abbreviated as 'ra'): Allah's Messenger (ṣallallahu alayhi wa 'alihi wa-sallam, abbreviated as 'saws') said, "Both in this world and in the Hereafter, I am the nearest of all the people to Essa (as), the son of Mary. The prophets are paternal brothers; their mothers are different, but their religion is one." [Bukhari]

Hadith: Narrated Ibn `Umar (ra): Allah's Messenger (saws) said, "Your period (i.e. the Muslims' period) in comparison to the periods of the previous nations, is like the period between the `Asr prayer and sunset. And your example in comparison to the Jews and the Christians is like the example of a person who employed some laborers and asked them, 'Who will work for me till midday for one Qirat each?' The Jews worked for half a day for one Qirat each. The person asked, 'Who will do the work for me from midday to the time of the `Asr (prayer) for one Qirat each?' The Christians worked from midday till the `Asr prayer for one Qirat. Then the person asked, 'Who will do the work for me from the `Asr till sunset for two Qirats each?' "The Prophet (saws) added, "It is you (i.e. Muslims) who are doing the work from the `Asr till sunset, so you will have a double reward. The Jews and the Christians got angry and said, 'We have done more work but got less wages.' Allah said, 'Have I been unjust to you as regards your rights?' They said, 'No.' So Allah said, "Then it is My Blessing which I bestow on whomever I like." [Bukhari]

The Qur'an

The *Qur'an* is the final revelation which completes earlier revealed scriptures, just as the Prophet Muhammad (saws) taught the same essential message as the many prophets before him, including Adam, Nuh, Musa, Ibrahim, and Eassa (peace be upon them all). According to Islamic teachings, Muslims must say "صَلَّى اللهُ عَلَيْهِ وَسَلَّمَ" *sallalu-alaihi-o-sallam* (abbreviated as 'saws') whenever they hear or say the Prophet's (saws) name. Similarly, Muslims say *radi allahu anhu* meaning *may Allah have mercy on him* (abbreviated as 'ra') for men and رضي الله عنه *radiallahu anha* meaning *may Allah have mercy on her for women* whenever they say or hear companions of Prophet (saws). The Quran clarifies what humanity needs to know from now until the Day of Judgment, and it will remain preserved from loss and distortion. The Quran was first revealed to Muhammad (saws) by the angel Jibril in a cave on the mountain of Hira in Makkah, and then over a period of twenty-three years (lunar months) until his death.

There are many themes and ideas explored in the Quran, but the major ones include:

- The Oneness of Allah Subhanahu Wa Ta'ala
- The importance of worship and obedience to Allah SWT
- The existence of an Afterlife and the Day of Judgment
- Guidance and wisdom for leading a righteous and moral life
- The creation of the universe and all living things
- The role of prophets and revelation in guiding humanity
- The consequences of good and evil actions
- The significance of social justice and fairness

The word "Subhanahu wa ta'ala" الله سبحانه وتعالى is Arabic, and is translated as "Glory to Him, the most High" or "Glory to Him, the Exalted." In reciting (Allah's name, SWT indicates an act of devotion to Allah. "SWT" appears in the Quran in several verses viz. Ch 16:1, Ch 17:43, Ch 30:40, Ch 39:67 and Ch 30:40.)

The abovementioned themes are connected to each other throughout the Quran and serve as a guide for Muslims on how to live their lives in accordance with the will of Allah SWT.

Essential to learning the history of the Quran is the study of the stages of its revelation, which is usually referred to by the term 'Tanzeel' of the Quran, the 'sending down' of the Quran from the Heavens to the Earth. 'Tanzeel' is derived from the Arabic root 'Nuzool', which means the descent or the movement from a high place down to a lower one. This is exactly what happened in the process of revelation where the Angel Jibril used to come down from the Heavens with a varying number of verses of the Quran to deliver to Prophet Muhammad (saws). The Quran was revealed in a single blessed night in the month of Ramadan that is called the 'Night of Power, or Decree'. Revelation lasted for about 23 years (Lunar years) in which the Quran was sent down in response to the development of events and in accordance with the sequence needed to complete the delivery of the Message of Allah SWT. The Quran is divided into 114 'Surahs' (Chapters) of unequal length and number of verses are more than 6200. First surah is surah Al-Fatiha and the last surah is surah An-Nas. The longest surah and the shortest surah in the Quran are Al-Baqarah and Al-Kawthar respectively.

The Quran was first revealed to the Messenger of the Allah (saws) in the cave of Hira when he was 40 years old. It is evident that the Holy Quran is the miracle of the Prophet Muhammad (saws). He never studied in any school (because the Creator of the Universe was his Teacher.) And who else on the earth would teach the Prophet (saws) who would guide and teach the mankind with wish of Allah SWT) and yet had the ability to recite the Holy verses to his people so they would worship One Allah and become Muslims.

The revelation in Makkah had been for 13 years while it had been for 10 years in Al Madinah. For this reason, some chapters of the Holy Quran are Makkeyah, i.e., related to Makkah, and the others are Madaneyah - related to Al-Madinah. The first verse revealed to the Prophet Muhammad (saws), as it is mentioned above, in the cave of Hira by Jibril the angel, was: *"Recite in the name of your Lord who created -"* *[Al-Alaq:Verse 1]*

On the other hand, most of the Muslim theologians agreed that the last verse of the Holy Quran that was revealed to the Prophet Muhammad (saws) was: *"And fear a Day when you will be returned to Allah. Then every soul will be compensated for what it earned, and they will not be treated unjustly."* *[Al-Baqarah, Ch 2: 281]*

The present arrangement of the Quran is not the work of later generations, but was made by the Prophet (saws) under Allah's direction. Whenever a surah was revealed, the Prophet (saws) called his scribes to whom he instructed them where to place it in relation to the other surahs. The Prophet (saws) followed the same order of surahs and verses when reciting during salat.

Hadith or Sunnah

Islam has given two reliable pathways for the guidance of mankind. One of them is the clear Verses of the Qur'an while the other is Sunnah or Hadith, which are quite consistent with the first. The Qur'an is the message, and the Hadith is the explanation of the message by the Messenger (saws) himself. The Qur'an makes it abundantly clear that the function of the Messenger (saws) is merely not to deliver the revelation from Allah SWT to us. Rather, he (saws) was entrusted with the most important task of explaining and illustrating the same. Allah SWT says:

We have sent down the Book to you, only because you may explain to them what they differed about, and (so that it may be) guidance and mercy for a people who believe. (Surah an-Nahl, Ch 16:64; interpretation of the meaning)

Much of Islam will remain mere abstract concepts without Hadith. To explain and interpret its basic and brief teachings, the Qur'an has itself mentioned the need for *Sunnah* and the Prophet's (saws) model lifestyle. Allah SWT says:

O you who believe, obey Allah and obey the Messenger and those in authority among you. Then, if you quarrel about something, revert it back to Allah and the Messenger, if you believe in Allah and the Last Day. That is good, and the best at the end. (Surah an-Nisa, Ch 4:59; interpretation of the meaning)

The latter explains the former. The *Sunnah* is an indispensable guide to understand the commandments and passages of Qur'an. Without *Hadith*, the entire faith and the entire *Shariah* (Islamic Law) will become no better than a riddle. The explanatory material relating to *Shari'ah*, as found in *Hadiths*, was also given to the Prophet (saws) by Allah through the angel Jibril. This is why Qur'an is called Revelation Recited. There are many verses where Allah SWT commanded to follow the Prophet (saws) and some of these are as follows (interpretation of the meaning):

- o *Say, O Prophet, "If you sincerely love Allah, then follow me; Allah will love you and forgive your sins. For Allah is All-Forgiving, Most Merciful." (Ch 3:31)*
- o *These entitlements are the limits set by Allah. Whoever obeys Allah and His Messenger will be admitted into Gardens under which rivers flow, to stay there forever. That is the ultimate triumph! (Ch 4:13)*
- o *Whoever obeys the Messenger has truly obeyed Allah. But whoever turns away, then know that We have not sent you O Prophet as a keeper over them. (Ch 4:80)*
- o *Obey Allah and His Messenger and do not dispute with one another, or you would be discouraged and weakened. Persevere! Surely Allah is with those who persevere. (Ch 8:46)*

- o *For whoever obeys Allah and His Messenger, and fears Allah and is mindful of Him, then it is they who will truly triumph. (Ch 24:52)*
- o *........Whoever obeys Allah and His Messenger, He will admit him to the gardens beneath which rivers flow. But whoever turns away, He will punish him with a painful punishment. (Ch 48:17)*

Presently, throughout the world including India, Pakistan and Bangladesh, there are people who believe that only the Qur'an is sufficient for a Muslim. They themselves call them Qur'anist. Qur'anist rejects all Hadiths and believe that obedience to the prophet (saws) means obedience to the Qur'an. Quranists believe that the Quran is clear, complete, and that it can be fully understood without hadith or sunnah. Therefore, they use the Quran itself to interpret the Quran. Following hadiths prove that belief of Quranists is false and baseless. We must follow the Holy Book and the Sunnah of the prophet (saws). We would never know how to pray, how to fast during Ramadan, how to pay zakat, or make pilgrimage without the illustration found in Hadith, and these acts of worship would remain as abstract rules in the Quran.

Hadith: Miqdam bin Ma'dikarib Al-Kindi (ra) narrated that: The Messenger of Allah (saws) said: "Soon there will come a time that a man will be reclining on his pillow, and when one of my hadiths is narrated he will say: 'The Book of Allah is (sufficient) between us and you. Whatever it states is permissible, we will take as permissible, and whatever it states is forbidden, we will take as forbidden.' Verily, whatever the Messenger of Allah (saws) has forbidden is like that which Allah has forbidden." [Sunan Ibn Majah]

Hadith: Abu Hurairah (ra) narrated that: The Prophet (saws) said: "Whoever obeys me, obeys Allah; and whoever disobeys me, disobeys Allah." [Sunan Ibn Majah]

Hadith: Narrated Abu Huraira (ra): Allah's Messenger (saws) said, "All my followers will enter Paradise except those who refuse." They said, "O Allah's Messenger (saws)! Who will refuse?" He (saws) said, "Whoever obeys me will enter Paradise, and whoever disobeys me is the one who refuses (to enter it)." [Bukhari]

Hadith: Abu Dawud also reported from al-'Irbad ibn Sariyah, may Allah be pleased with him, that "the Messenger of Allah (saws) led us in prayer one day, then he turned to us and exhorted us strongly . . . (he said), 'Pay attention to my sunnah (way) and the way of the Rightly-guided Caliphs after me, adhere to it and hold fast to it.'" [Abu Dawud]

Hadith: Narrated Jabir bin `Abdullah (ra): Some angels came to the Prophet (saws) while he was sleeping. Some of them said, "He is sleeping." Others said, "His eyes are sleeping but his heart is awake." Then they said, "There is an example for this companion of yours." One of them said, "Then set forth an example for him." Some of them said, "He is sleeping." The others said, "His eyes are sleeping but his heart is awake." Then they said, "His example is that of a man who has built a house and then offered therein a banquet and sent an inviter (messenger) to invite the people. So whoever accepted the invitation of the inviter, entered the house and ate of the banquet, and whoever did not accept the invitation of the inviter, did not enter the house, nor did he eat of the banquet." Then the angels said, "Interpret this example to him so that he may understand it." Some of them said, "He is sleeping." The others said, "His eyes are sleeping but his heart is awake." And then they said, "The houses stand for Paradise and the call maker is Muhammad (saws); and whoever obeys Muhammad (saws), obeys Allah; and whoever disobeys Muhammad (saws), disobeys Allah. Muhammad (saws) separated the people (i.e., through his message, the good is distinguished from the bad, and the believers from the disbelievers). [Bukhari]

The Arabic word *Hadith* means: conversation, account, narrative, report, and also novel or modern. But as a technical term, however, it means the deeds, utterances, circumstances and matters of Allah's Messenger (saws) or, in other words, whatever has come down to us concerning Allah's Messenger (saws); and his mission (through his Companions and their followers). *Hadith* may be verbal, or practical or just implied (that is, when the Prophet (saws) did not object to something, thereby giving his implied approval). However, some include even the Prophet's (saws) physical descriptions, natural disposition and habits. Following is a list of Hadith collections, which contain the sayings, acts or validly or invalidly, ascribed to the Prophet (saws), and collected by Muhaddiths. *Kutub al-Sittah*, commonly known as 'six authentic books' of Hadith are: Sahih al-Bukhari, Sahih al-Muslim, Sunan Abu Dawood, Sunan at-Tirmizi, Sunan an-Nasa'i and Sunan Ibn Majah. In addition, there are other books on Hadiths among many others viz. Muwatta Imam Malik, Musnad Ahmad ibn Hanbal, Mustadrak Al Hakim, Musannaf Ibn

Abi Shaybah, Musannaf Ibn Abdur Rajjak, Sunan al-Kubra lil Bayhaqi, Sunan al-Daraqutni, Sahih ibn Hibban. Hadiths of al-Bukhari and al-Muslim are considered to be 100% authentic (sahih).

Iman or faith

Iman is usually translated in English as *faith* or belief, and faith in turn signifies acceptance without proof or argument, without reference to reason or thought, knowledge or insight. In order to acquire Iman in Allah SWT, it is necessary to first reject every authority other than Allah. Each person is to determine what the Quran says as truth based on their own personal reasoning ability and should reject the authority of anyone who would attempt to tell them what the Quran says. Mu'min is one who accepts truth in such a way that it ensures his own peace and helps him to safeguard the peace and security of the rest of mankind. Allah SWT gives a comprehensive definition of Iman and in the Qur'an:

Righteousness is not (merely) that you turn your faces to the East and the West; but righteousness is that one believes in Allah and the Last Day and the angels and the Book and the Prophets, and gives wealth, despite (his) love for it, to relatives, and to orphans, the helpless, the wayfarer, and to those who ask, and (spends) in (freeing) slaves and observes the Salah (prayers) and pays Zakah-and (the act of) those who fulfil their covenant when they enter into a covenant, and, of course, those who are patient in hardship and suffering and when in battle! Those are the ones who are truthful, and those are the God - fearing. (Ch 2: 177: interpretation of meaning)

The person who believes is a believer (Mu'min). In another place, Allah SWT provides a clear definition of a true believer in Surah Anfal (interpretation of meaning):

The true believers are only those whose hearts tremble at the remembrance of Allah, whose faith increases when His revelations are recited to them, and who put their trust in their Lord. They are those who establish prayer and donate from what We have provided for them. It is they who are the true believers. (Ch 8: 2-4)

Summarising, qualities of true believers are:

I. When Allah is mentioned, he feels a fear in his heart, and thus implements His orders and abstains from His prohibitions.

II. Faith increases when revelations are recited to them.

III. 'Believers hope in none except Allah, direct their dedication to Him alone, seek refuge with Him alone, invoke Him alone for their various needs and supplicate to Him alone. They know that whatever He wills, occurs and that whatever He does not will never occurs, that He alone is the One Who has the decision in His kingdom, without partners; none can avert the decision of Allah and He is swift in reckoning.' (Ibn Kasir)

IV. He establishes Salat.

V. He pays Zakat or sadaqa.

Iman has to be individually acquired. Each of us consciously try to acquire knowledge and understanding by using our own intellect in the light of the revelation given in the Qur'an, so that Iman can enter our hearts. Several characteristics of Iman from the Qur'an are as follows (interpretation of the meaning):

- *Iman is not to accept it with the tongue but to accept it with the heart. (Ch 2:8-9)*
- *To accept everything which the Qur'an says as truth is Iman. (Ch2:26)*
- *In order to acquire Iman in Allah, it is necessary to first reject every authority other than Allah. (Ch 2:25-26)*
- *Iman will lead human beings from darkness towards light. (Ch 2:257)*
- *In matters of Iman, one's profession is irrelevant. (Ch 26: 111-112)*
- *Unless Iman enters the heart, it cannot be called Iman. One can only say that one has surrendered to Islam. (Ch 49:14)*
- *Allah does not discard anyone's Iman. (Ch 2:143)*

The Messenger of Allah (saws) said, "It (Iman) is that you believe in Allah and His angels and His Books and His Messengers and in the Last Day, and in qadar (fate), both in its good and in its evil aspects...." [al-Bukhari & Muslim]. Belief in Allah includes recognizing, affirming, testifying and believing that there is only one almighty, Allah; believing in His Names and Attributes as mentioned in the Quran and Sunnah.

Believing in angels means one has to believe in the existence of who belong to the unseen world, believing in their names that have been explicitly stated in the Quran and Hadiths, believing in their attributes and believing in the actions they perform.

Belief in Books sent down by Allah to His Messengers means believing the Quran (revealed to Prophet Muhammad saws), Tawrat (revealed to Prophet Musa PBH), Injil (revealed to Prophet Essa PBH) and Zabur (revealed to Prophet Dawud PBH) amongst others. A messenger is chosen by Allah to receive revelation from Him and pass that revelation on to his people. Muslims believe in all the Prophets sent by Allah from Adam (as) until Muhammad (saws) who is the last Prophet. Last day of judgement is the day on which every person is considered for every single deed of theirs, and rewarded with Jannah (Paradise) or punished with Jahannam (Hellfire). Belief in the Last day should make a believer rush to do good deeds and stay away from sins, repent constantly and seek Allah's forgiveness.

Qadar is the fate both in its good and its evil aspects. Qadar means Allah's decree of all things from eternity, and His knowledge that they will come to pass at the times that are known to Him and in the specific manner that He has decreed and willed. In Sahih Muslim it is narrated that Ibn 'Umar (ra) heard that some people were denying al-qadar. He said: "If I meet these people I will tell them that I have nothing to do with them and they have nothing to do with me. By the One by Whom 'Abdullah ibn 'Umar (ra) swore, if one of them had gold equivalent to Mount Uhud and he spent it, Allah would not accept it from him unless he believed in al-qadar." [A part of the Hadith from Muslim] What is visible to us of it, we believe in, and what Allah has hidden from us, we accept and believe in. We do not dispute with Allah concerning His actions and rulings with our limited intellect and knowledge, rather we believe in Allah's complete justice and wisdom, and that Allah is not to be asked about what Allah SWT does.

Prophet (saws) said: "Allah decided the decrees of creation fifty thousand years before He created the heavens and the earth. He said: And His Throne is above the water." [Muslim] Now, the question can be: If things are decreed, then how can a person be called to account for them? Why does Allah destine for some who commits sins and go to Hell? Why does Allah destine for some who commits good and go to

Paradise? The answer is like this: Allah is ar-Rahman, He is ar-Rahim. He is Al-Muqsit (in Arabic: ٱلْمُقْسِطُ), The One who is most fair and just. He recognizes and provides rewards beyond measure for any good, however small. He is The One who leads mankind to justice and harmony. Allah is Al-Adl (in Arabic: ٱلْعَدْلُ), The one who rectifies and sets matters straight in a just and equitable manner. He always delivers absolute justice through His wisdom without failure. Man has the free wills and options by which he can choose good or bad, he can choose whether to obey or not, whether to believe or disbelieve. Allah SWT provided us ear, eye and intellect (sense organs) for taking decision. Allah SWT says:

Say, O Prophet, "He is the One Who brought you into being and gave you hearing, sight, and intellect. Yet you hardly give any thanks." (Ch 67:23; interpretation of meaning)

And say, "The truth is from your Lord. Now, whoever so wills may believe and whoever so wills may deny." Surely, We have prepared for the unjust a fire, whose tent will envelop them. And if they will beg for help, they shall be helped with water like oily dregs that will scald the faces. Vile is the drink, and evil is the Fire as a resting-place. (Ch 18:29; interpretation of meaning)

If a person choses right path, he will be rewarded otherwise will be punished not obeying Allah. Allah SWT says:

Has there not reached them the news of those before them, the people of Nuh and 'Ad and Thamud and the people of Ibrahim and the people of Madyan, and (the news) of the towns overturned? Their messengers came to them with clear signs; so, Allah was not such as would wrong them, but they have been doing wrong to their own selves. (Ch 9:70; interpretation of meaning)

Allah as a creator knows what we will do, what he will choose and what his ultimate destiny is. Allah has shown us clear and straight path by sending Messengers and Books. Allah says:

"Verily, We showed him the way, whether he be grateful or ungrateful." (Ch 76:3; interpretation of the meaning)

There is a very famous Hadith in sahih al-Bukhari and sahih al-Muslim, that is sometimes referred to as 'Hadith of Jibril' which is as follows.

Hadith: Abu Hurairah (ra) said: One day the Messenger of Allah (saws) appeared before the people and there came to him a man who said: 'O Messenger of Allah (saws), what is faith (iman)?' He (saws) said: 'To believe in Allah, His Angels, His Book, the meeting with Him, and His Messengers, and to believe in the Resurrection Hereafter.' He said: 'O Messenger of Allah (saws), what is Islam?' He (saws) said: 'Islam is to worship Allah and not associate anything with Him, to establish the prescribed Salat, to pay the obligatory *Zakat,* and to observe fast (The month of) Ramadan.' He said: 'O Messenger of Allah (saws), what is Al-Ihsan?' He (saws) said: 'It is to worship Allah as though you can see Him, for although you cannot see Him, He indeed sees you.' He said: 'O Messenger of Allah (saws), when is the Hour? He (saws) said: 'The one who is asked about it does not know more than the one who is asking. But I shall tell you of its portents: When the slave woman gives birth to her mistress, that is one of its portents. When the barefoot and naked become the leaders of the people, that is one of its portents. When the herdsmen of sheep compete in the construction of lofty buildings, that is one of its portents. The Hour is one of the five things that no one knows except Allah.' Then he recited: "Verily, Allah, with Him (Alone) is the knowledge of the Hour, He sends down the rain, and knows that which is in the wombs. No person knows what he will earn tomorrow, and no person knows in what land he will die. Verily, Allah is All-Knower, All-Aware (of things)." He (Abu Hurairah ra) said: Then the man went away, and the Messenger of Allah (saws) said: 'Bring the man back to me.' They went to bring him back, but they did not see anything. The Messenger of Allah (saws) said: "That was Jibril, who came to teach the people their religion." [Muslim]

Declaration of faith

It is to be mentioned that the sentence *"I bear witness that none has the right to be worshipped but Allah, and that Muhammad* (saws) *is the Messenger of Allah"* is known as declaration of faith (*Shahadah*) and the Arabic version is as follows:

اَشْهَدُ اَنْ لَا اِلٰهَ اِلَّا اللّٰهُ وَ حْدَهُ لَا شَرِيْكَ لَهُ وَ اَشْهَدُ اَنَّ مُحَمَّدًا عَبْدُهُ وَ رَسُوْلُهُ

Ashhadu alla ilaha illallahu wahdahu la sharika lahu wa-ash-hadu anna Muhammadan abduhoo wa rasooluhu. (*I bear witness that there is none worthy of worship except Allah. He is One and has no partner. And I bear witness that Muhammad* (saws) *is His Servant and Messenger.*) The declaration of faith or *Shahadah* carries the spirit of Islam.

Hadith: 'Ubadah bin As-Samit (ra) said: The Messenger of Allah (saws) said: 'Whoever says: I bear witness that none has the right to be worshipped but Allah alone [with no partner] and that Muhammad (saws) is His slave and Messenger, and that 'Essa (as) is the slave of Allah, the son of His maidservant, a Word which He bestowed upon Mariam and a Spirit from (created by) Him, and that Paradise is true and that Hell is true,' Allah will admit him through whichever of the eight gates of Paradise he wants. [Muslim]

Rewards for Imaan

o   One who dies believing in Tawhid will definitely enter Paradise.

Hadith: It was narrated that 'Usman (ra) said: The Messenger of Allah (saws) said: "Whoever dies knowing (and acknowledging) that there is none worthy of worship except Allah, he will enter Paradise." [Muslim]

Hadith: It was narrated that Abdullah (ra) said: The Messenger of Allah (saws) said: 'No one will enter Paradise who has even a mustard-seed's weight of arrogance in his heart, and no one will enter Hell who has even a mustard-seed's weight of faith in his heart.' [Sunan Ibn Majah]

Hadith: Aishah (ra) narrated that the Messenger of Allah (saws) said: "The believer is not distressed by the prick of a thorn or what is worse (or greater) than that, except that by it Allah raises him in rank and removes sin from him." [Tirmizi]

Hadith: Narrated 'Ubada bin As-Samit (ra): I, along with a group of people, gave the pledge of allegiance to Allah's Messenger (saws). He (saws) said, "I take your Pledge on the condition that you (1) will not join partners in worship with Allah, (2) will not steal, (3) will not commit illegal sexual intercourse, (4) will not kill your offspring, (5) will not slander, (6) and will not disobey me when I order you to do good.

Whoever among you will abide by his pledge, his reward will be with Allah, and whoever commits any of those sins and receives the punishment in this world, that punishment will be an expiation for his sins and purification; but if Allah screens him, then it will be up to Allah to punish him if He will or excuse Him, if He will." [Bukhari]

Hadith: Narrated Anas (ra): I was informed that the Prophet (saws) had said to Mu'az (ra), "Whosoever will meet Allah without associating anything in worship with Him will go to Paradise." Mu'az (ra) asked the Prophet (saws), "Should I not inform the people of this good news?" The Prophet (saws) replied, "No, I am afraid, lest they should depend upon it (absolutely). [Bukhari]

- o One who is Content with Allah as His Lord, Islam as his Religion and Muhammad (saws) as his Prophet, then he is a believer, even if he commits major sins.

Hadith: It was narrated from Al-Abbas bin 'Abdul-Muttalib (ra) that he heard the Messenger of Allah (saws) says: "He has found the taste of faith who is content with Allah as his Lord, Islam as his religion and Muhammad (saws) as his Prophet." In Arabic:

رَضِيتُ بِاللهِ رَبَّاً، وَبِالْإِسْلَامِ دِيناً، وَبِمُحَمَّدٍ صَلَّى اللهُ عَلَيهِ وَسَلَّمَ نَبِيّاً

Raditu Billahi Rabban wa bil Islami dinan wa bi Muhammadin sallAllahu 'alayhi wa sallama Nabiyyan. [Muslim]

Number of Branches of Imaan

It was narrated from Abu Hurairah (ra) that the Prophet (saws) said: "Faith has seventy-odd branches, and modesty (Al-Haya') is a branch of faith." [Muslim] It was narrated that Abu Hurairah (ra) said: The Messenger of Allah (saws) said: 'Faith has seventy-odd' - or 'sixty odd-branches, the best of which is saying *La ilaha illallah,* and the least of which is removing something harmful from the road, and modesty (Al-Haya') is a branch of faith." [Muslim]

Features of Faith

- o A phrase that sums up Islam

It was narrated that Sufyan bin 'Abdullah As- Saqafi (ra) said: I said: 'O Messenger of Allah (saws), tell me something about Islam that I will not need to ask anyone about after you,' - according to the *Hadith* of Abu Usamah: 'other than you' - He (saws) said: "Say: I believe in Allah, then adhere firmly to that." [Muslim]

o   To love the Messenger (saws) is a part of faith

Narrated Abu Huraira (ra): Allah's Messenger (saws) said, "By Him in Whose Hands my life is, none of you will have faith till he loves me more than his father and his children." [Bukhari]

It was narrated that Anas bin Malik (ra) said: The Messenger of Allah (saws) said: 'None of you is a believer until I am dearer to him than his son, his father and all of mankind.' Messenger of Allah (saws) said: "Whoever believes in Allah and the Last Day, let him speak good or else remain silent; whoever believes in Allah and the Last Day, let him honour his neighbour; whoever believes in Allah and the Last Day, let him honour his guest." [Muslim]

o   What part of it is the best

It was narrated from 'Abdullah bin 'Amr (ra) that a man asked the Messenger of Allah (saws): "What part of Islam is the best?" He (saws) said: "To feed others, and to greet with *Salam* those whom you know and those whom you do not know." [Muslim]

'Abdullah bin 'Amr bin Al-A's (ra) said: A man asked the Messenger of Allah (saws): 'Which of the Muslims is the best?' He (saws) said: 'The one from whose tongue and hand the Muslims are safe.' [Muslim]

o   Sweetness of faith

It was narrated from Anas (ra) that the Prophet (saws) said: "There are three characteristics, whoever attains them has found the sweetness of faith: When Allah and His Messenger (saws) are dearer to him than others than them, when he loves a man and does not love him except for the sake of Allah, and when he would hate to return to disbelief after Allah has saved him from it, as he would hate to be thrown into the fire." [Bukhari, Muslim]

o   Forbidding evil is part of faith; faith increases and decreases

It was narrated that Tariq bin Shihab - and this is the *Hadith* of Abu Bakr (one of the narrators) - said: "The first one to start with the Khutbah on the day of 'Eid, before the prayer, was Marwan. A man stood up and said: '(Shouldn't) the prayer (come) before the Khutbah?' He said: 'What was there has been left.' Abu Sa'eed (ra) said: 'This man has done his duty. I heard the Messenger of Allah (saws) say: "Whoever among you sees an evil action, let him change it with his hand (by taking action); if he cannot, then with his tongue (by speaking out); and if he cannot, then with his heart (by hating it and feeling it is wrong), and that is the weakest of faith." [Muslim]

- o Loving the believers is part of faith and spreading salam is a means of attaining faith

It was narrated that Abu Hurairah (ra) said: The Messenger of Allah (saws) said: 'You will not enter Paradise until you (truly) believe, and you will not (truly) believe until you love one another. Shall I not tell you of something which, if you do it, you will love one another? Spread (the greeting of) Salam amongst you.' [Muslim]

- o Clarifying that faith decreases because of disobedience and negating it from the one committing the act of disobedience

It was narrated from Abu Hurairah (ra) that the Prophet (saws) said: 'No adulterer is a believer at the time he is committing adultery; no thief is a believer at the time he is stealing; no drinker of wine is a believer at the time he is drinking it; but repentance may be accepted afterwards.' [Muslim]

- o That Islam started as something strange, and will revert to being something strange, and it will retreat between the two Masajid

It was narrated that Abu Hurairah (ra) said: The Messenger of Allah (saws) said: "Islam began as something strange and will revert to being something strange, so glad tidings to the strangers." [Muslim]

- o The disappearance of faith at the end of Time

It was narrated from Anas (ra) that the Messenger of Allah (saws) said: "The Hour will not begin so long as it is said on earth: Allah, Allah." [Muslim] Narrated Abu Said Al-Khudri (ra): Allah's Messenger (saws) said, "A time will soon come when the best property of a Muslim will be sheep which he will take on the top of mountains and the places of rainfall (valleys) so as to flee with his religion from afflictions." [Bukhari]

- o Permissibility of concealing one's faith in the case of fear

It was narrated that Huzaifah (ra) said: We were with the Messenger of Allah saws) and He (saws) said: 'Tell me how many people have professed Islam.' We said: 'O Messenger of Allah (saws), do you fear for us while we are between six hundred and seven hundred strong?' He (saws) said: 'You do not know, perhaps you will be tested.' He said:

'And we were tested, until some of us performed Salat only in secret.' [Muslim]

o   The grades in superiority of the believers will be according to their good deeds

Narrated Abu Said Al-Khudri (ra): The Prophet (saws) said, "When the people of Paradise will enter Paradise and the people of Hell will go to Hell, Allah will order those who have had faith equal to the weight of a grain of mustard seed to be taken out from Hell. So, they will be taken out but (by then) they will be blackened (charred). Then they will be put in the river of Haya' (rain) or Hayat (life) (the Narrator is in doubt as to which is the right term), and they will revive like a grain that grows near the bank of a flood channel. Don't you see that it comes out yellow and twisted?" [Bukhari]

> o   If one does not embrace Islam truly but does so by compulsion or for fear of being killed (then that man is not a believer)

Narrated Sa'd (ra): Allah's Messenger (saws) distributed (Zakat) amongst (a group of) people while I was sitting there but Allah's Messenger (saws) left a man whom I thought the best of the lot. I asked, "O Allah's Messenger (saws)! Why have you left that person? By Allah I regard him as a faithful believer." The Prophet (saws) commented: "Or merely a Muslim." I remained quiet for a while, but could not help repeating my question because of what I knew about him. And then asked Allah's Messenger (saws), "Why have you left so and so? By Allah! He is a faithful believer." The Prophet (saws) again said, "Or merely a Muslim." And I could not help repeating my question because of what I knew about him. Then the Prophet (saws) said, "O Sa'd! I give to a person while another is dearer to me, for fear that he might be thrown on his face in the Fire by Allah." [Bukhari]

o   To be ungrateful to one's husband.

Narrated Ibn 'Abbas (ra): The Prophet (saws) said: "I was shown the Hell-fire and that the majority of its dwellers were women who were ungrateful." It was asked, "Do they disbelieve in Allah?" (or are they ungrateful to Allah?) He (saws) replied, "They are ungrateful to their husbands and are ungrateful for the favours and the good (charitable deeds) done to them. If you have always been good (benevolent) to one of them and then she sees something in you (not of her liking), she will say: I have never received any good from you." [Bukhari] o   Sins are from ignorance and a sinner is not a disbeliever unless he worships others along with Allah SWT

Narrated Al-Ma'rur: At Ar-Rabadha: I met Abu Zar (ra) who was wearing a cloak, and his slave, too, was wearing a similar one. I asked about the reason for it. He replied, "I abused a person by calling his mother with bad names." The Prophet (saws) said to me, 'O Abu Zar! Did you abuse him by calling his mother with bad names? You still have some characteristics of ignorance. Your slaves are your brothers and Allah has put them under your command. So whoever has a brother under his command should feed him of what he eats and dress him of what he wears. Do not ask them (slaves) to do things beyond their capacity (power) and if you do so, then help them.' [Bukhari]

o   To establish the (Nawafil - voluntary) prayers on the night of Qadr is a part of faith

Narrated Abu Huraira (ra): Allah's Messenger (saws) said, "Whoever establishes the prayers on the night of Qadr out of sincere faith and hoping to attain Allah's rewards (not to show off) then all his past sins will be forgiven." [Bukhari]

o   Fighting in Allah's Cause is a part of faith

Narrated Abu Huraira (ra): The Prophet (saws) said, "The person who participates in (Holy battles) in Allah's cause and nothing compels him to do so except belief in Allah and His Apostles (saws), will be recompensed by Allah either with a reward, or booty (if he survives) or will be admitted to Paradise (if he is killed in the battle as a martyr). Had I not found it difficult for my followers, then I would not remain behind any sariya (brigade, quadron) going for Jihad and I would have loved to be martyred in Allah's cause and then made alive, and then martyred and then made alive, and then again martyred in His cause." [Bukhari]

o   To accompany the funeral processions (up to the place of burial) is a part of faith

Narrated Abu Huraira (ra): Allah's Messenger (saws) said, "(A believer) who accompanies the funeral procession of a Muslim out of sincere faith and hoping to attain Allah's reward and remains with it till the funeral prayer is offered and the burial ceremonies are over, he will return with a reward of two Qirats. Each Qirat is like the size of the (Mount) Uhud. He who offers the funeral prayer only and returns before the burial, will return with the reward of one Qirat only." [Bukhari] o   Killing a Muslim is Kufr

Narrated Abdullah (ra): The Prophet (saws) said, "Abusing a Muslim is Fusuq (evil doing) and killing him is Kufr (disbelief)." [Bukhari]

o   Prohibition of controversy About the Qur'an

Narrated Abu Hurairah (ra): The Prophet (saws) said: "Controverting about the Qur'an is disbelief." [Sunan Abu Dawud]

o   Criticizing people's lineage and crying for deceased

It was narrated that Abu Hurairah (ra) said: "The Messenger of Allah (saws) said: There are two things that are common among people that are disbelief (Kufr): Slandering people's lineage and wailing for the deceased." [Muslim]

o   Saying 'we got rain because of the stars' is kufr

It was narrated that Zaid bin Khalid Al Juhani (ra) said: The Messenger of Allah (saws) led us in Fajr Prayer at Al-Hudaybiyah, after it had rained during the night. When he finished, He (saws) turned to the people and said: 'Do you know what your Lord said?' They said: 'Allah and His Messenger (saw) know the best.' He (saws) said: 'He (Allah) said, "This morning some of My slaves believe in Me and some disbelieve. As for the one who said 'We got rain by the bounty and mercy of Allah,' he is a believer in Me and a disbeliever in the stars. But as for the one who said, 'We got rain by virtue of such and such a star,' he is a disbeliever in Me and a believer in the stars." [Muslim]

o   Whoever dies upon disbelief, no good deed will benefit him

It was narrated that 'Aishah (ra) said: I said: 'O Messenger of Allah (saws), during the Jahiliyyah (pre-Islamic period), Ibn Jud'an used to uphold the ties of kinship and feed the poor. Will that benefit him at all?' He (saws) said: 'It will not benefit him, because he did not say (even for) one day: 'Lord forgive me my sins on the Day of Judgment.' [Muslim]

A person who embraces Islam sincerely

Narrated Abu Sa'id Al Khudri (ra): Allah's Messenger (saws) said, "If a person embraces Islam sincerely, then Allah SWT shall forgive all his past sins, and after that starts the settlement of accounts, the reward of his good deeds will be ten times to seven hundred times for each good deed and one evil deed will be recorded as it is unless Allah SWT forgives it." [Bukhari] Imran b. Husain (ra) reported: Verily the

Messenger of Allah (saws) said: "Seventy thousand men of my Ummah would enter Paradise without rendering account. They (the companions of the Holy Prophet saws) said: Who would be those, Messenger of Allah (saws)? He (saws) said: They would be those who neither practise charm, nor take forecasts (fortune telling), nor do they cauterise, but they repose their trust in their Lord." [Muslim]

Narrated Abu Huraira (ra): Allah's Messenger (saws) said: "The example of a believer is that of a fresh green plant the leaves of which move in whatever direction the wind forces them to move and when the wind becomes still, it stands straight. Such is the similitude of the believer: He is disturbed by calamities (but is like the fresh plant he regains his normal state soon). And the example of a disbeliever is that of a pine tree (which remains) hard and straight till Allah SWT cuts it down when He will." [Bukhari]

Status of the Prophet (saws) on Judgement Day

Narrated Abu Sa`id Al-Khudri (ra): Allah's Messenger (saws) said, "Nuh (as) will be called on the Day of Resurrection and he will say, 'Labbaik and Sa`daik, O my Lord!' Allah SWT will say, 'Did you convey the Message?' Nuh (as) will say, 'Yes.' His nation will then be asked, 'Did he convey the Message to you?' They will say, 'No Warner came to us.' Then Allah SWT will say (to Nuh), 'Who will bear witness in your favour?' He will say, 'Muhammad (saws) and his followers.' So they (i.e. Muslims) will testify that he conveyed the Message. And the Apostle (saws) will be a witness over yourselves, and that is what is meant by the Statement of Allah: *"Thus We have made of you a just and the best nation that you may be witnesses over mankind and the Apostle (Muhammad) will be a witness over yourselves."* (Ch 2:143) [Bukhari]

Seven great destructive sins (al-Kabira)

Narrated Abu Huraira (ra): The Prophet (saws) said: Avoid the seven great destructive sins. The people enquire: O Allah's Messenger (saws)! What are they? He (saws) said:

i)   To join others in worship along with Allah (i.e shirk),

ii)   to practice witchcraft,

iii)　　　to kill the life which Allah has forbidden except for a just cause, (according to Islamic law),

iv)　　　to eat up Riba (usury or interest),

v)　　　to eat up an orphan's wealth,

vi)　　　to give back to the enemy and fleeing from the battlefield at the time of fighting, and

vii)　　　to accuse, chaste women, who never even think of anything touching chastity and are good believers." [Bukhari]

Witchcraft involves worshipping Jinns and is therefore, shirk. Similarly, fornication/adultery, theft, drinking intoxicants, Sodomy, cursing parents, to kill one's offspring for fear that he might share his food with him, to commit adultery with one's neighbour's wife, invoke any other God along with Allah, suicide, eating swine, believing in fortune teller and astrologer, believing in omen etc are also major sins among others.

Sin is that Allah SWT dislikes. Sin is sometimes classified as major sin (Kabira) and minor sin (Saghira) based on the Book, Sunnah and consensus of scholars. Abu Bakrah (ra) reported: The Prophet (saws) said: "Shall I inform you of the severest of the major sins?" He (saws) repeated these three times, and then said: "Associating partners with Allah, mistreatment of parents." He was reclining, and then sat up and said: "And indeed the false statement and the false testimony." He kept repeating this so many times that we wished he should be quiet. [Bukhari, Muslim]

Although exact definition of major and minor sin is a matter of debate, scholars are of the opinion that sin that is accompanied by warning of punishment or there is a mention of a curse is a major sin. Otherwise it is a minor sin and no punishment is specified in this world or the hereafter. Minor sins should not be taken lightly. It is narrated from Abdullah ibn Mas'ud (ra) that the Messenger of Allah (saws) said: "Beware of these sins that are regarded as insignificant, for they will accumulate until they destroy a man." [Musnad Ahmad] It is not permissible to regard minor sins as insignificant, because continuing in a minor sin is a major sin. Allah says (interpretation of meaning):

"If you avoid the great sins which you are forbidden to do, We shall remit from you your (small) sins, and admit you to a Noble Entrance (i.e. Paradise)" (Ch 4:31)

There are several Hadiths on this subject of this verse. Narrated Salman Al-Farsi (ra): The Prophet (saws) said, "Whoever takes a bath on Friday, purifies himself as much as he can, then uses his (hair) oil or perfumes himself with the scent of his house, then proceeds (for the Jumu'ah prayer) and does not separate two persons sitting together (in the mosque), then prays as much as (Allah has) written for him and then remains silent while the Imam is delivering the Khutbah, his sins in-between the present and the last Friday would be forgiven." [Bukhari] It was narrated that Humran said: When 'Usman (ra) performed wudu, he said: 'By Allah, I am going to tell you a Hadith which, by Allah, were it not for a Verse in the Book of Allah, I would not tell it to you. I heard the Messenger of Allah (saws) say: "No man performs wudu and does it well, then performs Salat, but he will be forgiven for whatever (sins) come between that and the Salat which follows it." [Muslim] The sins forgiven here are basically minor sins. Detail description about major sins based on the Qur'an and Sunnah is available in the book titled 'The 70 Major Sins in Islam', written by a great Islamic scholar and historian, Imam Sams Uddeen Zahnawi (1274-1348 AD), available free for download at www.islambasics.com.

Muslim should not call another Muslim a disbeliever

Ibn 'Umar (ra) reported the Messenger of Allah (saws) as saying: "If any believing man calls another believing man an unbeliever (Kafir), if he is actually an infidel (disbeliever), it is all right; if not, he will become an infidel." [Sunan Abu Dawud]

Satan tries to destroy Iman

Narrated Abu Huraira (ra): Allah's Messenger (saws) said: Satan comes to one of you and says, 'Who created so-and-so? till he says, who has created your Lord?' So, when he inspires such a question, one should seek refuge with Allah and give up such thoughts. [Bukhari and Muslim]

Munafiq (hypocrite)

In Islam, *munafiqun* (hypocrites), or false Muslims are a group decried in the Quran as outward Muslim who were inwardly concealing disbelief (kufr) and actively sought to destabilize the Muslim community. Munafiq is a person who in public and in community shows that he is a Muslim but rejects Islam or propagates against it either in his heart or among the enemies of Islam.

The 63rd chapter of the Quran is titled as Al-Munafiqun. This chapter deals with the phenomenon of hypocrisy; it criticizes hypocrisy and condemns the hypocrites; the deceit of the hypocrites of Madinah is exposed and scolded. The Prophet (saws) is warned to beware of trusting the hypocrites; the hypocrites are cursed and declared sinners; the hypocrites were threatened with expulsion from Madinah. Verses of Al-Munafiqun (Chapter 63) and Surah An-Nisa (Chapter 4) are reproduced which are as follows (interpretation of the meaning):

- *When the hypocrites come to you O Prophet , they say, "We bear witness that you are certainly the Messenger of Allah"— and surely Allah knows that you are His Messenger—but Allah bears witness that the hypocrites are truly liars. (Ch 63:1)*
- *They have made their false oaths as a shield, hindering others from the Way of Allah. Evil indeed is what they do! (Ch 63:2)*
- *This is because they believed and then abandoned faith. Therefore, their hearts have been sealed, so they do not comprehend. (Ch 63:3)*
- *When you see them, their appearance impresses you. And when they speak, you listen to their impressive speech. But they are just like worthless planks of wood leaned against a wall . They think every cry is against them. They are the enemy, so beware of them. May Allah condemn them! How can they be deluded from the truth ? (Ch 63:4)*
- *When it is said to them, "Come! The Messenger of Allah will pray for you to be forgiven," they turn their heads in disgust , and you see them O Prophet turn away in arrogance. (Ch 63:5)*
- *It is the same whether you pray for their forgiveness or not, Allah will not forgive them. Surely Allah does not guide the rebellious people. (Ch 63:6)*

o *What has happened to you that you have two minds about the hypocrites even though Allah has reverted them, owing to the sins that they earned? Do you want to lead those to the right way whom Allah let go astray? And he whom Allah lets go astray, for him you can never find a way. (Ch 4:88)*

Characteristics of hypocrites

Hypocrisy is a spiritual disease. A person's heart could be overflowing with hypocrisy yet be unaware to it due to its hidden but delicate nature. We may frequently assume that we are acting correctly but truly be away from the mark. There are many characteristics of hypocrisy described in the book of Hadiths and some of them are listed below:

o Three/Four characteristics

Hadith: Narrated 'Abdullah bin 'Amr (ra): The Messenger of Allah (saws) said: "There are *four* characteristics, whoever has them all is a pure hypocrite, and whoever has one of its characteristics, he has one of the characteristics of hypocrisy, until he gives it up: when he speaks, he lies, when he makes an agreement, he betrays it, when he makes a promise, he breaks it, and when he disputes, he resorts to obscene speech. In the narration of Sufyan (one of the narrators) it is: And if he has one of them, he has one of the characteristics of hypocrisy," [Muslim]

Hadith: Narrated Abu Hurairah (ra): The Messenger of Allah (saws) said: "The signs of the hypocrite are *three*: When he speaks he lies, when he makes a promise he breaks it, and when he is entrusted with something he betrays that trust." [Muslim]

o Love of the Ansar is a part of faith and a sign thereof; hating them is a sign of hypocrisy

Hadith: It was narrated that 'Abdullah bin 'Abdullah bin Jabir (ra): I heard Anas (ra) say: The Messenger of Allah (saws) said: "The sign of the hypocrite is hatred of the *Ansar,* and the sign of the believer is love of the *Ansar.*" [Muslim]

Hadith: Narrated Al-Bara (ra): I heard the Prophet (saws) saying (or the Prophet (saws) said), "None loves the Ansar but a believer, and none hates them but a hypocrite. So, Allah will love him who loves them, and He will hate him who hates them." [Muslim]

The Muhajirin and Ansar are the Companions of the Messenger of Allah (saws). They are the best of this ummah and the best of humanity after the Prophets (saws). Muhajirin are the ones who became Muslim before the conquest of Makkah and migrated to join the Messenger (saws) in Madinah, where they settled. They left behind their homelands, their wealth and their families in support of this religion. Ansar are the people of Madinah who welcomed the Messenger (saws) and the Muhajirin. They gave them refuge in Madinah and shared their wealth with them, not withholding anything from them out of miserliness, and they strove in Allah's cause, offering their wealth and their lives.

- Hypocrites are in the lowest levels of Hell

"The hypocrites are in the lowest levels of Hell and you will not find anyone to help them". [An-Nisa, Ch 4:145]

- Hypocrites are double faced

Hadith: Narrated Abu Huraira (ra): Allah's Messenger (saws) said, "The worst of all mankind is the double-faced one, who comes to some people with one face and to others, with another face." [Bukhari]

As stated earlier, hypocrisy or disbelief is internal, and one should not call or allege any Muslim brother/sister a hypocrite or a disbeliever. Following Hadiths may be referred to in this regard.

Hadith: It was narrated from Ibn 'Umar (ra): The Messenger of Allah (saws) said: Any man who says to his brother: "O disbeliever," it will apply to one of them. Either it is as he said, otherwise it will come back to him. [Muslim]

Hadith: Usamah bin Zaid (ra) narrated: The Messenger of Allah (saws) sent us to A1-Huraqah of Juhainah, where we attacked the people in the morning and defeated them. A man from among the Ansar and I caught one of their men, and when we overpowered him, he *said: La ilaha illallah.* The *Ansar* left him alone but I stabbed him with my spear and killed him. When we came back, news of that reached the Prophet (saws) and he said to me: 'O Usamah, did you kill him after he said *La ilaha illallah?*' I said: 'O Messenger of Allah (saws), he was only trying to protect himself.' He (saws) said: 'Did you kill him after he said *La ilaha illallah?*' and he kept repeating it until I wished that I had not become Muslim before that day." [Muslim]

Pillars of Islam (arkan al-Islam)

The most important Islamic practices are the Five Pillars of Islam. The five pillars of Islam are:

Sahadah: *The declaration of faith in one almighty Allah and His messenger (peace be upon him).*

Salat: *The ritual prayer required of every Muslim five times a day throughout their lifetime.*

Zakat: *The act of giving a portion of a Muslim's wealth to those in need throughout their lifetime.*

Sawm: *The act of fasting during the holy month of Ramadan.*

Hajj: *The sacred pilgrimage to Makkah required of every Muslim at least once in their lifetime if it is within their means.*

Five pillars of Islam work with one another to bring peace and submission to Allah SWT, into the lifestyle of every Muslim. Monotheism and belief in Prophet Muhammad (saws) as the last messenger of Allah is the central Pillar of Islam around which everything else encircles, and reciting the *Shahadah* in prayer each day reminds Muslims of this integral belief. *Salat* occurs five times a day, and offers five different opportunities to remember Allah SWT and our purpose of life in this world. While charity is greatly encouraged to be a part of everyday Muslim life, it is obligatory to offer *Zakat* (alms) once a year, ensuring that wealth is continuously redistributed to those who need it. In the month of Ramadan, every Muslim abstains from food, drink and sexual relations for a period of time each day. Every year, by the *Sawm*, Muslims control over their human needs. Without these distractions, Muslims can instead nurture good conduct and their connection to Allah. During the *Hajj* (pilgrimage), Muslims wear the same simple clothes and perform the same ritual acts of devotion to Allah. Uncovered of worldly distinction, people are recapped that all are equal before Allah. Five pillars of Allah are confirmed from many Hadiths and some of these are as follows:

Hadith: It was narrated that Anas bin Malik (ra) said: We were forbidden to ask the Messenger of Allah (saws) about anything (needlessly), so it pleased us when a man came from the desert people and said: 'O Muhammad (saws), your messenger has come to us telling us that you claim that Allah has sent you.' the Messenger of Allah (saws) said: 'He spoke the truth.' He said: 'Who created the heavens?' He (saws) said: 'Allah.' He said: 'Who created the earth?' He (saws) said: 'Allah.' He said: 'Who raised these mountains and created whatever there is in them?' He (saws) said: 'Allah.' He said: 'By the One Who created the heavens and created the earth, and raised up these mountains, has Allah sent you?' The Messenger of Allah (saws) said: 'Yes.' He said: 'Your messenger claimed that we have to offer *five prayers* each day and night.' The Messenger of Allah (saws) said: 'He spoke the truth.' He said: 'By the One Who has sent you, is it Allah Who enjoined that upon you?' He (saws) said: 'Yes.' He said: 'Your messenger claimed that we must give *Zakat* from our wealth.' The Messenger of Allah (saws) said: 'He spoke the truth.' He said: 'By the One Who has sent you, is it Allah Who enjoined that upon you?' He (saws) said: 'Yes.' He said: 'Your messenger claimed that we must fast the month of *Ramadan* each year.' The Messenger of Allah (saws) said: 'He spoke the truth.' He said: 'By the One Who has sent you, is it Allah Who enjoined that upon you?' He (saws) said: 'Yes.' He said: 'Your messenger claimed that we must perform *pilgrimage to the House*, whoever is able to bear the journey.' The Messenger of Allah (saws) said: 'He spoke the truth.' He turned to leave, then he said: 'By the One Who has sent you with the truth, I shall not do more than this or less.' The Prophet (saws) said: 'If he is speaking the truth, he will enter Paradise." [Muslim].

Hadith: It was narrated from Ibn 'Umar (ra) that the Prophet (saws) said: "Islam is built on five (pillars): Singling out Allah, establishing the Salat, paying the Zakat, fasting (during the month of) Ramadan and Hajj." A man said: "Hajj and fasting Ramadan?" He (Ibn 'Umar) said: "No; fasting Ramadan and Hajj." This is how I heard it from the Messenger of Allah (saws). [Muslim]

Virtue of five pillars

It was narrated from Abu Suhail, from his father, that he heard Talhah bin 'Ubaidullah (ra) say: A man from the people of Najd came to the Messenger of Allah (saws) with unkempt hair. We could hear him talking loudly but we could not understand what he was saying until he came closer. He was asking about Islam. The Messenger of Allah (saws) said to him: 'Five prayers each day and night.' He said: 'Do I have to do anything else' He said: 'No, unless you do it voluntarily.' He said: 'And fasting the month of Ramadan.' He said: 'Do I have to do anything else?' He said: 'No, unless you do it voluntarily.' And the Messenger of Allah (saws) mentioned Zakat to him, and he said: 'Do I have to do anything else?' He said: 'No, unless you do it voluntarily.' The man left saying: 'By Allah, I will not do any more than this or any less.' The Messenger of Allah (saws) said: 'He will achieve salvation, if he is speaking the truth.' [Sunan an-Nasa'i]

Purpose of Creation

Allah SWT says in the Qura'n:
We have not created the heavens and earth and everything in between without purpose—as the disbelievers think. So woe to the disbelievers because of the Fire! (Ch 38:27; interpretation of meaning)
Purpose of the creation of the heavens and the earth, and of life and death is for testing. Whoever obeys Him, He will reward him, and whoever disobeys Him, He will punish him. Allah says (interpretation of the meaning):

- *I did not create jinn and humans except to worship Me. (Ch 51:56)*
- *the One who created death and life, so that He may test you as to which of you is better in his deeds. And He is the All-Mighty, the Most-Forgiving, (Ch 67:2)*
- *He is the One who created the heavens and the earth in six days, while His throne was on water, so that He might test you as to who among you is better in deed. And if you say, "You shall be raised after death," the disbelievers will surely say, "This is nothing but sheer magic." (Ch 11:7)*

Allah SWT announces the qualities of creation (human being) in this world so that he will be rewarded Hereafter. Allah SWT says:
Surely, Muslim men and Muslim women, believing men and believing women, devout men and devout women, truthful men and truthful women, patient men and patient women, humble men and humble women, and the men who give Sadaqah (charity) and the women who give Sadaqah, and the men who fast and the women who fast, and the men who guard their private parts (against evil acts) and the women who guard (theirs), and

the men who remember Allah much and the women who remember (Him) - for them, Allah has prepared forgiveness and a great reward. (Ch 33:35; interpretation of meaning)

When souls were created, Allah SWT took an oath from all of us that we will only worship Him. This is the covenant in Islam.

And remember when your Lord brought forth from the loins of the children of Adam their descendants and had them testify regarding themselves. Allah asked, "Am I not your Lord?" They replied, "Yes, You are! We testify." He cautioned, "Now you have no right to say on Judgment Day, 'We were not aware of this.' [al-A'raf Ch 7:172].

There is a narration from Ubayy b. Ka'b (ra), who has given the substance of what he had heard from the Prophet (saws): Allah gathered all human beings, divided them into different groups, granted them human form and the faculty of speech, made them enter into a covenant, and then making them witnesses against themselves He asked them: 'Am I not your Lord?' They replied: 'Assuredly you are Our Lord.' Then Allah told them: 'I call upon the sky and the earth and your own ancestor, Adam, to be witness against you lest you should say on the Day of Judgement that you were ignorant of this. Know well that no one other than Me deserves to he worshipped and no one other than Me is your Lord. So do not ascribe any partner to Me. I shall send to you My Messengers who will remind you of this covenant which you made with Me. I shall send down to you My Books.' In reply all said: 'We witness that You are Our Lord and our Deity. We have no lord or deity other than You.' [Musnad Ahmad]

Abu Huraira (ra) reported Allah's Messenger (saws) as saying: The mother of every person gives him birth according to his true nature. It is subsequently his parents who make him a Jew or a Christian or a Magian. Had his parents been Muslim he would have also remained a Muslim. Every person to whom his mother gives birth (has two aspects of his life); when his mother gives birth, Satan strikes him but it was not the case with Mariam and her son (Issa). [Muslim]

Knowledge

Ibn Sina, an Islamic scholar defines knowledge as 'the understanding or discernment of something, which is the reality reflecting itself in the intelligent which has been constantly observing what it is.' Man is able to receive all sort information with the help of knowledge. We have to seek (Islamic) knowledge mainly for two reasons: either we do not know or we do not know correctly. Both the reasons come under the category 'negligence'. In the language of Mathematics, negligence is the 'lower bound' of 'Boundary of Islam' and is also a crossing of boundary along the backward direction. And crossing of boundary is the transgression. Anas (ra) reported: The Messenger of Allah, peace and blessings be upon him, said, "Two deeds are quickly punished in the world: transgression and disrespect to parents." [al-Mustadrak Hakim] Thus, it mandatory for every Muslim to have correct knowledge of Islam. Anas ibn Malik (ra) reported: The Messenger of Allah (saws) said: Seeking knowledge is an obligation upon every Muslim. [Sunan Ibn Majah]

The first verse of the Qur'an is 'reading' by which we can acquire knowledge. Allah says:

Read with the name of your Lord who created (everything), (Ch 96:1; interpretation of meaning)

The scholars occupy a noble status in Islam, and which is higher than the position of others in this world and in the Hereafter. Allah says (interpretation of the meaning):

- *Allah will elevate those of you who are faithful, and raise those gifted with knowledge in rank. (Ch 58:11)*
- *Say, "Can those who know and those who do not know become equal?" (Ch 39:9)*

At the battle of Badr, seventy people of the opponent were taken prisoner. These prisoners of war were literate people from Makkah. The Prophet (saws) declared that if one prisoner teaches ten Muslims, he will be set free. This was the first school of Islam started by the Prophet (saws). The Prophet (saws) said: "Whoever follows a path in the pursuit of knowledge, Allah will make a path to Paradise easy for him." [Bukhari]

Virtue of learning and teaching of knowledge

Abu Huraira (ra) reported: The Messenger of Allah (saws) said: Whoever travels a path in search of knowledge, Allah will make easy for him a path to Paradise. People do not gather in the houses of Allah, reciting the book of Allah and studying it together, but that tranquillity will descend upon them, mercy will cover them, angels will surround them, and Allah will mention them to those near him. [Muslim]

Abu Darda (ra) reported: The Messenger of Allah (saws) said: Verily, the angels lower their wings for the seeker of knowledge. The inhabitants of the heavens and earth, even the fish in the depths of the water, seek forgiveness for the scholar. The virtue of the scholar over the worshiper is like the superiority of the moon over the stars. The scholars are the inheritors of the Prophets. They do not leave behind gold or silver coins, but rather they leave behind knowledge. Whoever has taken hold of it has been given an abundant share. [Abu Dawud]

Mu'awiyah (ra) reported: The Messenger of Allah, peace and blessings be upon him, said: If Allah intends goodness for someone, he gives him understanding of the religion. [Bukhari]

Abu Musa (ra) reported: The Prophet (saws) said: Verily, the parable of the guidance and knowledge that Allah Almighty sent with me is the likeness of rain falling upon the earth. Among them is a good group which receives the water and thus there is abundant growth of herbage and grass. Among them is a barren land which retains the water and thus Allah benefits people from it; they drink from it and graze their animals. And it falls upon another group which is only abysmal; it does not retain water, nor does herbage grow. Such is the parable of one who understands the religion of Allah and benefits from what Allah sent with me; he learns and he teaches. Such is the parable of one who does not raise his head and does not accept the guidance Allah sent with me. [Bukhari]

Abdullah ibn Mas'ud (ra) reported: The Prophet (saws) said: There is no envy but in two cases: a man whom Allah has given wealth and he spends it rightly, and a man whom Allah has given wisdom and he judges and teaches with it. [Bukhari]

Abdullah ibn Amr (ra) reported: The Prophet, peace and blessings be upon him, said: Convey from me, even a single verse. Narrate from the children of Israel, for there is no blame in it. Whoever deliberately lies about me, let him take his seat in Hellfire. [Bukhari]

Abu Huraira (ra) reported: The Messenger of Allah, peace and blessings be upon him, said: Whoever calls to guidance will have a reward similar to those who follow him, without detracting from their rewards at all. Whoever calls to misguidance will have sin upon him similar to those who follow him, without detracting from their sins at all. [Muslim]

Amr ibn 'Awf (ra) reported: The Messenger of Allah, peace and blessings be upon him, said: Know that whoever revives a tradition from my Sunnah if it has died out after me, he will have a reward like those who act upon it without diminishing any of their rewards. Whoever innovates a misguided deviation not pleasing to Allah and his messenger (saws), he will have a sin like those who act upon it without diminishing any of the people's burdens. [Tirmizi]

Anas ibn Malik (ra) reported: The Messenger of Allah, peace and blessings be upon him, said: Whoever goes out seeking knowledge is in the way of Allah until he returns. [Tirmizi]

Abu Huraira (ra) reported: The Messenger of Allah, peace and blessings be upon him, said: Whoever enters our mosque in order to teach goodness, or to learn it himself, he is striving in jihad in the way of Allah. Whoever enters it for another reason, he is viewing what does not belong to him. [Musnad Aḥmad]

Religion is easy

Allah SWT says (interpretation of meaning):
Say, O people of the Book, be not excessive in your religion unjustly, and do not follow the desires of a people who have already gone astray, misled many and lost the right path. (Al-Ma'idah, Ch 5:77)
In regards to fasting in Ramadan, Allah SWT says (interpretation of the meaning):
Allah intends for you ease, and He does not want to make things difficult for you. (Ch 2:185)
'Allah SWT allowed such persons, out of His mercy and to make matters easy for them, to break the fast when they are ill or traveling, while the fast is still obligatory on the healthy persons who are not traveling.' (Ibn Kasir)
It is important that we learn Islam and we learn it properly. It is neither harsh nor difficult. There is nothing in Islam that is impractical. The Prophet (saws) advised the ummah to perform religious activities as well as worldly affairs in a way that both are done. We should not be

extremist nor negligent. We should not exaggerate in matters of religion. Allah SWT made Islam easy for the ummah so that we are not overburdened. The Prophet (saws) that "Religion is very easy and whoever overburdens himself in his religion will not be able to continue in that way. So, you should not be extremists, but try to be near to perfection and receive the good tidings that you will be rewarded; and gain strength by worshipping in the mornings, the afternoons, and during the last hours of the nights." [Bukhari] Another teaching of the Prophet (saws) is that "Make things easy for the people, and do not make it difficult for them, and make them calm (with glad tidings) and do not repulse (them)." [Bukhari]

Hadith: Abu Hurairah (ra) narrated that the Messenger of Allah (saws) said: "Take on only as much as you can do of good deeds, for the best of deeds is that which is done consistently, even if it is little." [Sunan Ibn Majah]

Hadith: It was narrated that Ibn 'Abbas (ra) said: '…… Then he (saws) said: 'O people, beware of exaggeration in religious matters for those who came before you were doomed because of exaggeration in religious matters.' [a part of the Hadith from Sunan Ibn Majah]

Hadith: Narrated Aishah (ra) said: "I do not know that the Messenger of Allah (saws) recited the whole Quran in one night, or prayed Qiyam (Salat) until morning, or ever fasted an entire month, except Ramadan." [Sunan an-Nasai]

Hadith: Narrated Anas (ra): We were with 'Umar (ra) and he said, "We have been forbidden to undertake a difficult task beyond our capability (i.e. to exceed the religious limits e.g., to clean the inside of the eyes while doing ablution). [Bukhari]

Hadith: Narrated Anas bin Malik (ra): A group of three men came to the houses of the wives of the Prophet (saws) asking how the Prophet (saws) worshipped (Allah), and when they were informed about that, they considered their worship insufficient and said, "Where are we from the Prophet (saws) as his past and future sins have been forgiven." Then one of them said, "I will offer the prayer throughout the night forever." The other said, "I will fast throughout the year and will not break my fast." The third said, "I will keep away from the women and will not marry forever." Allah's Messenger (saws) came to them and said, "Are you the same people who said so-and-so? By Allah, I am more submissive to

Allah and more afraid of Him than you; yet I fast and break my fast, I do sleep and I also marry women. So he who does not follow my tradition in religion, is not from me (not one of my followers)." [Bukhari]

Hadith: Narrated `Abdullah bin `Amr (ra): Allah's Messenger (saws) entered upon me and said, "Have I not been informed that you offer prayer all the night and fast the whole day?" I said, "Yes." He (saws) said, "Do not do so; offer prayer at night and also sleep; fast for a few days and give up fasting for a few days because your body has a right on you, and your eye has a right on you, and your guest has a right on you, and your wife has a right on you. I hope that you will have a long life, and it is sufficient for you to fast for three days a month as the reward of a good deed, is multiplied ten times, that means, as if you fasted the whole year." I insisted (on fasting more) so I was given a hard instruction. I said, "I can do more than that (fasting)". The Prophet (saws) said, "Fast three days every week." But as I insisted (on fasting more) so I was burdened. I said, "I can fast more than that." The Prophet (saws) said, "Fast as Allah's prophet Dawud (as) used to fast." I said, "How was the fasting of the prophet Dawud (as)?" The Prophet (saws) said: "One half of a year (i.e. he used to fast on alternate days)." [Bukhari]

Hadith: Narrated Ibn Abbas (ra): "I spent a night with the Prophet (saws). When he woke up from his sleep (in the latter part of the night for prayer) he came to his ablution water. He took the tooth-stick and used it. He (saws) then recited the verse: "Verily in the creation of the heavens and the earth and the alternation of the night and the day are tokens (of His Sovereignty) for men of understanding" (Ch 3:190). He (saws) recited these verses up to the end of the chapter or he finished the whole chapter. He (saws) then performed ablution and came to the place of prayer. He (saws) then said two rak'ahs of prayer. He (saws) then lay down on the bed and slept as much as Allah wished. He (saws) then got up and did the same. He (saws) then lay down and slept. He (saws) then got up and did the same. Every time he (saws) used the tooth-stick and offered two rak'ah of prayer. He (saws) then offered the prayer known as witr. Fudail on the authority of Husain reported the wording: He (saws) then used the tooth-stick and performed ablution while he (saws) was reciting the verses: "Verily in the creation of the heaves and the earth..." until he (saws) finished the Chapter." [Sunan Abu Dawud]

Hadith: Hisham said: I went to 'A'isha (ra) and said, "Mother of the faithful, tell me about the nature of Allah's Messenger (saws)." She asked, "Do you not recite the Qur'an?" On my replying that I certainly did, she said, "The Prophet's (saws) nature was the Qur'an." I said, "Mother of the faithful, tell me about the witr of Allah's Messenger (saws)." She replied, "I used to prepare his tooth stick and his water for ablution, and Allah would rouse him to the extent He wished during the night. He (saws) would use the tooth stick, perform ablution, and pray nine rak'as, sitting only during the eighth of them, then he would make mention of Allah, praise and supplicate Him, then he (saws) would get up without uttering the salutation and pray the ninth. After that he (saws) would sit, make mention of Allah, praise and supplicate Him, then utter a salutation loud enough for me to hear. He (saws) would then pray two rak'as sitting after uttering the salutation, and that made eleven rak'as, sonny. But when Allah's Messenger saws grew old and became fleshy he (saws) observed a witr of seven, doing in the two rak'as, as he (saws) had done formerly, and that made nine, sonny. When Allah's prophet prayed a prayer he (saws) liked to keep on observing it, but when sleep or pain made it impossible for him to get up during the night; he (saws) prayed twelve *rak'as* during the day. I am not aware of Allah's prophet (saws) having recited the whole Qur'an in a night, or praying through a whole night till morning, or fasting a complete month, except Ramadan." [Mishkat]

Thus, Prophet (saws) used to sleep during night after performing respective prayers. So, we should also follow the moderate path. Moderation in religion means that one does not exaggerate and go beyond the limit set by Allah SWT and trying to do more that Prophet (saws) did. Moderation in religion means following the example of the Prophet (saws). At the same time, one must take care that he does not neglect it and fall short of the limit set by Allah SWT. So, brothers and sisters! Don't make the religion complicated which will in turn complicate your life. What is meant by saying that Islam is easy is not that it is in accordance with one's desires and opinions, but that it is easy in accordance with what the Shari'ah has brought. To comprehend essence of Islam easily, it is necessary to study commandments of Almighty Allah and sayings of the Prophet (saws) recorded in the form of authentic Hadiths. Islam is easy.

2. Purification

The Arabic word 'Tahaarah' (purification) denotes purity and cleanliness. Washing the hands, face, cleaning the nose and mouth, washing the entire body during bath, and cleaning oneself after relieving oneself (i.e. after toilet) are all things that do not require actually any law to prescribe them. Rather it is sufficient for a human being to have a sound human nature in order to clean body parts, and to keep them free from impurity. Purification also prevents us from many diseases. The Muslim is required to stand before the Lord in prayer. Allah SWT is the most deserving that people should make themselves clean. In Islam, there is a linking between the outward and the inward purity (Shirk is the impurity of soul). Both types of purification are a means of attaining the love of Allah SWT, as Allah SWT says (that means):

- o *Indeed, Allah loves those who are constantly repentant and loves those who purify themselves* [Ch 2: 222].
- o *In it there are men who love to observe purity and Allah loves those who maintain purity.* [Ch 9:108]
- o *O you who have believed, indeed the polytheists are unclean, so let them not approach al-Masjid al-Haram after this, their [final] year. And if you fear privation, Allah will enrich you from His bounty if He wills. Indeed, Allah is knowing and wise.* [Ch 9:28]

Types of impurity and purification

There are mainly three types of impurity in Islam. These may be summarized as follows:

1. Impurity due to tangible dirtiness: This includes mud, urine, dung, stool etc. According to the majority of scholars, such dirtiness is purified by proper washing with pure water. In case of a dog, and a pig as well as what comes from them, this is washed seven times, including once with dust. The scholars provided different views regarding some details.

2. Minor impurity: There are some ceremonial impurities that requires *wudu* (ablution) or *ghusl* (complete bath) and comes under minor impurity. Examples are: prostatic fluid coming out from the excretory organs, urine, excrement, unconsciousness due to sleeping, fainting, intoxication etc.

3. Major impurity: It is a state of sexual impurity which requires both *wudu* and *ghusl*. Examples are: wet dreams by men and women, sexual relationship, end of menstruation period or bleeding of woman after giving birth.

Wudu (wet ablution)

Wuḍu, Arabic: الوضو is the Islamic procedure for cleansing parts of the body, a type of ritual purification or ablution. Wudu is compulsory for salat. The four mandatory acts of Wudu are: washing the face, the arms, wiping the head, then washing feet, and doing these in order, without any big breaks between them. Wudu is also compulsory for tawaf around the Kaba. Following Hadiths may be referred to in this context.

Hadith: Aishah (ra) said: "When he [the Prophet saws] wanted to do tawaf, he (saws) did wudu." And he (saws) said: "Learn from me your rituals (of Hajj and 'Umrah)." [Muslim].

Steps of wudu

Make intention to perform wudu, and say "Bismillah" (in the name of Allah) before starting wudu. Intention is the Islamic concept of performing an act for the sake of Allah. To perform wudu, one should centre oneself and focus seriously on what one is doing. With regard to what is to be said at the beginning, the only thing that has been narrated is to mention the name of Allah by saying Bismillah (in the name of Allah). The Prophet (saws) said: "There is no wudu for one who does not mention the name of Allah in it." [Tirmizi]

Steps of wudu are as follows:

- *Wash your hands*. Wash both the hand three times. Make sure to wash in between your fingers and all the way up to your wrists.

- *Take water into your mouth.* Use your right hand to cup water into your mouth three times. Gargle it at least once.

- *Inhale water into your nose.* Use your right hand to cup water and inhale it into your nose and blow out three times. Sniff sharply without taking too much water into your nose and choking yourself.
- *Wash your face.* Wash your face three times by spreading your hands from your right ear to the left, and from the hairline to the chin.
- *Wash your lower arms from wrists to elbows, leaving no part dry.* From your wrist to your elbow, wash your right arm with your left hand three times and then wash your left arm with your right hand three times.
- *Clean your head.* Using your wet hands, gently wipe the entire head once, from the forehead to the back of the head, and wipe it again forward from the back of the head to the forehead.
- *Wipe your ears inside and out.* Use your thumb to clean behind your ears from the bottom upward. This is done one time.
- *Wash both of your feet.* Clean up to the ankles and be sure water goes between the toes. Use your finger and go through each toe to eliminate anything between. Start with your right foot and scrub each foot three times.

In Wudu, washing should be performed one after another, so one should know the order of the steps. If there is a mistake in the order, one has to begin wudu from the beginning once again.

Recite the du'a after wudu

A number of hadiths have been narrated concerning du'a after wudu. Narrated 'Umar ibn al-Khattab (ra): The Messenger of Allah (saws) said: "There is no one among you who does wudu and does it well, then says, *Ashhadu an la ilaha ill-Allah wahdahu la sharika lah, wa ashhadu anna Muhammadan 'abduhu was rasuluhu* (I bear witness that there is no god except Allah Alone, with no partner or associate, and I bear witness that Muhammad is His slave and Messenger) but the eight gates of Paradise will be opened for him and he will enter through whichever one he wants." [Muslim] There is no authentic proof that the Prophet (saws) recited any du'a during wudu whilst washing or wiping his limbs, etc.

Wudu performed by the Prophet (saws) for salat

Humran, the freed slave of 'Usman (ra) narrated that 'Usman bin 'Affan (ra) called for water for wudu, to perform wudu. He washed his hands three times, then he rinsed his mouth and nose, then he washed his face three times, then he washed his right hand up to the elbow three times, then he washed his left hand in like manner. Then he wiped his head, then he washed his right foot up to the ankle three times, then he washed his left foot in like manner. Then he said: I saw the Messenger of Allah (saws) performing wudu as I have done it, then the Messenger of Allah (saws) said: "Whoever performs wudu as I have done it, then stands up and prays two Rak'ah in which he does not let his mind wander, he will be forgiven his previous sins." (One of the narrators) Ibn Shihab said: Our scholars used to say: "This is the most complete wudu that anyone may do for the Salat." [Muslim]

Hadith: It was narrated from 'Amr bin Yahya bin 'Umarah, from his father, from 'Abdullah bin Zaid bin 'Asim Al-Ansari (ra) who was a Companion of the Prophet (saws) he said: It was said to him: Perform wudu for us as the Messenger of Allah (saws) did it. He called for a vessel (of water) and poured some of it onto his hands and washed them three times. Then he put his hand in and brought it out, and rinsed his mouth and nose using one handful, and he did that three times. Then he put his hand in and brought it out and washed his face three times. Then he put his hand in and brought it out and washed his hands up to the elbows, washing each one twice. Then he put his hand in and brought it out and wiped his head, moving his hands forwards and backwards. Then he washed his feet up to the ankles. Then he said: "This is how the Messenger of Allah (saws) performed Wudu." [Muslim]

Hadith: It was narrated from Abu Hurairah (ra) that the Prophet (saws) said: "When one of you wakes up from sleep, let him not put his hand in the vessel until he has washed it three times, for he does not know where his hand was during the night." [Muslim]

Washing each part thrice

It was narrated that Shaqiq bin Salamah said: I saw 'Usman and 'Ali (ra) performing ablution, washing each part three times, and they said: 'This is how the Messenger of Allah (saws) used to perform ablution.' [Sunan Ibn Majah]

It was narrated from 'Amr bin Shu'aib from his father, from his grandfather, that: A Bedouin came to the Prophet (saws) and asked him about ablution. He showed him how to perform it washing each part of the body three times. Then he said: "This is the ablution, and whoever does more than this, has done evil, transgressed the limits and wronged himself." [Sunan Ibn Majah]

No salat is accepted without wudu

It was narrated from Simak bin Harb, that Mus'ab bin Sa'd said: Abdullah bin 'Umar (ra) came to visit Ibn 'Amir when he was sick and he said: 'Won't you supplicate to Allah for me, O Ibn 'Umar (ra)? He said: I heard the Messenger of Allah (saws) say: "No salat is accepted without wudu (purification), and no charity (is accepted) that comes from Ghulul," and you were the governor of Al-Basrah. (Ghulul means Goods stolen from the spoils of war prior to their authorized distribution.) [Muslim]

Abu Hurairah (ra) narrated from the Messenger of Allah (saws) and he quoted several ahadith, including: The Messenger of Allah (saws) said: "The Salat of one of you will not be accepted when he commits Hadath, until he performs wudu. [Muslim] (Hadath means those occurrences which invalidates wudu such as farting, defecation etc)

Virtues of wudu

The virtues of wudu and other obligation are described in many Hadiths. Some of them are listed below.

Hadith: Abu Malik at-Ash'ari (ra) reported: The Messenger of Allah (saws) said: Cleanliness is half of faith and al-Hamdu Lillah (all praise and gratitude is for Allah alone) fills the scale (Meejan), and Subhan Allah (Glory be to Allah) and al-Hamdu Lillah fill up what is between the heavens and the earth, and prayer is a light, and charity is proof (of one's faith) and endurance is a brightness and the Holy Qur'an is a proof on your behalf or against you. All men go out early in the morning and sell themselves, thereby setting themselves free or destroying themselves. [Muslim]

Hadith: It was narrated that Humran said: When 'Usman (ra) performed wudu he said: 'By Allah, I am going to tell you a Hadith which, by

Allah, were it not for a Verse in the Book of Allah, I would not tell it to you. I heard the Messenger of Allah (saws) say: "No man performs wudu and does it well, then performs Salat, but he will be forgiven for whatever (sins) come between that and the Salat which follows it." [Muslim]

Hadith: It was narrated from Abu Hurairah (ra) that the Prophet (saws) said: "When any one of you cleans himself with pebbles, let him use an odd number, and when any one of you performs Wudu, let him put water in his nostrils, then let him blow it out." [Muslim]

Hadith: It was narrated that 'Abdullah bin 'Amr (ra) said: We came back with the Messenger of Allah (saws) from Makkah to Al-Madinah, and when we were at an oasis on the way, some people hastened at the time of 'Asr and performed wudu in a hurry. We came to them and their heels were visibly dry and had not been touched by water. The Messenger of Allah (saws) said: "Woe to the heels from the Fire! Do wudu properly." [Muslim]

Hadith: It was narrated from Abu Hurairah (ra) that the Messenger of Allah (saws) said: "When a Muslim performs wudu and washes his face, every sin that he looked at with his eyes comes out from his face with the water - or with the last drop of the water. When he washes his hands, every sin that he committed with his hands comes out from his hands with the water - or with the last drop of the water. When he washes his feet, every sin to which he walked with his feet comes out from his feet with the water - or with the last drop of the water - until he emerges cleansed of sins." [Muslim]

Hadith: It was narrated from Nu'aim bin 'Abdullah that he saw Abu Hurairah (ra) performing wudu. He washed his face and his hands almost up to the shoulders, then he washed his feet up to the calves. Then he said: I heard the Messenger of Allah (saws) say: "On the Day of Resurrection, my Ummah will come with glimmering faces and limbs because of the traces of wudu, so whoever among you is able to increase the brightness of his face, let him do so." [Muslim]

Hadith: It was narrated from Abu Hurairah (ra) that the Messenger of Allah (saws) said: "My Cistern (Hawd) will be larger than the distance between Aylah and 'Adan. It will be whiter than snow and sweeter than honey mixed with milk, and its vessels are more numerous than the stars.

I will block the people from approaching it as a man blocks the people's camels from approaching his cistern." They said: "O Messenger of Allah (saws), will you recognize us on that Day?" He (saws) said: "Yes, you will have a feature that none of the other nations will have. You will come to me with glimmering faces and limbs because of the traces of Wudu." [Muslim]

Hadith: It was narrated that 'Uqbah bin 'Amir (ra) said: We were charged with taking care of the camels. When my turn came, I brought them back in the evening and found the Messenger of Allah (saws) standing up, addressing the people. I caught up with him when he (saws) was saying: "There is no Muslim who performs wudu and does it well, then stands and prays two *Rak'ah* in which his heart is focused as he faces the *Qiblah,* but Paradise will be due to him." I said: 'How good this!' Someone who was in front of me said: 'What came before it was even better.' I looked and saw that it was 'Umar (ra). He said: I see that you have just come; he said: "There is no one among you who performs wudu and does it completely - or he said *Fayusbighu* – then *says: 'Ash-hadu An la ilaha illallah, Wa Anna Muhammadan 'Abduhu Wa Rasuluh* (I bear witness that none has the right to be worshipped but Allah and that Muhammad (saws) is His slave and Messenger),' but the eight gates of Paradise will be opened to him, and he will enter through whichever one he wishes." [Muslim]

Saying 'Bismilllah' when performing ablution

It was narrated that Abu Sa'eed bin Zaid (ra) said: The Messenger of Allah (saws) said: "There is no prayer for one who does not have ablution, and there is no ablution for one who does not mention the Name of Allah (before it)." [Sunan Ibn Majah]

Wudu is valid after eating

It was narrated from Ibn 'Abbas (ra) that the Messenger of Allah (saws) got dressed, then he came out to offer Salat. A gift of bread and meat was brought to him and he ate three mouthfuls, then he led the people in prayer, and he did not touch any water (i.e. he did not perform wudu). [Muslim]

It was narrated that Abu Rafi (ra) said: "I bear witness that I used to grill sheep liver for the Messenger of Allah (saws), then he prayed and he did not perform wudu." [Muslim]

It was narrated from Az-Zuhri, from 'Ubaidullah bin 'Abdullah, from Ibn 'Abbas (ra) that the Prophet (saws) drank some milk, then he called for some water and rinsed out his mouth and said: "There is some greasiness in it" [Muslim]

Wudu after eating camel meat and lamb meat

It was narrated from Jabir bin Samurah (ra) that a man asked the Messenger of Allah (saws): "Should I perform wudu after eating lamb?" He (saws) said: "If you wish, then perform wudu, and if not, then do not do it." He said: "Should I perform wudu after eating camel meat?" He (saws) said: "Yes, perform wudu after eating camel meat." He said: "Can I offer prayer in sheep pens (*i.e. a small area of ground with a fence around it, used for keeping sheep together for a short time*)?" He (saws) said: "Yes." He said: "Can I pray in the area where camels rest?" He (saws) said, "No." [Muslim]

When someone has doubt about farting

It was narrated from Sa'eed, and 'Abbad bin Tamim, from his paternal uncle, that a complaint was made to the Prophet (saws) about when one thinks that something has happened while he is praying. He (saws) said: "Do not stop until you hear a sound or notice a smell." [Muslim]

Wudu due to flowing blood and vomiting

According to Islamic teachings, flowing blood can disrupt the state of wudu. There is a disagreement among scholars regarding this issue. Imam Abu Hanifah and Imam Ahmad were of the view that they invalidate wudu. They quoted a number of texts as evidence. For example: The words of the Prophet (saws) to the woman who was suffering from *istihaadah* (non-menstrual vaginal bleeding): "That is from a vein, so do wudu for every prayer." They said: The reason why wudu is required may be that it is bleeding from a vein, and this applies to every kind of bleeding. It is therefore recommended by some scholars to repeat the wudu if bleeding is excessive from a body part.

There is no evidence that vomiting invalidate wudu. Imam Shafai believed that vomiting does not invalidate wudu because there is no evidence of it. On the other hand, the Hanafi and Hanbali consider that if someone vomits a mouthful, it would break the wudu.

Wudu after deep sleep, fainting

Deep sleep is considered to break wudu. When one falls into a deep sleep, he become unconscious; and according to Islamic law, this is considered a breaking point. So, after waking up from a deep sleep, one has to perform Wudu again before engaging in any act of worship, such as prayer. This ruling is based on the belief that during deep sleep, one cannot control over bodily functions such as farting.

Fainting renders wudu invalid. According to Islamic scholars, fainting breaks wudu regardless of the duration of unconsciousness. When a person faints and becomes unconscious, he loses control of bodily functions, so wudu should be performed again when they regain consciousness.

Wudu after touching between the couples

Touching between the couples does not break wudu. Following Hadith from al-Bukhari narrated by A'isha (ra) is relevant.

Hadith: Narrated Aishah (ra): I used to stretch my legs towards the Qibla of the Prophet (saws) while he (saws) was praying; whenever he (saws) prostrated, he (saws) touched me, and I would withdraw my legs, and whenever he (saws) stood up, I would re-stretch my legs. [Bukhari]

Permissibility of performing all the prayers with one wudu

It was narrated from Sulaiman bin Buraidah, from his father, that the Prophet (saws) prayed all the prayers on the day of the Conquest (of Makkah) with one wudu, and he wiped over his Khuff. 'Umar (ra) said to him: "Today you have done something that you did not do before." He (saws) said: "I did it deliberately, O 'Umar." [Muslim]

Ablution with left over water

It was narrated from Kabshah bint Ka'b, who was married to one of the sons of Abu Qatadah (ra), that: She poured water for Abu Qatadah to perform ablution. A cat came and drank the water, and he tilted the vessel for it. She started looking at it (in surprise) and he said: O daughter of my brother, do you find it strange? The Messenger of Allah (saws) said: "They (cats) are not impure, they are of those who go around among you." [Sunan Ibn Majah]

Ablution with seawater

It was narrated that Mughirah bin Abu Burdah, who was from the tribe of Banu 'Abdud-Dar, said that: He heard Abu Hurairah (ra) say: A man came to the Messenger of Allah (saws) and said: "O Messenger of Allah saws, we travel by sea and carry a small amount of water with us. If we use it for ablution, we will become thirsty. Can we perform ablution with seawater?" The Messenger of Allah (saws) said: "Its water is a means of purification, and its dead meat is permissible. (i.e. the fish found dead in the sea)." [Sunan Ibn Majah]

Touching private parts

Qais bin Talq Al-Hanafi narrated that his father said: I heard the Messenger of Allah (saws) being asked about touching the penis. He (saws) said: "That does not require ablution, because it is a part of you (your body)." [Sunan Ibn Majah]

Running fingers through the beard and wiping head

It was narrated from 'Usman (ra) that: The Messenger of Allah (saws) performed ablution and ran his fingers through his beard. [Sunan Ibn Majah] It was also narrated that 'Usman bin 'Affan (ra) said: "I saw the Messenger of Allah (saws) performing ablution and he wiped his head once." [Sunan Ibn Majah]

Left hand should to sniff water into the nose?

It was narrated that 'Ali (ra) called for (water for) wudu, then he rinsed his mouth and nose, and he sniffed up water and blew it out using his left hand. He did that three times, then he said: "This is how the Prophet of Allah (saws) purified himself." [Sunan an-Nasai]

Concerning wiping the ears

It was narrated from Ibn 'Abbas (ra) that: The Messenger of Allah (saws) wiped his ears, putting his forefingers in his ears and wiping the back of them with his thumbs, so he wiped them inside and out. [Sunan Ibn Majah]

Running the fingers between the toes

It was narrated that Mustawarid bin Shaddad (ra) said: I saw the Messenger of Allah (saws) performing ablution, and he ran his little finger between his toes. [Sunan Ibn Majah]

Asim bin Laqit bin Saabirah narrated that his father said: The Messenger of Allah (saws) said: "Perform ablution properly and let the water run between your fingers." [Sunan Ibn Majah]

It was narrated from Miqdam bin Ma'dikarib (ra) that: The Messenger of Allah (saws) performed ablution; so he washed his feet three times. [Sunan Ibn Majah]

Cleaning the inside of the eyes

Narrated Anas (ra): We were with `Umar (ra) and he said: We have been forbidden to undertake a difficult task beyond our capability (i.e. to exceed the religious limits e.g., to clean the inside of the eyes while doing ablution). [Bukhari]

Sprinkling water after ablution

It was narrated from Hakam bin Sufyan As-Sawri that: He saw the Messenger of Allah (saws) perform ablution then take a handful of water and sprinkle it over his private area to remove any doubts about urine drippings. [Sunan Ibn Majah]

Wiping over the khuff (leather socks)

It was narrated that Hammam said: Jarir (ra) urinated, then he performed wudu and wiped over his khuff. It was said: Do you do that? He said: Yes; I saw the Messenger of Allah (saws) urinated, then he performed wudu and wiped over his khuff. Al A'mash said: "Ibrahim said: They were impressed by this Hadith, because Jarir (ra) accepted Islam after Surat Al-Ma'idah was revealed." [Muslim]

It was narrated that Shuraih bin Hani' said: I came to Aishah (ra) and asked her about wiping over the khuff. She said: You should go to Ali Ibn Abi Talib (ra) and ask him, for he used to travel with the Messenger of Allah (saws). So we asked him and he said: The Messenger of Allah (saws) set a limit of three days and their nights (i.e., three nights) for the traveller, and one day and night for one who is not travelling. [Muslim]

It was narrated from 'Urwah bin Al Mughirah, from his father, that he helped the Prophet (saws) to perform wudu. He performed wudu and wiped over his khuff, then he said: "I put them on while my two feet were Tahir (clean or pure)." [Muslim]

Narrated Al-Mughira bin Shu'ba (ra): I helped the Prophet (saws) in performing ablution and he passed his wet hands over his khuffs and prayed. [Bukhari]

Parts of the earth purify each other

It was narrated that Umm Salamah (ra), the wife of the Prophet (saws), said: I am a woman whose hem is lengthy, and I may walk through a dirty place. The Messenger of Allah (saws) said: That which comes after it purifies it. [Sunan Ibn Majah]

Tayammum or dry ablution

Tayammum refers to the act of cleansing without using water where there is no known source of water nearby. Occasionally, it is used to replace both wudu and Ghusl (except Junub *i.e.* in a state of sexual impurity), only in exceptional circumstances. Since it is performed without water, it is called 'dry ablution.'

Hadith: It was narrated that Aishah (ra) said: We went out with the Messenger of Allah (saws), on one of his journeys, and when we were in Al-Baida' or in Dhat Al-Jaish - a necklace of mine broke (and fell off). The Messenger of Allah (saws) started to look for it, and the people did likewise. They were not near any water source and they did not have any water with them. The people came to Abu Bakr (ra) and said: Do you not see what Aishah (ra) has done? She has delayed the Messenger of Allah (saws) and the people with him. They are not near any water source and they do not have any water with them. Abu Bakr (ra) came and the Messenger of Allah (saws) was resting his head on my thigh and had gone to sleep. He (Abu Bakr) said: 'You have delayed the Messenger of Allah (saws) and the people. They are not near any water source and they do not have any water with them.' Abu Bakr (ra) scolded me, and said whatever Allah willed he should say. He started poking me in the side with his hand, and nothing prevented me from moving except the fact that the Messenger of Allah (saws) was resting on my thigh. The Messenger of Allah (saws) slept until morning came and there was no water. Then Allah revealed the Verse of *Tayammum,* so they performed *Tayammum.* Usaid bin Hudair (ra) who was one of the leaders said: This is not the first of your blessings, O family of Abu Bakr! Aishah (ra) said: We made the camel that I had been riding get up, and we found the necklace underneath it. [Muslim]. The verse of *Tayammum* that was revealed is as follows (interpretation of the meaning):

"But if you are ill or on a journey, or any of you comes after answering the call of nature, or you have been in contact with women (i.e. sexual intercourse), and you find no water, then perform Tayammum with clean earth and rub therewith your faces and hands" [Al-Maa'idah: 6]

The way in which tayammum is done is to say Bismillah with the intention of doing tayammum, then to strike the ground once with the palms of the hands, then to wipe the right hand with the palm of the left, and the left hand with the palm of the right, then to wipe the face with both hands.

Regarding dry ablution

It was narrated from 'Ammar bin Yasir (ra) that: When they did dry ablution with the Messenger of Allah (saws), he commanded the Muslims to strike the dust with the palms of their hands, and they did not pick up any dust. Then they wiped their faces once, then they struck the dust with their palms once again and wiped their hands. [Sunan Ibn Majah]

"The earth has been made for me a Masjid and a thing to purify"

Narrated Jabir bin `Abdullah (ra): Allah's Messenger (saws) said, "I have been given five things which were not given to any amongst the Prophets before me. These are:

1. Allah made me victorious by awe (by His frightening my enemies) for a distance of one month's journey.

2. The earth has been made for me (and for my followers) a place for praying and a thing to perform Tayammum. Therefore, my followers can pray wherever the time of a prayer is due.

3. The booty has been made Halal (lawful) for me (and was not made so for anyone else).

4. Every Prophet used to be sent to his nation exclusively but I have been sent to all mankind.

5. I have been given the right of intercession (on the Day of Resurrection.) [Bukhari]

Defecating or urinating

It was narrated from 'Abdur Rahman bin Yazid, from Salman (ra) that it was said to him: "Your Prophet (saws) has taught you everything, even how to defecate?" He said: "Yes. He (saws) forbade us to face towards the *Qiblah* when defecating or urinating, or to clean ourselves with our right hands, or to clean ourselves with less than three pebbles, or to clean ourselves with dung or bones." [Muslim]

It was narrated from 'Abdullah bin Abi Qatadah that his father said: The Messenger of Allah (saws) said: "None of you should hold his private part in his right hand when he is urinating, nor wipe himself with his right hand after defecating, or breathe into the vessel (while drinking)." [Muslim]

It was narrated from Abu Hurairah (ra) that the Messenger of Allah (saws) said: "Beware of the two things that provoke curses." They said: "What are the two things that provoke curses, O Messenger of Allah (saws)?" He (saws) said: "The one who relieves himself in the street where people pass, or in places where they seek shade." [Muslim]

It was narrated from Anas bin Malik (ra) that the Messenger of Allah (saws) entered a garden, and a boy who was the youngest among us followed him with a jug of water. He placed it beside a lote-tree, and the Messenger of Allah (saws) relieved himself then came out to us, having cleaned himself with that water. [Muslim]

It was narrated from Abu Hurairah (ra) that the Prophet (saws) said: "None of you should urinate into standing water and then wash himself with it." [Muslim]

It was narrated that 'Abdullah bin Ja'far (ra) said: "The Messenger of Allah (saws) made me ride behind him one day, and he told me a secret which I will never tell to any of the people. When relieving himself, the Messenger of Allah (saws) liked to find a place where he was well concealed, a hill or a cluster of date-palms." [Muslim]

Anas bin Malik (ra) said: "While we were in the *Masjid* with the Messenger of Allah (saws), a Bedouin (Tribe) came and stood and urinated in the *Masjid.* The Companions of the Messenger of Allah (saws) said: 'Stop, stop!' The Messenger of Allah (saws) said: 'Do not interrupt him; let him be.' So they left him alone until he had finished urinating. Then the Messenger of Allah (saws) called him and said to him: 'These Masajid are not for any of this urine and filth; rather they are for the remembrance of Allah, the Mighty and Sublime, and Salat, and reading the Qur'an,' or as the Messenger of Allah (saws) said it. Then he ordered a man from the people to bring a bucket of water and pour it over it." [Muslim]

It was narrated that 'Aishah (ra) said: "A nursing baby was brought to the Messenger of Allah (saws) and the baby urinated in his lap; he (saws) called for water and poured it over it." [Muslim] It was also narrated from Umm Mihsan (ra) that she brought a son of hers who was not yet eating regular food to the Messenger of Allah (saws) and placed him in his lap, and he urinated. He (saws) did not do any more than to sprinkle water over it. [Muslim]

Urinating while standing

It was narrated that Huzaifah (ra) said: "I was with the Prophet (saws) and we came to a garbage-dump of some people. He (saws) urinated standing, and I started to go away. He (saws) said: 'Come closer (to shield).' So I came closer until I was standing (behind him) at his heels, then he (saws) performed wudu and wiped over his khuff. [Muslim] This was an exceptional case where the place was a dirty one. The Prophet (saws) used to urinate while sitting and it is therefore Sunnah. Narrated Aishah (ra): "Whoever tells you that the Prophet (saws) used to urinate standing up, do not believe him. He (saws) only ever used to urinate sitting down." [Tirmizi]

Moreover, if one urinates while standing, drops of urine will splash on the person including his clothes and foot which will make him impure. It is obligatory to take precaution while urinating. It was narrated that Ibn 'Abbas (ra) said: The Messenger of Allah (saws) passed by two graves, and he said: "They are being punished, but they are not being punished for anything great (i.e., it was not difficult to avoid). One of them used to walk around spreading malicious gossip, and the other did not protect himself from his urine." He (saws) called for a palm branch, split it in two, then planted one piece on one grave and the other on the other grave. Then he (saws) said: "Perhaps it (the punishment) will be reduced for them so long as this does not dry out." [Muslim].

Usage of stones for cleaning without anything else

It was narrated from 'Aishah (ra) that the Messenger of Allah (saws) said: "When any one of you goes to the Gha'it (toilet to defecate), let him take with him three stones and clean himself with them, for that will suffice him." [Sunan an-Nasai]

Greeting during urinating

It was narrated from Ibn 'Umar (ra) that a man passed by when the Messenger of Allah (saws) was urinating. He greeted him, but he (saws) did not return the greeting. [Muslim]

Urine of infants

It was narrated that 'Ali (ra) said: The Messenger of Allah (saws) said: "The urine of a boy is to be sprinkled with water and the urine of a girl is to be washed." Qatadah said: "That is if they are not yet eating solid food; if they are eating solid food then their urine is to be washed in both cases." [Musnad Ahmad]

Toilet etiquette

Entering Toilet

It was narrated from Anas (ra) that when the Messenger of Allah (saws) entered the area in which he relieved himself, he would say: *"Allahumma, inni a 'auju bika minal-khubusi wal-khaba'is* (O Allah, I seek refuge in You from the male and female devils.)" In Arabic:

اللَّهُمَّ إِنِّي أَعُوذُ بِكَ مِنَ الْخُبُثِ وَالْخَبَائِثِ

[Muslim]

What should be said when coming out the Toilet

Yusuf bin Abi Burdah narrated: I heard my father say: I entered upon 'Aishah (ra), and I heard her say: When the Messenger of Allah (saws) exited the toilet, he would say: "Ghufranaka (I seek Your forgiveness)." [Sunan Ibn Majah]

Remembrance of Allah while in the toilet

Urwah narrated from 'Aishah (ra) that: The Messenger of Allah (saws) used to remember Allah in all circumstances. [Sunan Ibn Majah]

Distancing oneself for defecating outside

It was narrated that Mugirah bin Shu'bah (ra) said: "Whenever the Prophet (saws) went to relieve himself, he would go far away." [Sunan Ibn Majah]

It was narrated that 'Abdullah bin Ja'far (ra) said: The thing that the Prophet (saws) most liked to conceal himself behind when relieving himself was a hillock or a stand of date-palm trees. [Sunan Ibn Majah]

Ibrahim bin Jarir narrated from his father that: The Prophet of Allah (saws) entered an undergrowth and relieved himself, then Jarir (ra) brought him a small water skin from which he cleansed himself, then he wiped his hand in the dirt. [Sunan Ibn Majah]

Junub or the state of sexual impurity

Janabat is a ritual impurity caused by the discharge of semen or by sexual intercourse; and the person is called a *junub*. It does not make any difference whether this discharge is while awake or in a wet-dream. In case of sexual intercourse, both *wudu* and ghusl become compulsory on both the man and the woman.

Junub cannot offer salat

O believers! Do not approach prayer while intoxicated until you are aware of what you say, nor in a state of full impurity—unless you merely pass through the mosque —until you have bathed. But if you are ill, on a journey, or have relieved yourselves, or been intimate with your wives and cannot find water, then purify yourselves with clean earth, wiping your faces and hands. And Allah is Ever-Pardoning, All-Forgiving. (Surah an-Nisa', Ch 4:43; interpretation of meaning)

O believers! When you rise up for prayer, wash your faces and your hands up to the elbows, wipe your heads, and wash your feet to the ankles. And if you are in a state of full impurity, then take a full bath. But if you are ill, on a journey, or have relieved yourselves, or have been intimate with your wives and cannot find water, then purify yourselves with clean earth by wiping your faces and hands. It is not Allah's Will to burden you, but to purify you and complete His favour upon you, so perhaps you will be grateful. (Surah al-Ma'ida, Ch 5:6; interpretation of meaning).

Ghusl is optional for Junub for going to sleep

It was narrated from 'Aishah (ra) that if the Messenger of Allah (saws) wanted to sleep while he was Junub, he would perform wudu as for prayer before going to sleep. [Muslim]

It was narrated from Ibn 'Umar (ra) that 'Umar (ra) consulted the Prophet (saws) and said: "Can one of us go to sleep while he is Junub?" He (saws) said: "Yes. Let him perform wudu and then go to sleep, until he does Ghusl whenever he wishes." [Muslim]

It was narrated that 'Abdullah bin Abi Qais said: I asked 'Aishah (ra) about the War of the Messenger of Allah (saws) and he mentioned the Hadith. I said: "What did he (saws) do in the case of Janabah? Did he (saws) perform Ghusl before he (saws) slept, or sleep before he (saws) performed Ghusl?" She said: "He (saws) would do both. Sometimes he (saws) performed Ghusl and then slept, and sometimes he (saws) would perform wudu and sleep." I said: "Praise be to Allah Who has made the matter flexible." [Muslim]

Procedure of Ghusl in case of Janabat

It was narrated that 'Aishah (ra) said: "When the Messenger of Allah (saws) performed Ghusl in the case of Janabah, he would start by washing his hands, then he would pour water with his right hand into his left and wash his private part. Then he would perform wudu as for prayer. Then he would take water (and pour it over his head) and make it reach the roots of his hair, using his fingers. When he saw that it was thoroughly wet, he would pour three handfuls of water over his head. Then he would pour water over the rest of his body, then he would wash his feet." [Muslim]

It was narrated that 'Aishah (ra) said: "The Messenger of Allah (saws) performed *Ghusl* in a vessel like a *Faraq,* and he and I used to perform *Ghusl* using a single vessel." According to the *Hadith* of Sufyan: "With a single vessel." Qutaibah said: Sufyan said: "The *Faraq is* three *Sa* (a measure that equals four *Mudd;* about 3kg." [Muslim]

It was narrated from Jubair bin Mut'im that mention of Ghusl for *Janabah* was made in the presence of the Prophet (saws) and he said: "As for me, I pour water over my head three times." [Muslim]

It was narrated that Umm Salamah (ra) said: I said: "O Messenger of Allah (saws), I am a woman with tightly braided (interwoven) hair; should I undo it for Ghusl from Janabah?" He (saws) said: "No; it is sufficient for you to pour three handfuls of water over your head, then pour water over you, and you will become pure." [Muslim]

It was narrated that Shaqiq said: I was sitting with 'Abdullah and Abu Musa when Abu Musa said: 'O Abu' Abdur-Rahman! If a man becomes sexually impure and cannot find any water for a month, what do you think he should do about offerings salat?' 'Abdullah said: 'He should not do Tayammum even if he does not find water for a month.' Abu Musa said: 'What about this Verse in Surat Al-Ma'idah: "...and you find no water, then perform *Tayammum* with clean earth...'? 'Abdullah said: 'If they were granted a concession because of this Verse, soon they would do *Tayammum* with clean earth if they found the water too cold.' Abu Musa said to 'Abdullah: 'Have you not heard what 'Ammar (ra) said? "The Messenger of Allah (saws) sent me on an errand and I became sexually impure. I could not find any water, so I rolled in the dust like an animal, then I came to the Messenger of Allah (saws) and told him about that. He (saws) said: 'It would have been sufficient for you to do like this with your hands' - then he struck the ground with his hands once, then wiped the left hand over the right, and the back of his hands and his face." 'Abdullah said: 'Did you not notice that 'Umar (ra) was not convinced by the words of 'Ammar (ra)?" [Muslim]

As per Hanafi school of thought, there are three requisites for an obligatory ghusl to be valid: to rinse one's mouth with gargle, to pass water in the nostrils (up to last part of nose), to pour water over the entire body once. It is argued that wudu and gusl is achieved in this manner.

Purification after wet dream

When a man or a woman discharges semen or vaginal fluid in a dream while sleeping is called wet dream. Some people wake up in the process, but others may not. A wet dream is often the result of a sexual dream, but not always. Wet dreams typically begin during puberty. By the process of wet dream, one becomes sexually impure and both wudu and ghusl is compulsory.

Hadith: It was narrated from Qatadah that Anas bin Malik (ra) told them that Umm Sulaim (ra) narrated, that she asked the Prophet of Allah (saws) about a woman who sees in her dreams what a man sees. The Messenger of Allah (saws) said: If a woman sees that, let her perform Ghusl. Umm Salamah (ra) said: "I felt shy because of that, and I said: 'Does that really happen?" The Prophet of Allah (saws) said: "How else does resemblance (of the child to either parent) happen? The water of the man is thick and white, and the water of the woman is thin and yellow. Whichever of them prevails, or comes first, the resemblance will be (to that parent)." [Muslim]

The ruling on clothes with semen

It was narrated from 'Alqamah and Al-Aswad that a man stayed at 'Aisah's (ra) house, and in the morning, he washed his garment. 'Aishah (ra) said: "It would have been sufficient, if you saw it (the semen), to wash that place, and if you did not see it, to sprinkle water around it, for I remember scratching the garment (at the place of semen) of the Messenger of Allah (saws) thoroughly, then he performed Salat in it." [Muslim]

The Messenger of Allah (saws) used to wash off the semen. As for Ibn Al-Mubarak and 'Abdul-Wahid, according to their Hadith she (Aishah) said: "I used to wash it from the garment of the Messenger of Allah (saws)." [Muslim]

The impurity of menstrual blood and how to wash it

It was narrated that Asma (ra) said: "A woman came to the Prophet (saws) and said: "Menstrual blood may get onto the clothes of any one of us; what should she do with it?" He (saws) said: "She should scratch it (when it is dry), then rub it with water, then wash it, then pray in it." [Muslim]

Prohibition of performing ghusl in standing water

It was narrated from Abu As-Sa'ib, the freed slave of Hisham bin Zuhair that he heard Abu Hurairah (ra) saying: The Messenger of Allah (saws) said: "None of you should perform Ghusl in standing water when he is Junub (in a state of sexual impurity)." He said: "What should he do, O Abu Hurairah?" He said: "Let him scoop it out in handfuls." [Muslim]

Other issues of impurity

Purification after dog licking

It was narrated that Abu Hurairah (ra) said: The Messenger of Allah (saws) said: "The purification of the vessel of one of you, if a dog licks it, is to wash it seven times, the first time with mud." [Muslim]

It was narrated that Ibn Al-Mughaffal (ra) said: The Messenger of Allah (saws) ordered the killing of dogs, then he said: "What is the problem with them (the people) and the dogs?" Then he (saws) granted a concession with regard to hunting dogs and sheep dogs, and said: "If a dog licks the vessel of one of you, let him wash it seven times and rub it with mud the eighth time." [Muslim]

The quantity of water that does not become unclean

It was narrated from 'Ubaidullah bin 'Abdullah bin 'Umar that his father said: I heard the Messenger of Allah (saws) being asked about water in the wilderness that is frequented by beasts and predators. The Messenger of Allah (saws) said: "If the water reaches the amount of two Qullahs, nothing can make it impure (Najis)." [Sunan Ibn Majah]

Two Qullahs is approximately 204 litres of water.

Shaking hands with Junub

It was narrated from Abu Rafi' that: Abu Hurairah (ra) was met by the Prophet (saws) in one of the streets of Al-Madinah when he was in a state of sexual impurity, so he slipped away. The Prophet (saws) missed him, so when he came (later on), he (saws) said: "Where were you O Abu Hurairah?" He said: "O Messenger of Allah (saws), you met me when I was in a state of sexual impurity, and I did not want to sit with you until I had a bath." The Messenger of Allah (saws) said: "The believer does not become impure." [Sunan Ibn Majah]

Fitrah (sound human nature)

Fitrah means human nature of believing one God. It was narrated from Abu Hurairah (ra) that the Prophet (saws) said: "The *Fitrah* is five things" - or "five things are part of the *Fitrah*" –"Circumcision, shaving the pubes, clipping the nails, plucking the armpit hairs, and trimming the moustache." [Muslim]

Hadith: It was narrated that Anas bin Malik (ra) said: "A time limit was set for us for trimming the moustache, clipping the nails, plucking the armpit hairs and shaving the pubes: that was not to be left for more than forty days." [Muslim]

Hadith: It was narrated from Ibn 'Umar (ra) that the Prophet (saws) said: "Trim the moustache and let the beard grow." [Muslim]

Hadith: It was narrated that Zaid bin Arqam (ra) said: The Messenger of Allah (saws) said: "Whoever does not trim his moustache, he is not from one of us." [Sunan an-Nasai]

Hadith: Narrated Abu Huraira (ra): Allah's Messenger (saws) said, "Abraham did his circumcision with an adze* at the age of eighty." [Bukhari]

*a type of cured blade axe

Menstruation

Menstruation (also known as a period) is the periodical discharge of blood and mucosal tissue from inner lining of uterus of woman. Menstruation is triggered by falling progesterone (natural hormone) levels and is a sign that pregnancy has not occurred. The first period, a point in time known as menarche, usually begins between the ages of 12 and 15. The typical length of time between the first day of one period and the first day of the next is between 21 and 31 days with the average being 28 days. Bleeding usually lasts around 2 to 7 days. Periods stop during pregnancy. Menstruation ceases after menopause, which usually occurs between 45 and 55 years of age. Symptoms in advance of menstruation that do interfere with normal life are called pre-menstrual syndrome. Some women however, experience premenstrual syndrome such as bloating, abdomen pain, feeling tired, irritability, and mood changes etc. Allah SWT mentions about menstruation in the Quran (interpretation of the meaning):

"They ask you O Prophet about menstruation. Say, "Beware of its harm! So keep away, and do not have intercourse with your wives during their monthly cycles until they are purified. When they purify themselves, then you may approach them in the manner specified by Allah. Surely Allah loves those who always turn to Him in repentance and those who purify themselves." (Ch 2:222)

Salat is exempted for menstruating woman

Narrated `Aisha (ra): Fatima bint Abi Hubaish (ra) used to have bleeding in between the periods, so she asked the Prophet (saws) about it. He (saws) replied, "The bleeding is from a blood vessel and not the menses. So give up the prayers when the (real) menses begins and when it has finished, take a bath and start praying." [Bukhari]

Menstruating woman cannot offer fast

Narrated Abu Sa`id Al-Khudri (ra): Once Allah's Messenger (saws) went out to the Musalla (to offer the prayer) of `Id-al-Adha or Al-Fitr prayer. Then he passed by the women and said, "O women! Give alms, as I have seen that the majority of the dwellers of Hell-fire were you (women)." They asked, "Why is it so, O Allah's Messenger (saws)?" He (saws) replied, "You curse frequently and are ungrateful to your husbands. I have not seen anyone more deficient in intelligence and religion than you. A cautious sensible man could be led astray by some of you." The women asked, "O Allah's Messenger (saws)! What is deficient in our intelligence and religion?" He said, "Is not the evidence of two women equal to the witness of one man?" They replied in the affirmative. He (saws) said, "This is the deficiency in her intelligence. Isn't it true that a woman can neither pray nor fast during her menses?" The women replied in the affirmative. He (sa) said, "This is the deficiency in her religion." [Bukhari]

Fasting left during Ramadan is to be made up

A'isha (ra) reported: If one amongst us had to break fasts (of Ramadan due to natural reasons, i. e. menses) during the life of the Messenger of Allah (saws), she could not find it possible to complete them so long she had been in the presence of Allah's Messenger (saws) till Sha'ban commenced. [Bukhari]

Salat during menses not to make up

It was narrated from Mu'adhah that a woman asked, "Aishah (ra): "Should one of us make up the prayers that she misses during her menses?" 'Aisah (ra) said: "Are you a Hariiriyyah (a town in Iraq)? One of us would menstruate during the time of the Messenger of Allah saws, then she was not ordered to make up (the prayers)." [Muslim]

Sexual intercourse not allowed during menstruation

Sabit narrated from Anas (ra), that among the Jews, when a woman menstruated, they would not eat with her or stay with her in their houses. The Companions of the Prophet asked the Prophet saws (about that), and Allah, the Mighty and Sublime, revealed (that means): "They ask you concerning menstruation. Say: "That is an *Adha* (a harmful thing), therefore, keep away from women during menses..." until the end of the Verse. The Messenger of Allah (saws) said: "Do everything except (sexual) intercourse." News of that reached the Jews and they said: "This man does not want to leave any of our affairs, but he differs from us therein." Usaid bin Hudair and 'Abbad bin Bishr (ra) came and said: "O Messenger of Allah (saws), the Jews are saying such and such. Why don't we have intercourse with them (the women)?" The face of the Messenger of Allah (saws) changed until we thought that he was angry with them, but when they went out, a gift of milk was sent to the Prophet (saws). He (saws) sent someone to bring them back and gave them (some of that milk) to drink, and they knew that he was not angry with them. [Muslim]

Touching a menstruating woman above the izar

It was narrated that 'Aishah (ra) said: "If one of us was menstruating, the Messenger of Allah (saws) would tell her to put on a waist-wrapper *(Izar),* then he would touch her." [Muslim]

It was narrated that 'Aishah (ra) said: "If one of us was menstruating, the Messenger of Allah (saws) would tell her to put on a waist-wrapper if her menstrual flow was heavy, then he would touch her. She said: 'Who among you can control his desire as the Messenger of Allah (saws) did?" [Muslim]

Lying down with a menstruating woman under a single cover

It was narrated that Kuraib, the freed slave of Ibn 'Abbas (ra): I heard Maimunah (ra), the wife of the Prophet (saws), say: "The Messenger of Allah (saws) used to lie down with me, when I was menstruating, with a garment between me and him." [Muslim]

Household works

It was narrated that 'Aishah (ra) said: "I used to wash the head of the Messenger of Allah (saws) while I was menstruating." [Muslim]

It was narrated that 'Aishah (ra) said: "The Messenger of Allah (saws) used to lean his head out towards me when I was in my room, and I would comb his hair while I was menstruating." [Muslim]

It was narrated that 'Aishah (ra) said: "The Messenger of Allah (saws) told me to pass him the palm-fibre mat from the *Masjid.* I said: "I am menstruating." He (saws) said: "Give it to me; the menstruation is not in your hand." [Muslim]

Menstruating woman can share food

It was narrated that 'Aishah (ra) said: "I would drink while I was menstruating, then I would pass it to the Prophet (saws) and he (saws) would put his mouth at the place where my mouth had been and drink. And I would nibble meat from the bone while I was menstruating, then I would pass it to the Prophet (saws) and he (saws) would put his mouth where my mouth had been." Zuhair (one of the narrators) did not mention "and drink." [Muslim]

One may recline menstruating woman's lap and recite Qur'an

It was narrated that 'Aishah (ra) said: "The Messenger of Allah (saws) used to recline in my lap when I was menstruating, and recite Qur'an." [Muslim]

If menstrual blood gets on clothes

It was narrated from Asma' bint Abi Bakr (ra) that a woman asked the Messenger of Allah (saws) about menstrual blood that gets on clothes. He (saws) said: "Scratch it, then rub it with water, then sprinkle water over it, and pray in it." [Sunan an-Nasai]

Ghusl after menses

It was narrated from Safiyyah and she narrates from 'Aishah (ra) that Asma (ra) asked the Prophet (saws) about Ghusl following menses. He (saws) said: "Let one of you take her water and Sidr (lote tree) leaves and clean herself well, then let her pour water over her head and rub it vigorously, so that it will reach the roots of her hair. Then let her pour the water over herself, then take a piece of cloth scented with musk and purify herself." Asma (ra) said: "How should she purify herself?" He (saws) said: *"Subhan-Allah* (Glorious is Allah)! Purify yourself with it." 'Aishah (ra) said as if she whispered it to her - "Follow the traces of blood." And she asked him about *Ghusl* in the case of *Janabah.* He (saws) said: "Let her take water and clean herself well or clean herself thoroughly, then let her pour water over her head and rub it so that it reaches the roots of the hair, then let her pour water over herself." 'Aishah (ra) said: "How good the woman of the *Ansar* were! They did not let shyness prevent them from understanding their religion properly." [Muslim]

Note: There is a difference between ghusl after sexual impurity and ghusl after menses. Prophet (saws) prescribed rubbing the hair and applying perfume in case of ghusl after menses. One has to say Bismillah before wudu and ghusl according to majority of the jurist. Rinsing the mouth and nose is essential in ghusl, as is the view of the Hanafis and Hanbalis.

Istiazah

It was narrated that 'Aishah (ra) said: Fatimah bint Abi Hubaish (ra) came to the Prophet (saws) and said: O Messenger of Allah (saws), I am a woman who suffers from Istiazah (prolonged vaginal bleeding) and I do not become pure. Should I give up As-Salat?" He (saws) said: "No, rather that is from a vein and is not menstruation. When the time of your menstruation arrives, stop praying, and when it is ends, wash the blood from yourself and offer As-Salat." [Muslim]

It was narrated from Umm Salamah (ra) that a woman suffered constant bleeding at the time of the Messenger of Allah (saws), so Umm Salamah (ra) consulted the Prophet (saws) for her. He (saws) said: "Let her count the number of nights and says that she used to menstruate each month before this happened to her, and let her stop praying for that amount of time each month. Then when that is over let her perform Ghusl, then let her use a pad, and pray." [Sunan an-Nasai]

Mazi (Prostatic Fluid)

Mazi it is a thin white sticky fluid which is discharged due to sexual stimulation, e.g. thinking about sexual acts, or kissing or the like. It was narrated that Ibn 'Abbas (ra) said: Ali bin Abi Talib (ra) said: "I sent al-Miqdad bin Al-Aswad (ra) to the Messenger of Allah (saws), to ask him about the prostatic fluid that comes out of a man, and how he should deal with it." The Messenger of Allah (saws) said: "Perform Wudu and sprinkle (wash) your private part." [Muslim]

Nifas

The word nifas is usually translated as "post-natal bleeding." The blood which is discharged from a woman's womb after a miscarriage is also nifas. Umm Salamah (ra) narrated: "The time of waiting for Nifas during the time of Allah's Messenger saws was 40 days. We used to cover our faces with reddish-brown Wars." [Tirmizi]

According to the scholars, including the four imams, there is no minimum limit for nifas. Whenever a woman becomes pure from nifas, she has to do ghusl and pray and fast. Nifas may be vary from person to person. It is unanimously agreed upon among the scholars that the nufasaa' does not pray for forty days unless she sees blood stoppage before the end of 40 days period. She should then perform ghusl (ablution of the whole body) and she resumes praying. The majority of the religious scholars say that a woman does pray even if she continues to notice blood after the forty days period expires.

Performing ghusl after nifas (postnatal bleeding)

It was narrated from Jabir bin 'Abdullah (ra), in the Hadith of Asma' bint 'Umair (ra) [Wife of Abu Bakr], when she gave birth in Zul-Hulaifah*, that the Messenger of Allah (saws) said to Abu Bakr (ra): "Tell her to perform Ghusl and enter Ihram." [Sunan an Nasai]

(*during Hajj pilgrimage)

Summary

1. For tangible impurity such as sticking of dung etc, do cleanse it by washing.

2. For salat and tawaf, wudu is compulsory.

3. After intention, one has to say 'Bismillah' before starting wudu.

4. After wudu, say *'Ashhadu an la ilaha ill-Allah wahdahu la sharika lah, wa ashhadu anna Muhammadan 'abduhu was rasuluhu'*. In Arabic: أَشْهَدُ أَنْ لَا إِلَهَ إِلَّا اللهُ وَحْدَهُ لَا شَرِيكَ لَهُ وَأَشْهَدُ أَنَّ مُحَمَّداً عَبْدُهُ وَرَسُولُهُ

5. Sexual impurity is a major impurity that needs wudu and ghusl both.

6. Menstruation and post-natal bleeding also need wudu and ghusl. Prophet (saws) prescribed rubbing the hair and applying perfume in case of ghusl after menses.

7. Wet dream is a major impurity.

8. Salat missed during menses are not to make up. However, fasting during Ramadan missed due to menses are to be made up later on.

3. Salat

Azan

Azan is the Islamic call to public prayer in a Masjid recited by Muazzin (callers to prayer) at prescribed times of a day. A second call, known as the Iqamah, calls people within the mosque to line up for the beginning of the prayers.

Abdullah bin 'Umar (ra) said: When the Muslims came to Al- Madinah, they would gather and they would wait for the time for the prayer to come, but no one would watch and announce the times. One day they spoke about that. Some of them said: (to call the people for prayers) 'Use a bell like the bell of the Christians.' Some of them said: 'Use a horn like the horn of the Jews.' 'Umar (ra) said: 'It is better to send a man to call (the people) to prayer.' The Messenger of Allah (saws) said: "O Bilal, get up and give the call to prayer." [Muslim]

Hadith: It was narrated from Abu Mahzurah (ra) that the Prophet of Allah (saws) taught him this Azan: *Allah is the Greatest, Allah is the Greatest; I testify that there is no god but Allah, I testify that there is no god but Allah; I testify that Muhammad Is the Messenger of Allah, I testify that Muhammad is the Messenger of Allah, and it should be again repeated: I testify that there is no god but Allah, I testify that there is no god but Allah; I testify that Muhammad Is the Messenger of Allah, I testify that Muhammad is the Messenger of Allah. Come to the prayer (twice). Come to success (twice).* Ishaq added: *Allah is the Greatest, Allah is the Greatest; there is no god but Allah.* [Muslim]

Azan for Fajr prayer

It was narrated that Abu Mahdhurah (ra) said: I used to call the Azan for the Messenger of Allah (saws) and in the first Azan of Fajr I used to Say: *'Hayya 'ala al-falah, as-salatu khairun minan-nawm, as-salatu khairun minan-nawm, Allahu Akbar Allahu Akbar, la ilaha illallah* (Come to prosperity, prayer is better than sleep, prayer is better than sleep, Allah is the Greatest, Allah is the Greatest, there is none worthy of worship except Allah).' [Sunan an-Nasa'i]

One should respond to Azan

It was narrated from 'Abdullah bin 'Amr bin Al-As (ra) that he heard the Prophet (saws) say: "When you hear the Muazzin, say what he says, then send *Salat* (invoke a blessing) upon me, for whoever sends *Salat*[*] upon me, Allah will send *Salat* upon him tenfold. Then ask Allah to grant me *Al-Wasilah,* for it is a station in Paradise which only one of the slaves of Allah will attain, and I hope that I will be the one. Whoever asks for *Al-Wasilah* for me, (my) intercession will be permissible for him." [Muslim, Tirmizi]

[*]sending blessings on the Prophet (saws)

It was narrated from Jabir bin Abdullah (ra): Allah's Messenger (saws) said, "Whoever, after listening to the Azan (for the prayer) says, '*Allahumma rabba hadhihid-da'wat it-tammah was-salat il-qaimah, ati Muahmmadan al-wasilah wal-fadilah, wab'athu maqaman mahmudan alladhi wa'adtahu* (O Allah, the Lord of this complete call and of this prayer, which is going to be established! Give Muhammad Al-Wasilah (the highest position in Paradise only one of the slaves of Allah will attain) and Al-Fadila (the degree of superiority) and raise him to Al-Maqam-al-Mahmud (the praiseworthy station) which You have promised him,)' will be granted my intercession for him on the Day of Resurrection." [Bukhari, Sunan an-Nasai]. In Arabic, the dua is as follows:

اللَّهُمَّ رَبَّ هَذِهِ الدَّعْوَةِ التَّامَّةِ وَالصَّلاَةِ الْقَائِمَةِ، آتِ مُحَمَّدًا الْوَسِيلَةَ وَالْفَضِيلَةَ، وَابْعَثْهُ مَقَامًا مَحْمُودًا الَّذِي وَعَدْتَهُ

The Quran says (that means): "*It may be that your Lord will raise you to Maqam Mahmud (a station of praise and glory, i.e., the honour of intercession on the Day of Resurrection.*" (Ch 17:79; interpretation of meaning) *Maqam Mahmud* is the 'praised position' and honour given to no one else by Allah except to His final messenger (saws). The 'praised position' (Maqam Mahmud) is intercession before Allah so that He will start to judge between His slaves, and no one will be granted this except our Prophet (saws). Allah has raised some prophets more than others and that is His blessings and having mercy on mankind through their high ranks: "*We have chosen some of those messengers above others. Allah spoke directly to some, and raised some high in rank.*" (Ch 2:253) It is called al-maqam al-mahmud because all of creation will praise Prophet (saws) for that status, because his intercession will ease their distress on that terrible day of Judgement by initiation of the process of judgement by Allah SWT.

It was narrated that 'Umar bin A1-Khattab (ra) said: "The Messenger of Allah (saws) said: 'If the *Muazzin* says: *"Allahu akbaru Allahu akbar* and one of you says: *"Allahu akbaru Allahu akbar then he says:* *"Ashhadu an la illallah* and you *say: " Ashhadu an la illallah* then he says: *"Ashhadu anna Muhammadan Rasusl-Allah* and *you say: " Ashhadu anna Muhammadan Rasusl-Allah* then he says: *"Hayya 'ala s-salat* and you say: *"La hawla wa la quwwata illa Billah* then he says: *"Hayya 'alal-falah* and you say: *La hawla wa la quwwata illa Billah* then he says: *"Allahu akbaru Allahu akbar* and you say: *"Allahu akbaru Allahu akbar* then he says: *"La ilaha illallah* and one of you says: *"La ilaha illallah* from the heart, he will enter Paradise." [Muslim]

Saying Salah upon the Prophet (saws) after the azan

Abdullah bin 'Amr (ra) said: "I heard the Messenger of Allah (saws) say: 'When you hear the Mu'azzin then say what he says, and do Salah upon me, for whoever does Salah upon me once, Allah will Salah upon him ten (times). Then ask Allah to grant me Al-Wasilah, which is a position in paradise which only one of the slaves of Allah will attain, and I hope that I will be the one. Whoever asks for Al-Wasilah for me, will be entitled to my intercession." [Sunan an-Nasai] Salah means sending blessings (durud) upon the Prophet (saws).

To say after Azan

Sa'd bin Abu Waqqas (ra) reported: The Prophet (saws) said, "He who says after the Azan: *'Ash-hadu an la ilaha illallah Wah-dahu la sharika Lahu; wa ash-hadu anna Muhammadan 'abduhu wa Rasuluhu, radhitu Billahi Rabban, wa bi Muhammadin Rasulan, wa bil Islami Dinan* [I testify that there is no true god except Allah Alone; He has no partners and that Muhammad (saws) is His slave and Messenger; I am content with Allah as my Rubb, with Muhammad as my Messenger and with Islam as my Deen],' his sins will be forgiven." [Muslim, Sunan an-Nasai] In Arabic:

أَشْهَدُ أَنْ لاَ إِلَهَ إِلاَّ اللَّهُ وَحْدَهُ لاَ شَرِيكَ لَهُ وَأَنَّ مُحَمَّدًا عَبْدُهُ وَرَسُولُهُ رَضِيتُ بِاللَّهِ رَبًّا وَبِمُحَمَّدٍ رَسُولاً وَبِالإِسْلاَمِ دِينًا

Azan for one who is praying alone

It was narrated that 'Uqbah bin 'Amir (ra) said: I heard the Messenger of Allah (saws) say: "Your Lord is pleased with a shepherd high in the mountains who calls the Azan for the prayer and prays. Allah says: 'Look at this slave of Mine; he calls the Azan and Iqamah for the prayer and fears Me. I have forgiven My slave and admitted him to Paradise." [Sunan an-Nasai]

Honour of a Muazzin

Muawiyah (ra) reported: I heard the Messenger of Allah (saws) saying: "The Mu'azzin (callers to prayer) will have the longest necks on the Day of Resurrection." (They will be the more deserving of Allah's mercy and reward) [Muslim]

Ibn Umar (ra) reported: The Prophet (saws) said, "Allah forgives the callers to prayer when they end their call, and every creature on land or sea who hears his voice seeks forgiveness for him." [Musnad Aḥmad]

Narrated 'Abdul Rahman: Abu Sa'id Al-Khudri (ra) told my father, "I see you liking sheep and the wilderness. So whenever you are with your sheep or in the wilderness and you want to pronounce Azan for the prayer raise your voice in doing so, for whoever hears the Azan, whether a human being, a jinn or any other creature, will be a witness for you on the Day of Resurrection." Abu Sa'id (ra) added, "I heard it (this narration) from Allah's Apostle (saws)." [Bukhari]

Narrated Abu Huraira (ra): Allah's Apostle (saws) said, "If the people knew the reward for pronouncing the Azan and for standing in the first row (in congregational prayers) and found no other way to get that except by drawing lots they would draw lots, and if they knew the reward of the Zuhr prayer (in the early moments of its stated time) they would race for it (go early) and if they knew the reward of 'Isha' and Fajr (morning) prayers in congregation, they would come to offer them even if they had to crawl." [Bukhari]

How the Iqamah is to be recited

It was narrated that Abu Al-Musanna, the Mu'azzin of the Jami' Masjid, said: "I asked Ibn 'Umar (ra) about the Azan and he said: 'At the time of the Messenger of Allah (saws), the phrases of the Azan were recited twice and the phrases of Iqamah once, except that you should say (the phrase) Qad qamat is-salah (prayer is about to begin) "قَدْ قَامَتِ الصَّلَاةُ" twice. When we heard 'prayer is about to begin' we would perform Wudu and go out to pray.' [Sunan an-Nasai]

Saying the Phrases of the lqamah once

Narrated Anas (ra): Bilal (ra) was ordered to repeat the wording of the Azan for prayers twice, and to pronounce the wording of the Iqama once except "Qad-qamat-is-salat". [Bukhari]

Dua between azan and iqamah

Narrated Anas ibn Malik (ra): The Messenger of Allah (saws) said: "Du'a is not rejected between the Azan and iqamah, so engage in du'a (supplication)." [Tirmizi, Abu Dawud, Musnad Ahmad]

Azan after child birth

Narrated Abu Rafi (ra): I saw the Messenger of Allah (saws) uttering the call to prayer (Azan) in the ear of al-Hasan ibn Ali (ra) when Fatimah (ra) gave birth to him. [Sunan Abu Dawud]

Effect of Azan on Shaitan

It was narrated from Abu Hurairah (ra) that the Prophet (saws) said: "When the *Shaitan* hears the call to prayer, he runs away breaking wind so that he will not hear the sound. When it ends, he comes back and whispers (distractions), then when he hears the *Iqamah* he runs away so that he will not hear the sound, then when it ends, he comes back and whispers (distractions)." [Muslim]

Salat

On the authority of Abu Hurayrah (ra) from the Prophet (saws), who said: Allah (mighty and sublime be He) says: The first of his actions for which a servant of Allah will be held accountable on the Day of

Resurrection will be his prayers. If they are in order, then he will have prospered and succeeded: and if they are wanting, then he will have failed and lost. If there is something defective in his obligatory prayers, the Lord (glorified and exalted be He) will say: See if My servant has any supererogatory prayers with which may be completed that which was defective in his obligatory prayers. Then the rest of his actions will be judged in like fashion. [Tirmizi]

Salat or Salah is the daily ritual prayer instructed upon all Muslims as one of the five pillars of Islam. Salat is the soul of religion. Where there is no salat, there can be no purification of the soul. It aims at purifying both body and soul, for it finds no separation between them. It impresses upon one's mind that he is the humble servant of Allah SWT and his spiritual development and religious devotion lies in sincere and willing obedience to Allah. Daily five obligatory (fard) prayers are:

- salat al-Fajr (dawn),
- al-Zuhr (midday),
- al-Asr (afternoon),
- al-Maghrib (sunset), and
- al-Isha (evening).

Allah SWT says in the Qur'an (that means):

Observe the prayer from the decline of the sun until the darkness of the night and the dawn prayer, for certainly the dawn prayer is witnessed by angels. (Ch 17:78)

And rise at the last part of the night, offering additional prayers, so your Lord may raise you to a station of praise. (Ch 17:79)

So be patient 'O Prophet' with what they say. And glorify the praises of your Lord before sunrise and before sunset, and glorify Him in the hours of the night and at both ends of the day, so that you may be pleased 'with the reward'. (Ch 20:130)

Hadith: It was narrated from Abu Suhail, from his father, that he heard Talhah bin 'Ubaidullah (ra) say: A man from the people of Najd came to the Messenger of Allah (saws) with unkempt hair. We could hear him talking loudly but we could not understand what he was saying until he came closer. He was asking about Islam. The Messenger of Allah (saws) said to him: 'Five prayers each day and night.' He said: 'Do I have to do anything else?' He (saws) said: 'No, unless you do it voluntarily. He (saws) said: 'And fasting the month of Ramadan?' He said: 'Do I have to do anything else?' He (saws) said: 'No, unless you do it voluntarily.' And the Messenger of Allah (saws) mentioned Zakat to him, and he said: 'Do I have to do anything else?' He (saws) said: 'No, unless you do it voluntarily.' The man left saying: 'By Allah, I will not do any more than this or any less.' The Messenger of Allah (saws) said: 'He will achieve salvation, if he is speaking the truth.' [Sunan an-Nasa'i]

Islam has laid the greatest emphasis on the institution of Salat. It is enjoined upon every Muslim to pray five times a day. Abu Zar (ra) narrated: The Prophet (saws) said, " ....I again passed by Musa (as) and he said to me: Return to your Lord, for your followers will not be able to bear it. So I returned to Allah and He said, 'These are five prayers and they are all (equal to) fifty (in reward) for My Word does not change.' I returned to Musa (as) and he told me to go back once again. I replied, 'Now I feel shy of asking my Lord again.' Then Jibril took me till we "reached Sidrat-il-Muntaha (Lote-tree of the utmost boundary) which was shrouded in colours, indescribable. Then I was admitted into Paradise where I found small (tents or) walls (made) of pearls and its earth was of musk." [Part of the Hadith from Bukhari]

The scholars are unanimously agreed that the five daily prayers were not made obligatory until this night. Angel Jibril (as) on behalf of Allah SWT taught salat to Prophet (saws). Narrated Ibn Shihaab: Umar ibn 'Abd al-'Azeez delayed the prayer one day. 'Urwah ibn az-Zubayr entered upon him and told him that al-Mughirah ibn Shu'bah delayed the prayer one day when he was in Kufah, and Abu Masud al-Ansari (ra) entered upon him and said: What is this, O Mughirah (ra)? Do you not know that Jibril came down and prayed, and the Messenger of Allah (saws) prayed, then he prayed and the Messenger of Allah (saws) prayed, then he prayed and the Messenger of Allah (saws) prayed, then he prayed and the Messenger of Allah (saws) prayed, then he prayed and the Messenger of Allah (saws) prayed. Then he said: This is what has been enjoined upon me. 'Umar said to 'Urwah: Think what you are narrating, O 'Urwah! Is Jibril the one who taught the Messenger of Allah (saws) the times of the prayers? 'Urwah said: That is what Basheer ibn Abi Masud used to narrate from his father. [Bukhari, Muslim]

Before the Isra (Night Journey), the Prophet (saws) definitely used to pray, as did his companions, but there is a scholarly difference of opinion as to whether any kind of prayer was made obligatory before the five daily prayers or not.

Why salat is obligatory

Salat is made obligatory upon every adult Muslim. We are ordered to observe salat in all occasions, whether one is healthy or sick, whether one prays standing, sitting or lying down, whether one is traveling or not travelling. Salat is our key to success in this world and in the hereafter. Allah SWT says in the Holy Quran (interpretation of the meaning):

o   *"Successful indeed are the believers who are humble in their prayers" (Ch 23:1-2)*

o   *"and those who are properly observant of their prayers. These are the ones who will be awarded Paradise as their own They will be there forever" (Ch 23:9-11)*

o   *"Recite what has been revealed to you of the Book and establish prayer. Indeed, genuine prayer should deter one from indecency and wickedness. The remembrance of Allah is an even greater deterrent. And Allah fully knows what you all do". (Ch 29:45)*

o   *"And seek help in patience and Prayer; and truly it is hard except for those who prostrate before Me with sincerity - Who know that they have to meet their Lord, and that it is to Him they are to return." (Ch 2:45-46)*

Hadith: Narrated Jabir (ra) that the Prophet (saws) said: Between disbelief (kufr) and faith is abandoning the Salat. [Muslim, Tirmizi]

Hadith: Jabir bin 'Abdullah (ra) narrated that Allah's Messenger (saws) said: The key to Paradise is Salat, and the key to Salat is wudu'. [Tirmizi]

Hadith: Abu Huraira (ra) reported: The Messenger of Allah (saws) said, "The first action for which a servant of Allah will be held accountable on the Day of Resurrection will be his prayers. If they are in order, he will have prospered and succeeded. If they are lacking, he will have failed and lost. If there is something defective in his obligatory prayers, then the Almighty Lord will say: See if My servant has any voluntary prayers that can complete what is insufficient in his obligatory prayers. The rest of his deeds will be judged the same way." [Tirmizi, Sunan an-Nasai].

Hadith: The Prophet (saws) said: "Order your children to pray at the age of seven and beat them to do so at the age of ten and separate them (boys & girls) in their beds." [Sunan Abu Dawud and Tirmizi]

Hadith: Narrated Ibn Mas`ud (ra): A man kissed a woman (unlawfully) and then went to the Prophet (saws) and informed him. Allah revealed (that means): *And offer prayers perfectly at the two ends of the day and in some hours of the night (i.e. the five compulsory prayers). Verily! good deeds remove (annul) the evil deeds (small sins)* (Ch 11:114). The man asked Allah's Messenger (saws), "Is it for me?" He (saws) said, "It is for all my followers." [Bukhari]

Note: The sin referred here is minor sin (saghira)

Virtues of five daily prayers

It was narrated from Abu Hurairah (ra) that the Messenger of Allah (saws) said: "The (obligatory) five daily prayers, from one *Jumu'ah* to the next, are an expiation for whatever (minor sins) come in between, so long as one does not commit major sins." [Muslim]

Narrated Anas (ra): The Prophet (saws) said: My Lord says, "If My slave comes nearer to me for a span, I go nearer to him for a cubit; and if he comes nearer to Me for a cubit, I go nearer to him for the span of outstretched arms; and if he comes to Me walking, I go to him running." [Bukhari]

Narrated Abu Huraira (ra): I heard Allah's Messenger (saws) saying, "If there was a river at the door of anyone of you and he took a bath in it five times a day would you notice any dirt on him?" They said, "Not a trace of dirt would be left." The Prophet (saws) added, "That is the example of the five prayers with which Allah blots out (annuls) evil deeds." [Muslim]

Importance of learning Hadiths of Salat

The importance of learning Hadiths of Salat lies in the fact that any Salat offered not in accordance with the way the Prophet (saws) offered will be in vain and discarded. Following Hadith explains the purpose of this and is listed below.

Hadith: Malik (ra) reported: We came to the Prophet (saws) and stayed with him for twenty days and nights. We were all young and of about the same age. The Prophet (saws) was very kind and merciful. When he (saws) realized our longing for our families, he (saws) asked about our homes and the people there and we told him. Then he (saws) asked us to go back to our families and stay with them and teach them (the religion) and to order them to do good things. He (saws) also mentioned some other things which I have (remembered or [??]) forgotten. The Prophet (saws) then added, "Pray as you have seen me praying وَصَلُّوا كَمَا رَأَيْتُمُونِي أُصَلِّي and when it is the time for the prayer one of you should pronounce the Azan and the oldest of you should lead the prayer. [Bukhari]

The times of as-salat

Abdullah bin 'Amr (ra) reported the Prophet (saws) as saying: The time of the Zuhr prayer is as along as the time of the 'Asr prayer has not come; the time of the Asr prayer is as long as the sun has not become yellow; the time of the Maghrib prayer is as long as the twilight has not ended; the time of the Isha prayer is up to midnight; and the time of the Fajr prayer is as long as the sun has not risen. [Sunan Abu Dawud]

Satan says, 'The night is long, so keep on sleeping'

Narrated Abu Huraira (ra) that Allah's Messenger (saws) said, "During your sleep, Satan knots three knots at the back of the head of each of you, and he breathes the following words at each knot, 'The night is long, so keep on sleeping,' If that person wakes up and celebrates the praises of Allah, then one knot is undone, and when he performs ablution the second knot is undone, and when he prays, all the knots are undone, and he gets up in the morning lively and in good spirits, otherwise he gets up in low spirits and lethargic." [Bukhari]

Narrated 'Abdullah (ra): It was mentioned before the Prophet (saws) that there was a man who slept the night till morning (after sunrise). The Prophet (saws) said, "He is a man in whose ears (or ear) Satan had urinated." [Bukhari]

How to perform salat?

In early few years during the holy time of thr Prophet (saws), Qiblah was al-Aqsa. The Prophet (saws) had the wish of having K'aba as the Qiblah. This is described in the Qur'an (interpretation of the meaning):
We have been seeing you turning your face to the heavens. So, We will certainly assign to you a Qiblah that you would like. Now, turn your face in the direction of the Sacred Mosque (Al-Masjid-ul-Haram), and (O Muslims), wherever you are, turn your faces in its direction. Even those who have been given the Book know well that it is the truth from their Lord, and Allah is not unaware of what they do. (Ch 2:144)
Hadith: Narrated Al-Bara (ra): We prayed along with the Prophet (saws) facing Jerusalem for sixteen or seventeen months. Then Allah ordered him to turn his face towards the Qiblah (in Makkah): "And from whence-so-ever you start forth (for prayers) turn your face in the direction of (the Sacred Mosque of Makkah) Al-Masjid-ul Haram." (Ch 2:149) [Bukhari]
Note: This incidence happened in the Masjid Al Qiblatyn in Madinah.
Hadith: Narrated Ibn ʻUmar (ra): While some people were at Quba (offering) morning prayer, a man came to them and said, "Last night Qur'anic Verses have been revealed whereby the Prophet (saws) has been ordered to face the Ka'ba (at Makkah), so you too should face it." So they, keeping their postures, turned towards the Ka'ba. Formerly the people were facing Sham (Jerusalem) (Allah said): "And from whence-so-ever you start forth (for prayers), turn your face in the direction of the Sacred Mosque of Makkah (Al-Masjid-ul-Haram), and whence-so-ever you are, turn your face towards it (when you pray)." (Ch 2:150) [Bukhari]

Takbir in the beginning of salat (Takbir Tahrima)

Scholars have unanimously agreed that to raise the hands while saying the opening Takbir to begin the Salat is obligatory. Following are some Hadiths.
Hadith: It was narrated by Abu Hurairah (ra): "When the Messenger of Allah (saws) began his prayer, he (saws) raised his hands extensively." [Sunan Abu Dawud] Muhammad bin ʻAmr bin ʻAta said: I heard Abu Humaid As-Sa'idi (ra) say: When the Messenger of Allah (saws) stood

up for prayer, he (saws) would face the prayer direction, raise his hands, and say: "Allahu Akbar." [Sunan ibn Majah]

Placing hands

Narrated Sahl bin Sa`d (ra): The people were ordered to place the right hand on the left forearm in the prayer. Abu Hazim said, "I knew that the order was from the Prophet (saws)." [Bukhari] Waa'il ibn Hujr (ra) said: I prayed with the Messenger of Allah (saws) and he placed his right hand over his left hand on his chest. [Sahih Ibn Khuzaymah]

Raising the hands until they are level with the highest part of the ears

It was narrated from Malik bin Al-Huwairith (ra) that: He saw the Prophet (saws) raise his hands when he bowed, and when he raised his head from bowing, until they were in level with the highest part of his ears. [Sunan an-Nasai]

Sami'a Allahu Liman Hamidah

Abu Huraira (ra) reported: When the Messenger of Allah (saws) got up for prayer, he would say the takbir (Allahu -Akbar) when standing, then say the takbir when bowing. Then say: سَمِعَ اللَّهُ لِمَنْ حَمِدَهُ *Allah listened to him who praised him,* when coming to the erect position after bowing, then say while standing: رَبَّنَا وَلَكَ الْحَمْدُ *To Thee, our Lord, be the praise,* then recite the takbir when getting down for prostration, then say the takbir on raising his head, then say the takbir on prostrating himself, then say the takbir on raising his head. He would do that throughout the whole prayer till he would complete it, and he would say the takbir when he would get up at the end of two rak'as after adopting the sitting posture. Abu Huraira (ra) said: My prayer has the best resemblance amongst you with the prayer of the Messenger of Allah (saws). [Muslim]

It is obligatory to recite al-Fatihah in every rak'ah

It was narrated from 'Ubadah bin As-Samit (ra) that the Prophet (saws) said: "There is no prayer for the one who does not recite the Opening of the Book (Al-Fatihah)." [Muslim]

It was narrated from Abu Hurairah (ra) that the Messenger of Allah (saws) said: "When the Imam says *'Amin'* (at the end of Al-Fatiah) then say *'Amin,'* for if a person's saying *Amin* coincides with that of the angels, his previous sins will be forgiven." [Muslim]

Abu Huraira (ra) reported: The Messenger of Allah (saws) said: If anyone observes prayer in which he does not recite Umm al-Qur'an, it is deficient [he said these three times] and not complete. It was said to Abu Huraira (ra): At times we are behind the Imam. He said: Recite it inwardly, for he had heard the Messenger of Allah (saws) declare that Allah the Exalted had said: I have divided the prayer into two halves between Me and My servant, and My servant will receive what he asks. When the servant says: Praise be to Allah, the Lord of the universe, Allah the Most High says: My servant has praised Me. And when he (the servant) says: The Most Compassionate, the Merciful, Allah the Most High says: My servant has lauded Me. And when he (the servant) says: Master of the Day of judgment, He remarks: My servant has glorified Me. and sometimes He would say: My servant entrusted (his affairs) to Me. And when he (the worshipper) says: Thee do we worship and of Thee do we ask help, He (Allah) says: This is between Me and My servant, and My servant will receive what he asks for. Then, when he (the worshipper) says: Guide us to the straight path, the path of those to whom Thou hast been Gracious not of those who have incurred Thy displeasure, nor of those who have gone astray, He (Allah) says: This is for My servant, and My servant will receive what he asks for. Sufyan said: 'Ala bin Abdur Rahman bin Ya'qub narrated it to me when I went to him and he was confined to his home on account of illness, and I asked him about it. [Muslim]

Bismillahir-Rahmanir-Rahim should not be recited aloud

Muhammad bin Ja'far narrated from Shu'bah, who said: "I heard Qatadah narrate, that Anas (ra) said: I observed prayer along with the Messenger of Allah (saws) and with Abu Bakr (ra), Umar (ra) and Usman (ra), but I never heard any one of them reciting Bismillahir-Rahmanir-Rahim loudly." [Muslim]

Abda narrated: 'Umar ibn Khattab (ra) used to recite loudly these words: *Subhanaka Allahumma wa bi hamdika wa tabarakasmuka wa ta'ala jadduka wa la ilaha ghairuka.* Qatada informed in writing that Anas bin Malik (ra) had narrated to him: I observed prayer behind the Messenger of Allah (saws) and Abu Bakr and Umar and 'Usman. They started (loud recitation) with: Al-hamdu lillahi Rabbil al-'Alamin [All Praise is due to Allah, the Lord of the worlds] and did not recite Bismillahir- Rahmanir-Rahim (loudly) at the beginning of the recitation or at the end of it.

سُبْحَانَكَ اللَّهُمَّ وَبِحَمْدِكَ تَبَارَكَ اسْمُكَ وَتَعَالَى جَدُّكَ وَلاَ إِلَهَ غَيْرُكَ

[Glory and praise be to You, O Allah! Blessed be Your Name, and exalted be Your Majesty, and there is no God but You.]. [Muslim]

Abu Sa'id Al Khudri (ra) narrated: When Allah's Messenger (saws) stood for Salat during the night, he would say the Takbir (Allahu Akbar), then say: (*Subhanaka Allahumma wa bihamdika wa Tabarakasmuka wa Ta'ala Jadduka wa la ilaha ghairuk.*) 'Glorious You are O Allah, and with Your praise, and blesses is Your Name, and exalted is Your majesty, and none has the right to be worshipped but You' Then he would say: (*A'uzu Bilahi As-Sami'il-Alimi min Ash-Shaitanir-Rajimi, min Hamzihi Wa Nafkhihi wa Nafsihi.*) 'Allah is undoubtedly the greatest.' (Allahu Akbaru Kabira). Then he would say: 'I seek refuge in Allah the All-Hearing, the All-Knowing, from the cursed Shaitan, from his madness, his arrogance, and his poetry.' [Tirmizi]

Placing the right hand on the left

Wa'il bin Hujr (ra) reported: He saw the Messenger of Allah (saws) raising his hands at the time of beginning the prayer and reciting *takbir*, and according to Hammam (the narrator), the hands were lifted opposite to ears. He (saws) then wrapped his hands in his cloth and placed his right hand over his left hand. And when he (saws) was about to bow down, he (saws) brought out his hands from the cloth, and then lifted them, and then recited *takbir* and bowed down, and when (he came back to the erect position) he (saws) recited:" سَمِعَ اللَّهُ لِمَنْ حَمِدَهُ Allah listened to him who praised Him" And when he (saws) prostrated, he (saws) prostrated between his two palms. [Muslim]

The Tashah-hud in the Prayer

It was narrated that `Abdullah b. Mas`ud (ra) said: While observing prayer behind the Messenger of Allah (saws) we used to recite: Peace be upon Allah, peace be upon so and so. One day the Messenger of Allah (saws) said to us: Verily Allah is Himself Peace. When any one of you sit during the prayer, he should say:

التَّحِيَّاتُ لِلَّهِ وَالصَّلَوَاتُ وَالطَّيِّبَاتُ السَّلاَمُ عَلَيْكَ أَيُّهَا النَّبِيُّ وَرَحْمَةُ اللَّهِ وَبَرَكَاتُهُ السَّلاَمُ عَلَيْنَا وَعَلَى عِبَادِ اللَّهِ الصَّالِحِينَ

(*All services rendered by words, by acts of worship, and all good things are due to Allah. Peace be upon you, O Prophet, and Allah's mercy and blessings. Peace be upon us and upon Allah's upright servants*), for when he says this it reaches every upright servant in the heavens and the earth. (And say further):

أَشْهَدُ أَنْ لاَ إِلَهَ إِلاَّ اللَّهُ وَأَشْهَدُ أَنَّ مُحَمَّدًا عَبْدُهُ وَرَسُولُ

(*I testify that there is no god but Allah and I testify that Muhammad is His servant and Messenger*). Then he may choose any supplication which pleases him and offer it. [Muslim]

Sending Salat upon the Prophet (saws)

It was narrated that Abu Mas'ud Al-Ansari said: We were sitting in the company of Sa'id bin 'Ubida when the Messenger of Allah (saws) came to us. Bashir bin S'ad said: Allah has commanded us to bless you. Messenger of Allah (saws)! But how should we bless you? He (the narrator) said: The Messenger of Allah (saws) kept quiet (and we were so much perturbed over his silence) that we wished we had not asked him. The Messenger of Allah (saws) then said: (For blessing me) say:

اللَّهُمَّ صَلِّ عَلَى مُحَمَّدٍ وَعَلَى آلِ مُحَمَّدٍ كَمَا صَلَّيْتَ عَلَى آلِ إِبْرَاهِيمَ وَبَارِكْ عَلَى مُحَمَّدٍ وَعَلَى آلِ مُحَمَّدٍ كَمَا بَارَكْتَ عَلَى آلِ إِبْرَاهِيمَ فِي الْعَالَمِينَ إِنَّكَ حَمِيدٌ مَجِيدٌ . وَالسَّلاَمُ كَمَا قَدْ عَلِمْتُمْ " .

"O Allah, bless Muhammad and the members of his household as Thou didst bless the members of Ibrahim's household. Grant favours to Muhammad and the members of his household as Thou didst grant favours to the members of the household of Ibrahim in the world. Thou art indeed Praiseworthy and Glorious"; and salutation as you know. [Muslim]

It was narrated from Abu Hurairah (ra) that the Messenger of Allah (saws) said: "Whoever sends *Salat* upon me once, Allah will send *Salat* upon him tenfold." [Muslim] Ali (ra) said: "The Messenger of Allah (saws) said: The miser is the one who, when I am mentioned in his presence, does not send prayers upon me." [Tirmizi]

Narrated `Abdur-Rahman bin Abi Laila: Ka`b bin Ujrah met me and said, "Shall I not give you a present I got from the Prophet (saws)?" `Abdur- Rahman said, "Yes, give it to me." I said, "We asked Allah's Messenger (saws) saying, 'O Allah's Messenger (saws)! How should one (ask Allah to) send blessings on you, the members of the family, for Allah has taught us how to salute you (in the prayer)?' He said, 'Say: O Allah! Send Your Mercy on Muhammad and on the family of Muhammad, as You sent Your Mercy on Ibrahim and on the family of Ibrahim, for You are the Most Praise-worthy, the Most Glorious. O Allah! Send Your Blessings on Muhammad and the family of Muhammad, as You sent your Blessings on Ibrahim and on the family of Ibrahim, for You are the Most Praise-worthy, the Most Glorious.' [Bukhari]

Saying 'Rabbana wa Lakal-hamd'

It was narrated from Abu Hurairah (ra) that the Messenger of Allah (saws) said: When the *Imam* says: *'Sami'a Allahu liman hamidah* (Allah hears those who praise Him),' *say: 'Allahumma Rabbana lakal hamd* (O Allah, our Lord, to You be praise).' If a person's saying coincides that with the angels his previous sins will be forgiven. [Muslim]

Raful Yadain before and after bowing

'Raful' means to raise and 'Yadain' means two hands. According to authentic Hadiths, Raful-Yadain is a Sunnah of the Prophet (saws).

Hadith: It was narrated from Salim bin 'Abdullah that Ibn 'Umar (ra) said: When the Messenger of Allah (saws) stood up to offer Salat, he would raise his hands until they were level with his shoulders, then he (saws) would say the Takbir. When he (saws) wanted to bow, he (saws) did that, and when he (saws) rose from bowing he (saws) did that, but he (saws) did not do that when he (saws) lifted his head from prostrating. [Muslim]

Hadith: It was narrated from Abu Salamah that Abu Hurairah (ra) used to say the *Takbir* in his prayer every time he moved up or down. We said: O Abu Hurairah, what is this Takbir? He said: It is how the Messenger of Allah (saws) offered Prayers. [Muslim]

Hadith: Abdullah ibn 'Umar (ra) narrated: I saw that whenever Allah's Messenger (saws) stood for the prayer, he used to raise both his hands up to the shoulders, and used to do the same on saying the Takbir for bowing and on raising his head from it and used to say, "Sami'allaahu liman hamidah". But he did not do that (i.e. raising his hands) in prostrations. [Bukhari]

Hadith: It was narrated whenever Ibn 'Umar (ra) started the prayer with Takbir, he used to raise his hands: whenever he bowed, he used to raise his hands (before bowing) and also used to raise his hands on saying, "Sami'allahu liman hamidah", and he used to do the same on rising from the second rak'aat (for the 3rd rak'aat). Ibn 'Umar (ra) said: The Prophet (saws) used to do the same. [Bukhari]

Use of Siwak (Tooth- Stick) is a Sunnah

It was narrated from Abu Hurairah (ra) that the Prophet (saws) said: Were it not that it would be too difficult for the believers - according to the Hadith of (one of the narrators) Zuhair: "for my Ummah" - I would have commanded them to use the Siwak for every Salat. [Muslim]

It was narrated from A1-Miqdam bin Shuraih that his father said: I asked 'Aishah (ra): With what did the Prophet (saws) start when he entered his house? She said: With the Siwak. [Muslim] It was narrated that Hudhaifah (ra) said: When the Messenger of Allah (saws) got up to perform Tahajjud, he cleaned his mouth with the Siwak. [Muslim]

Praying with full focus and humbleness in it (*khushu*)

Khushu refers to humbleness, submissiveness, and gentleness within heart due to the consciousness of Allah's Greatness and Dignity while offering Salat. We must be attentive with concentration and we have to perform salat in a calm and unhurried manner, when prostrating and bowing, between the two prostrations, and after bowing when standing up again. Allah SWT says in the Qur'an (interpretation of meaning):

Successful indeed are the believers: those who humble themselves in prayer; (Ch 23:1-2)

Hadith: As narrated by Abu Huraira (ra): One day the Messenger of Allah (saws) led the prayer. Then turning (towards his Companions) he (saws) said: O you man, why don't you say your prayer well? Does the observer of prayer not see how he is performing the prayer, for he performs it for himself? By Allah, I see behind me as I see in front of me. [Muslim]

Hadith: Aishah (ra) narrated: I asked the Messenger of Allah (saws) about looking around during the Salat. He said: 'It is a portion which the Shaitan snatches during a man's prayer.' [Tirmizi]

Hadith: Abu Huraira (ra) reported: People should avoid lifting their eyes towards the sky while supplicating in prayer, otherwise their eyes would be snatched away. [Muslim]

Hadith: Narrated Abu Huraira (ra): The Prophet (saws) offered a prayer, and (after finishing) he said, "Satan came in front of me trying persistently to divert my attention from the prayer, but Allah gave me the strength to over-power him." [Bukhari]

While in Prayer, we should not think of anything outside of the prayer; rather our focus should be on the prayer, humbling ourselves before Allah SWT. One may try to achieve khushu by means of the following:

- For non-Arabs like us who do not know the meanings of the Qur'an or the azkaar, the best thing is to learn the meaning of verses of the Qur'an as much as possible, meaning of other azkaar like tasahud, salah etc. Then only one will not miss out the virtue of reflecting upon the meanings.

- Bear in mind that you are standing in front of Allah SWT in prayer. Allah can see you and is watching you as you pray. Bukhari and Muslim narrated from 'Abdullah ibn 'Umar (ra) that the Messenger of Allah (saws) saw some sputum on the wall of the Qiblah. He scratched it then he turned to the people and said: "If one of you is praying, let him not spit in front of him, for Allah is in front of him when he prays."

- Be attentive to make your prayer perfect so that reward of the prayer is not missed. 'Ammaar ibn Yaasir (ra) said: I heard the Messenger of Allah (saws) say: "A person may offer a prayer and nothing of it is recorded for him except one tenth of it, one ninth of it, one eighth of it, one seventh of it, one sixth of it, one fifth of it, one quarter of it, one third of it, or half of it." [Musnad Ahmad]

- Do not wander while praying. The Prophet (saws) said: "Allah is turning towards His slave so long as he does not look around, so when you pray, do not look around." [Musnad Ahmad]

- We should think that this could be my last prayer. Ad-Daylami narrated from Anas (ra:) The Prophet (saws) said: "Remember death when you pray, for if a man remembers death when he prays, he will strive to make his prayer good. Pray the prayer of a man who does not think that he will ever pray another prayer, and beware of any matter that may require you to offer an apology." [Musnad al-Firdaus]

Worst of thieves is the one who steals his prayer

Yahya related to me from Malik from Yahya ibn Said from an-Numan ibn Murra that the Messenger of Allah (saws) said, "What about drunkenness, stealing and adultery?" That was before anything had been revealed about them. They said, "Allah and His Messenger (saws) know best." He (saws) said, "They are excesses and in them is a punishment. And the worst of thieves is the one who steals his prayer." They said, "How does he steal his prayer, Messenger of Allah (saws)?" He (saws) replied, "He does not perform ruku or sajda properly." [Muwatta Imam Malik]

At the completion of salat

It was narrated that Jabir bin Samurah (ra) said: When we prayed with the Messenger of Allah (saws) we used to say (at the completion of prayers): *'As-salamu 'alaikum wa rahmatullah, as-salamu 'alaikum wa rahmatullah* (Peace be upon you and the mercy of Allah. Peace be upon you and the mercy of Allah), and he gestured with his hand to either side. The Messenger of Allah (saws) said: Why do you gesture with your hands as if they were the tails of restless horses? Rather it is sufficient for one of you to put his hand on his thigh then say the *Salam* to his brothers to his right and left. [Muslim]

Prolong time before bowing and in between two sajda

Sabit reported it on the authority of Anas (ra): While leading you in prayer I do not shorten anything in the prayer. I pray as I saw the Messenger of Allah (ra) leading us. He (Sabit) said: "Anas (ra) used to do that which I do not see you doing; when he lifted his head from bowing he stood up (so long) that one would say: He has forgotten (to bow down in prostration). And when he lifted his head from prostration, he stayed in that position, till someone would say: He has forgotten (to bow down in prostration for the second sajda)." [Muslim]

Reciting the Quran while bowing and prostrating

Ali bin Abi Talib (ra) reported: The Messenger of Allah (saws) forbade me to recite (the Qur'an) in a state of bowing and prostration. [Muslim]

What is to be said while bowing and prostrating

Abu Huraira (ra) reported: The Messenger of Allah (saws) said: The nearest a servant comes to his Lord is when he is prostrating himself, so make dua, supplication (in this state). [Muslim]

Huzaifah ibn al-Yaman (ra) reported: The Messenger of Allah (saws) said three times while bowing in prayer, "سُبْحَانَ رَبِّيَ الْعَظِيمِ *Glory to my Lord, the Almighty,*" and he said three times while prostrating in prayer, "سُبْحَانَ رَبِّيَ الْأَعْلَى *Glory to my Lord, the Most High.*" [Sunan Ibn Majah]

Ibn Mas'ud (ra) reported: The Prophet (saws) said, "When one of you bows in prayer, let him say three times in his bowing: سُبْحَانَ رَبِّيَ الْعَظِيمِ. He will have completed his bowing and that is the least of it. Let him say three times in his prostration: سُبْحَانَ رَبِّيَ الْأَعْلَى. He will have completed his prostration and that is the least of it." [Sunan al-Tirmizi]

Huzaifah (ra) reported: He prayed one night with the Messenger of Allah (saws) and he heard him when he announced the opening exaltation, "Allah is the greatest, O possessor of power, dominion, grandeur, and might." The Prophet (saws) said in his bowing, "سُبْحَانَ رَبِّيَ الْعَظِيمِ." When he raised his head from bowing, he said, "*To my Lord is all praise. To my Lord is all praise,*" and in his prostration, "سُبْحَانَ رَبِّيَ الْأَعْلَى" and between the two prostrations, "رَبِّي اغْفِرْ لِي رَبِّي اغْفِرْ لِي *Lord, forgive me. Lord, forgive me.*" The Prophet's (saws) standing, bowing, when he raised his head from bowing, his prostrations, and between his prostrations were nearly the same length. [Sunan an-Nasa'i]

Ibn Abbas (ra) reported: The Prophet peace and blessings be upon him, used to say between the two prostrations, "اللَّهُمَّ اغْفِرْ لِي وَارْحَمْنِي وَاجْبُرْنِي وَاهْدِنِي وَارْزُقْنِي *O Allah, forgive me, have mercy on me, restore me, guide me, and provide for me.*" [Sunan at-Tirmizi]

Abu Huraira (ra) reported: The Messenger of Allah (saws) used to say while prostrating himself: O Lord, forgive me all my sins, small and great, first and last, open and secret اللَّهُمَّ اغْفِرْ لِي ذَنْبِي كُلَّهُ دِقَّهُ وَجِلَّهُ وَأَوَّلَهُ وَآخِرَهُ وَعَلاَنِيَتَهُ وَسِرَّهُ[Muslim]

A'isha (ra) reported that the Messenger of Allah (saws) used to pronounce while bowing and prostrating himself: All Glorious, All Holy, Lord of the Angels and the Spirit. سُبُّوحٌ قُدُّوسٌ رَبُّ الْمَلاَئِكَةِ وَالرُّوحِ [Muslim]

Prostrating with the forehead and the nose

Abu Humaid As-Sa'idi (ra) narrated: "When the Prophet (saws) would prostrate, he placed his nose and his forehead on the ground, and he held his forearms away from his sides, and he placed his hands parallel to his shoulders." [Tirmizi]

A man should place his face between hands when he prostrates

Abu Ishaq narrated: I said to Al-Bara bin Azib (ra): "Where would the Prophet (saws) place his face when he prostrated?" He said: "Between his hands." [Tirmizi]

Prostrating on seven bones

Al-Abbas bin Abdul-Muttalib (ra) narrated that he heard Allah's Messenger (saws) saying: "When the worshipper prostrates with him: His face, his hands, his knees, and his feet." [Tirmizi]

Ibn Abbas (ra) narrated: "The Prophet (saws) ordered that one prostrate on seven bones and that he not gather his hair nor his garment." [Tirmizi]

The Sunnah of sitting in prayer

Tawus reported: We asked Ibn Abbas (ra) about sitting on the two feet in prayer and he said, "It is the Sunnah." We said to him, "We see it as difficult for a man to do." Ibn Abbas (ra) said, "Rather, it is the Sunnah of your Prophet, peace and blessings be upon him." [Muslim]

Abdullah ibn al-Zubayr (ra) reported: When the Messenger of Allah (saws) would sit in prayer, he would place his left foot between his thigh and shin, stretch his right foot, place his left hand on his left know, place his right hand on his right thigh, and point with his finger. In another narration, Abdullah (ra) said: The gaze of the Prophet (saws) would not go beyond his index finger. [Muslim]

Wa'il bin Hujr (ra) said: I arrived in Al-Madinah and I said, 'Let me look at the Salat of Allah's Messenger (saws).' When he (saws) sat - meaning for At-Tashahhud – he (saws) spread his left foot, and placed his left hand - meaning on his left thigh - and held his right foot erect. [Tirmizi]

Reciting the Qur'an in a prayer

Abdulla Ibn 'Abbas (ra) reported: The word of (Allah) Great and Glorious: *'And utter not thy prayer loudly, nor be low in it'* (Ch 17: 110) was revcaled as the Messenger of Allah (saws) was hiding himself in Makkah. When he (saws) led his Companions in prayer he raised his voice (while reciting the) Qur'an. And when the polytheists heard that, they reviled the Qur'an and Him Who revealed it and him who brought it. Upon this Allah SWT, said to His Apostle (saws): Utter not thy prayer so loudly that the polytheists may hear thy recitation and (recite it) not so low that it may be inaudible to your Companions. Make them hear the Qur'an, but do not recite it loudly and seek a (middle) way between these. Recite between loud and low tone. [Muslim]

Note: This instruction was discontinued under the changed conditions at Al-Madinah.

Moderation in prostration

Narrated 'Abdullah bin Malik Ibn Buhaina (ra): When the Prophet (saws) prayed, he used to separate his arms from his body so widely that the whiteness of his armpits was visible. [Bukhari]

Anas (ra) reported: The Messenger of Allah (saws) said: Observe moderation in prostration, and let none of you stretch out his forearms (on the ground) like a dog. [Muslim]

It was reported that Al-Bira' b. 'Azib (ra) said: The Messenger of Allah (saws) said, "When you prostrate yourself, place the palms of your hands on the ground and raise your elbows." [Muslim]

The virtue of prostration

Rabi'a bin Ka'b (ra) said: I was with Allah's Messenger (saws) one night and I brought him water and what he required. He (saws) said to me: Ask (anything you like). I said: I ask your company in Paradise. He (the Holy Prophet saws) said: Or anything else besides it. I said: That is all (what I require). He (saws) said: Then help me to achieve this for you by devoting yourself often to prostration. [Muslim]

Salat starts with *Allahu Akbar* and ends with *Assalamu aalaikum wa rahmatullah*

A'isha (ra) reported: The Messenger of Allah (saws) used to begin prayer with takbir (saying *Allahu Akbar*) and the recitation: "Praise be to Allah, the Lord of the Universe." When he bowed he neither kept his head up nor bent it down, but kept it between these extremes; when he raised his head after bowing he did not prostrate himself till he had stood erect; when he raised his head after prostration he did not prostrate himself again till he sat up. At the end of every two rak'ahs he recited the at-tahiyya; and he used to place his left foot flat (on the ground) and raise up the right; he prohibited the devil's way of sitting on the heels, and he forbade people to spread out their arms like a wild beast. And he used to finish the prayer with the *taslim (Assalamu alaikum wa rahmatullah).* According to the report of Ibn Numair from Abu Khalid: "And *he forbade 'Aqibi Saitan."* [Muslim]

Prophet Muhammad (saws) said, "The key to prayer is purification, its opening is to say Allahu Akbar, and its closing is to say al-salamu' alaykum." [Abu Dawud, Sunan Ibn Majah, Tirmizi, Musnad Ahmad]

Placing palms on thighs

Ali bin 'Abual-Rahman al-Mu'awi reported: 'Abdullah b. Umar (ra) saw me playing with pebbles during prayer. After finishing the prayer, he forbade me (to do it) and said: Do as the Messenger of Allah (saws) used to do. I said: How did Allah's Messenger (saws) do? He said that he (saws) sat at tasahhud, placed his right palm on the right thigh and closed all his fingers and pointed with the help of finger next to the thumb, and placed his left palm on his left thigh. [Muslim]

Du'a between the tashahhud and the taslim

Abu Huraira (ra) reported: The Messenger of Allah (saws) said: When any one of you utters tashah-hud (in prayer) he must seek refuge with Allah from four (trials) and should thus say: "O Allah! I seek refuge with Thee from the torment of the Hell, from the torment of the grave, from the trial of life and death and from the evil of the trial of Masih al-Dajjal." [Muslim]

It was narrated from Abu Bakr (ra) that he said to the Messenger of Allah (saws): Teach me a du'a that I may say in my prayer. He (saws) said: 'Say: O Allah, I have wronged myself greatly and no one forgives sins but you, grant me forgiveness from you and have mercy on me for you are the Forgiver the Most Merciful. [Bukhari, Muslim, Tirmizi, Musnad Ahmad]. Arabic dua is as follows:

اللَّهُمَّ إِنِّي ظَلَمْتُ نَفْسِي ظُلْمًا كَثِيرًا وَلَا يَغْفِرُ الذُّنُوبَ إِلَّا أَنْتَ فَاغْفِرْ لِي مَغْفِرَةً مِنْ عِنْدِكَ وَارْحَمْنِي إِنَّكَ أَنْتَ الْغَفُورُ الرَّحِيمُ

Remembrance after the prayer

It was narrated that Ibn 'Abbas (ra) said: We used to know that the prayer of the Messenger of Allah (saws) had ended from the Takbir (Allahu akbar). [Bukhari, Muslim]

Sauban (ra) reported: When the Messenger of Allah (saws) finished his prayer, he (saws) begged forgiveness three times and said: *O Allah! Thou art Peace, and peace comes from Thee; Blessed art Thou, O Possessor of Glory and Honour.*

اللَّهُمَّ أَنْتَ السَّلَامُ وَمِنْكَ السَّلَامُ تَبَارَكْتَ يَا ذَا الْجَلَالِ وَالْإِكْرَامِ

(Allahumma Antas-Salam wa minkas-salam. Tabarakta ya Dhal-jalali wal- ikram.)

Walid reported: I said to Auza'i: How is the seeking of forgiveness? He replied: You should say: I beg forgiveness from Allah, I beg forgiveness from Allah أَسْتَغْفِرُ اللهَ [Muslim]

Mughira bin Shu'ba (ra) wrote to Mu'awiya (ra): When the Messenger of Allah (saws) finished the prayer and pronounced salutation he uttered (this supplication):" *There is no god but Allah. He is alone, Who has no partner. To Him belongs the sovereignty and to Him praise is due and He is Potent over every. thing. O Allah! no one can withhold what Thou givest, or give what Thou withholdest, and the riches cannot avail a wealthy person with Thee.*" [Muslim]. In Arabic, it is as follows:

لَا إِلَهَ إِلاَّ اللَّهُ وَحْدَهُ لَا شَرِيكَ لَهُ لَهُ الْمُلْكُ وَلَهُ الْحَمْدُ وَهُوَ عَلَى كُلِّ شَيْءٍ قَدِيرٌ اللَّهُمَّ لَا مَانِعَ لِمَا أَعْطَيْتَ وَلَا مُعْطِيَ لِمَا مَنَعْتَ وَلَا يَنْفَعُ ذَا الْجَدِّ مِنْكَ الْجَدُّ

Abu Huraira (ra) reported Allah's Messenger (saws) as saying: If anyone extols Allah after every prayer thirty-three times (*Subhan Allah*), and praises Allah thirty-three times (*al hamdulillah*), and declares His Greatness thirty-three times (*Allahu akbar*), ninety-nine times in all, and says to complete a hundred: *There is no god but Allah, having no partner with Him, to Him belongs sovereignty and to Him is praise due, and He is Potent over everything*, لاَ إِلَهَ إِلاَّ اللَّهُ وَحْدَهُ لاَ شَرِيكَ لَهُ لَهُ الْمُلْكُ وَلَهُ الْحَمْدُ وَهُوَ عَلَى كُلِّ شَىْءٍ قَدِيرٌ his sins will be forgiven even If these are as abundant as the foam of the sea. [Muslim]

Between the opening takbir and the recitation of the Qur'an

Abu Huraira (ra) reported that Allah's Messenger (saws) used to observe, silence for a short while between the takbir (at the time of opening the prayer) and the recitation of the Qur'an. I said to him: O Messenger of Allah (saws), for whom I would give my father and mother in ransom, what do you recite during your period of silence between the takbir and the recitation? He said: I say (these words):" *O Allah, remove my sins from me as Thou hast removed the East from the West. O Allah purify me from sins as a white garment is purified from filth. O Allah! wash away my sins with snow, water, and ice.*" [Muslim] In Arabic it is as follows:

اللَّهُمَّ بَاعِدْ بَيْنِي وَبَيْنَ خَطَايَاىَ كَمَا بَاعَدْتَ بَيْنَ الْمَشْرِقِ وَالْمَغْرِبِ اللَّهُمَّ نَقِّنِي مِنْ خَطَايَاىَ كَمَا يُنَقَّى الثَّوْبُ الأَبْيَضُ مِنَ الدَّنَسِ اللَّهُمَّ اغْسِلْنِي مِنْ خَطَايَاىَ بِالثَّلْجِ وَالْمَاءِ وَالْبَرَدِ

Anas (ra) narrated: A man came breathless and entered the row of worshippers and said: *Praise be to Allah, much praised and blessed.* When the Messenger of Allah (saws) finished the prayer he (saws) said: Who amongst you uttered these words? The people remained silent. He (saws) said: Who amongst you uttered these words? He (saws) said nothing wrong. Then a man said: I came and had a difficulty in breathing, so I uttered them. He (saws) replied: I saw twelve angels facing one another as to who will take them up (to Allah). [Muslim]. In Arabic, it is as follows:

الْحَمْدُ لِلَّهِ حَمْدًا كَثِيرًا طَيِّبًا مُبَارَكًا فِيهِ

Gates of heaven opened for a good supplication (Du'a)
Ibn 'Umar (ra) reported: While we were praying with the Messenger of Allah (saws), one among the people said: *Allah is truly Great, praise be to Allah in abundance. Glory be to Allah in the morning and the evening.* The Messenger of Allah (saws) said: Who uttered such and such a word? A person among the people said: It is I, Messenger of Allah (saws) (who have recited these words). He (saws) said: It (its utterance) surprised me, for the doors of heaven were opened for it. Ibn 'Umar (ra) said: I have not abandoned them (these words) since I heard the Messenger of Allah (saws) saying this. [Muslim]. In Arabic, it is as follows:

اللَّهُ أَكْبَرُ كَبِيرًا وَالْحَمْدُ لِلَّهِ كَثِيرًا وَسُبْحَانَ اللَّهِ بُكْرَةً وَأَصِيلاً

The virtue of reciting the Qur'an in prayer and learning it
Abu Huraira (ra) reported Allah's Messenger (saws) as saying: Would any one of you like, when he returns to his family, to find there three large, fat, pregnant she-camels? We said: Yes. Upon this he (saws) said: Three verses that one of you recites in his prayer are better for him than three large, fat, pregnant she-camels. [Muslim]

Superiority of the Fajr and Asr prayer

Narrated Ibn 'Umar (ra): Allah's Messenger (saws) said, "Whoever misses the Asr prayer (intentionally) then it is as if he lost his family and property." [Bukhari]

As narrated Qais: Jarir (ra) said: We were with the Prophet (saws) and he looked at the moon: full-moon and said, "Certainly you will see your Lord as you see this moon and you will have no trouble in seeing Him. So if you can avoid missing (through sleep or business, etc.) a prayer before the sunrise (Fajr) and a prayer before sunset (Asr), you must do so." He (saws) then recited Allah's Statement: *And celebrate the praises Of your Lord before the rising of the sun and before (its) setting.* (Ch 50:39) Isma'il said, "Offer those prayers and do not miss them." [Bukhari]

As narrated by Abu Huraira (ra) that Allah's Messenger (saws) said: Angels come to you in succession by night and day and all of them get together at the time of the Fajr and Asr prayers. Those who have passed the night with you (or stayed with you) ascend (to the Heaven) and Allah asks them, though He knows everything about you well, "In what state did you leave my slaves?" The angels reply: "When we left them they were praying and when we reached them, they were praying." [Bukhari]

Sleeping before the Isha prayer

Narrated Abu Barza (ra): Allah's Messenger (saws) disliked to sleep before the Isha' prayer and to talk after it. [Bukhari]

Reward of Fajr and Isha

It was narrated that Abu Hurairah (ra) said that the Messenger of Allah (saws) said: "The most burdensome prayers for the hypocrites are the Isha' prayer and the Fajr prayer. If only they knew what (reward) there is in them, they would come to them even if they had to crawl." [Sunan Ibn Majah]

It is recommended to pray Asr early

Anas bin Malik (ra) reported: We used to offer the 'Asr prayer, then one would go to Quba' and reach there and the sun would be still high. [Muslim]

Salat facing the Qiblah

Narrated Anas bin Malik (ra): Allah's Messenger (saws) said, "Whoever prays like us and faces our Qibla and eats our slaughtered animals is a Muslim and is under Allah's and His Apostle's protection. So do not betray Allah by betraying those who are in His protection." [Bukhari]

Bara' bin `Azib (ra) narrated: Allah's Messenger (saws) prayed facing Baitul-Maqdis for sixteen or seventeen months but he loved to face the Ka`ba (at Makkah) so Allah revealed: "Verily, We have seen the turning of your face to the heaven!" (Ch 2:144) So the Prophet (saws) faced the Ka`ba and the fools amongst the people namely the Jews said, "What has turned them from their Qibla (Baitul-Maqdis) which they formerly observed?" (Allah revealed): Say: *To Allah belongs the East and the*

West. He guides whom he will to a straight path. (Ch 2:142) A man prayed with the Prophet saws (facing the Ka`ba) and went out. He saw some of the Ansar praying the Asr prayer with their faces towards Baitul-Maqdis, he said, "I bear witness that I prayed with Allah's Messenger saws facing the Ka`ba." So all the people turned their faces towards the Ka`ba. [Bukhari]

Offering the prayers at the stated times

Narrated Abdullah (ra): I asked the Prophet (saws), "Which deed is the dearest to Allah?" He (saws) replied, "To offer the prayers at their early stated fixed times." I asked, "What is the next (in goodness)?" He (saws) replied, "To be good and dutiful to your parents." I again asked, "What is the next (in goodness)?" He (saws) replied, "To participate in Jihad (religious fighting) in Allah's cause." `Abdullah (ra) added, "I asked only that much and if I had asked more, the Prophet (saws) would have told me more." [Bukhari]

Salat after returning from a journey

Narrated Jabir bin Abdullah (ra): I went to the Prophet (saws) in the mosque (the sub-narrator Mas`ar thought that Jabir had said, "In the forenoon.") He ordered me to pray two rak`at. He owed me some money and he repaid it to me and gave more than what was due to me. [Bukhari]

In severe heat, offer zuhr prayers when it becomes (a bit) cooler

Narrated Abu Huraira (ra): The Prophet (saws) said, "In very hot weather delay the Zuhr prayer till it becomes (a bit) cooler because the severity of heat is from the raging of the Hell-fire. The Hell-fire of Hell complained to its Lord saying: O Lord! My parts are eating (destroying) one another. So Allah allowed it to take two breaths, one in the winter and the other in the summer. The breath in the summer is at the time when you feel the severest heat and the breath in the winter is at the time when you feel the severest cold." [Bukhari]

Whatever direction to pray voluntary prayers on mount

It was narrated from Salim that his father said: "The Messenger of Allah (saws) used to pray voluntary prayers (Usabbih) while riding his mount, facing whatever direction it was facing, and he would pray Witr likewise, but he would not offer the prescribed prayers (Fard Salat) on it." [Sunan an-Nasai]

No voluntary prayers after fajr and asr

Abu Sa'id al-Khudri (ra) reported: The Messenger of Allah (saws) said, "There is no prayer after the morning prayer until the sun has risen, and there is no prayer after the afternoon prayer until the sun has set." [Bukhari, Muslim]
Narrated Ibn 'Umar (ra): I pray as I saw my companions praying. I do not forbid praying at any time during the day or night except at sunset and sunrise. [Bukhari]

The prayer of the one sitting down

Abdullah bin Buraidah said: 'Imran b. Hussain (ra) asked the Prophet (saws) about the prayer a man offers in sitting condition. He (saws)replied: His prayer in standing condition is better than his prayer in sitting condition, and his prayer in sitting condition is half the prayer he offers in standing condition, and his prayer in lying condition is half the prayer he offers in sitting condition. [Sunan Abu Dawud]

Prayer of a sick person

Yahya related to me from Malik from Nafi that Abdullah ibn Umar (ra) used to say, "When a sick man is unable to prostrate, he should motion with his head, and not raise anything to his forehead." [Muwatta Imam Malik]

Reciting aloud in as-subh prayer

Ibn 'Abbas (ra) reported: The Messenger of Allah (saws) neither recited the Qur'an to the Jinn nor did he see them. The Messenger of Allah (saws) went out with some of his Companions with the intention of going to the bazaar of 'Ukaz and there had been (at that time) obstructions between Satans and the news from the Heaven, and there were flung flames upon them. So Satan went back to their people and they said: What has happened to you? They said: There have been created obstructions between us and the news from the Heaven. And there have been flung upon us flames. They said: It cannot happen but for some (important) event. So they traversed the eastern parts of the earth and the western parts and find out why is it that there have been created obstructions between us and the news from the Heaven. So they went forth and traversed the easts of the earth and its wests. Some of them proceeded towards Tihama and that is a Nakhl towards the bazaar of 'Ukaz and he (the Holy Prophet saws) was leading his Companions in the morning prayer. So when they heard the Qur'an, they listened to it attentively and said: It is this which has caused obstruction between us and news from the Heaven. They went back to their people and said: O our people, we have heard a strange Qur'an which directs us to the right path; so we affirm our faith in it and we would never associate anyone with our Lord. And Allah, the Exalted and Glorious, revealed to His Apostle Muhammad (saws). "It has been revealed to me that a party of Jinn listened to it." (Ch 72:1). [Muslim]

The recitation for Zuhr and Asr

Abu Qatada (ra) reported: The Messenger of Allah (saws) led us in prayer and recited in the first two rak'ahs of the noon and afternoon prayers Surat al-Fatiha and two (other) surahs. And he would sometimes recite loud enough for us the verses. He (saws) would prolong the first rak'ah more than the second. And he acted similarly in the morning prayer. Abu Qatada reported it on the authority of his father. [Muslim]
The Messenger of Allah (saws) would recite in the first two rak'ahs of the noon and afternoon prayers the opening chapter of the Book (Surah al-Fatiha) and another surah. He would sometimes recite loud enough to

make audible to us the verse and would recite in the last two rak'ahs Surat al-Faitiha (only). [Muslim]

Salat in congregation

Anas ibn Malik (ra) said: The Messenger of Allah (saws) said, "Whoever prays for forty days with the congregation, always being present for the first takbeer, it will be written that he will be safe from two things: he will be safe from the Fire and safe from hypocrisy. [Tirmizi]

While entering the mosques etc. one should start with the right foot

Narrated `Aisha (ra): The Prophet (saws) used to start everything from the right (for good things) whenever it was possible in all his affairs; for example: in washing, combing or wearing shoes. [Bukhari]

One should offer two Rak'a (Tahayyat-al-Masjid) before sitting

Narrated Abu Qatada Al-Aslami (ra): Allah's Messenger (saws) said, "If anyone of you enters a mosque, he should pray two rak`at before sitting." [Bukhari, Muslim]

Narrated Jabir bin `Abdullah (ra): A person entered the mosque while the Prophet (saws) was delivering the Khutba on a Friday. The Prophet (saws) said to him, "Have you prayed?" The man replied in the negative. The Prophet (saws) said, "Get up and pray two rak`at." [Bukhari]

Yahya related to me from Malik from Abu'n Nadr, the slave of Umar ibn Ubaydullah, that Abu Salama ibn Abd ar-Rahman asked him, "Didn't I see your master sit down before praying after he had entered the mosque?" Abu'n-Nadr said, "By that he meant Umar ibn Ubaydullah, and he was finding fault with him for sitting down before praying after he had come into the mosque." Yahya said that Malik said, "It is good to do that but not obligatory." [Muwatta Imam Malik]

Prayer in congregation is one of the sunnah of guidance

Abdullah bin Mas'ud (ra) reported: I have seen the time when no one stayed away from prayer except a hypocrite, whose hypocrisy was well known, or a sick man, but if a sick man could walk between two persons (i.e. with the help of two persons with one on each side) he would come to prayer. And (further) said: The Messenger of Allah (saws) taught us the paths of right guidance, among which is prayer in the mosque in which the Azan is called. [Muslim]

Abu Huraira (ra) reported Allah's Messenger (saws) as saying: Prayer said in a congregation is twenty-five degrees more excellent than prayer said by a single person. [Muslim]

Abu Huraira (ra) reported: The Messenger of Allah (saws) found some people absenting from certain prayers and he (saws) said: I intend that I order (a) person to lead people in prayer, and then go to the persons who do not join the (congregational prayer) and then order their houses to be burnt by the bundles of fuel. If one amongst them were to know that he would find a fat fleshy bone he would attend the night prayer. [Muslim]

Abu Huraira (ra) reported Allah's Messenger (saws) as saying: The most burdensome prayers for the hypocrites are the night prayer and the morning prayer. If they were to know the blessings they have in store, they would have come to them, even though crawling, and I thought that I should order the prayer to be commenced and command a person to lead people in prayer, and I should then go along with some persons having a fagot of fuel with them to the people who have not attended the prayer (in congregation) and would burn their houses with fire. [Muslim]

Warning against missing congregational Asr prayer

Ibn Umar (ra) reported: The Messenger of Allah (saws) said, "Whoever misses the afternoon prayer, it is as if he had lost his family and his property." [Bukhari, Muslim]

One who hears azan should come to the Masjid

Abu Huraira (ra) reported: There came to the Messenger of Allah (saws) a blind man and said: Messenger of Allah (saws), I have no one to guide me to the mosque. He, therefore, asked Allah's Messenger's (saws) permission to offer prayer in his house. He (saws) granted him permission. Then when the man turned away he (saws) called him and said: Do you hear the call to prayer? He said: Yes. He (saws) said: Respond to it. [Muslim]

According to a version narrated by Abu Dawud and Ibn Majah he (saws) said: "I do not think there is any concession for you."

The virtue of praying 'Isha and Subh in congregation

Abd al-Rahman bin Abd 'Amrah reported: 'Usman bin 'Affan (ra) entered the mosque after evening prayer and sat alone. I also sat alone with him, so he said: O, son of my brother, I heard the Messenger of Allah (saws) say: He who observed the 'Isha' prayer in congregation, it was as if he prayed up to midnight, and he who prayed the morning prayer in congregation, it was as if he prayed the whole night. [Muslim]

Virtue of salat in congregation

Abu Huraira (ra) reported Allah's Messenger (saws) as saying: A man's prayer in congregation is more valuable than twenty degrees and some above them as compared with his prayer in his house and his market, for when he performs ablution doing it well, then goes out to the mosque, and he is impelled (to do so) only by (the love of congregational) prayer, he has no other objective before him but prayer. He does not take a step without being raised a degree for it and having a sin remitted for it, till he enters the mosque, and when he is busy in prayer after having entered the mosque. The angels continue to invoke blessing on him as long as he is in his place of worship. saying: O Allah, show him mercy, and pardon him! Accept his repentance (and the angels continue this supplication for him) so long as he does not do any harm in it, or as long as his ablution is not broken. [Muslim]

Jabir bin Abdullah (ra) reported: There were some plots vacant around the mosque. Banu Salama decided to shift (to this land) and come near the mosque (in Madinah). This (news) reached the Messenger of Allah (saws) and he said to them (Banu Salama): I have received (information) that you intend to shift near the mosque. They said: Yes, Messenger of Allah saws, we have taken this decision. Upon this he (saws) said: O Banu Salama, live in your houses, for your steps are recorded; live in your houses, for your steps are recorded. [Muslim]

Ata' bin Yasar reported, on the authority of Abu Huraira (ra), the Messenger of Allah (saws) as saying: He who went towards the mosque in the morning or evening, Allah would arrange a feast for him morning or evening in Paradise. [Muslim]

It is permissible to offer voluntary prayers in congregation

Anas b. Malik (ra) reported that his grandmother, Mulaika invited the Messenger of Allah (saws) to a dinner which she had prepared. He (saws) ate out of that and then said: Stand up so that I should observe prayer (in order to bless) you. Anas bin Malik (ra) said: I stood up on a mat (belonging to us) which had turned dark on account of its long use. I sprinkled water over it (in order to soften it), and the Messenger of Allah (saws) stood upon it, and I and an orphan formed a row behind him (saws) and the old woman was behind us, and the Messenger of Allah (saws) led us in two rak'ahs of prayer and then went back. [Muslim]

Straightening the rows during congregation

Abu Mas'ud (ra) narrated: The Messenger of Allah (saws) used to touch our shoulders in prayer and say: Keep straight, don't be irregular, for there would be dissension in your hearts. Let those who are the wisest and possessing intellect be closest to me, then those who are next to them, then those who are next to them. Abu Mas'ud (ra) said: Now-a-days there is much dissension amongst you. [Muslim]

It was narrated that Anas bin Malik (ra) said: "The Messenger of Allah (saws) said: 'Make your rows straight, for straightening the rows is part of the completion of the prayer." [Muslim]

Excellence of Azan and in the first row of salat

Abu Huraira (ra) reported: The Messenger of Allah (saws) said: If the people were to know what excellence is there in the Azan and in the first row, and they could not (get these opportunities) except by drawing lots, they would have definitely done that. And if they were to know what excellence lies in joining the prayer in the first takbir (prayer), they would have vied with one another. And if they were to know what excellence lies in the night prayer and morning prayer, they would have definitely come even if crawling (on their knees). [Muslim]

It was narrated from Abu Huraira (ra) that the Messenger of Allah (saws) said: The best rows for men are the first rows, and the worst ones the last ones, and the best rows for women are the last ones and the worst ones for them are the first ones. [Muslim]

Note: The above Hadith is applicable when there is no screening between men and women in a mosque. But nowadays, everywhere men and women have separate accommodation for prayer. So, in case of women, filling up the first row first without any gap will be applicable. This is the opinion of the scholars.

The prohibition of preceding the Imam

It was narrated that Abu Huraira (ra) said: The Messenger of Allah (saws) while teaching us (the principles of faith), said: Do not try to go ahead of the Imam, recite *takbir* when he recites it, and when he says: " وَلاَ الضَّالِّينَ Nor of those who err" you should say Amin, bow down when he bows down, and when he says: " سَمِعَ اللَّهُ لِمَنْ حَمِدَهُ Allah listens to him who praises Him" say: " اللَّهُمَّ رَبَّنَا لَكَ الْحَمْدُ O Allah, our Lord, to Thee be the praise". [Muslim]

Anas (ra) reported: The Messenger of Allah (saws) one day led us in the prayer. And when he completed the Prayer, he (saws) turned his face towards us and said: O People, I am your Imam, so do not precede me in bowing and prostration and in standing and turning (faces, i.e. in pronouncing salutation), for I see you in front of me and behind me, and then said: By Him in Whose hand is the life of Muhammad, if you could see what I see, you would have laughed little and wept much more. They said: What did you see, Messenger of Allah (saws)? He (saws) replied: (I saw) Paradise and Hell. [Muslim]

Abu Hurairah (ra) said: The Prophet Muhammad (saws) said: Does the one who raises his head before the Imam (does so) not fear that Allah may turn his head into the head of a donkey? [Muslim]

To offer Salat (prayers) in congregation while sitting

Narrated Anas bin Malik (ra): Allah's Apostle (saws) fell from a horse and got injured so he led the prayer sitting and we also prayed sitting. When he completed the prayer he (saws) said, "The Imam is to be followed; if he says Takbir then say Takbir, bow if he bows; raise your heads when he raises his head, when he says, 'Sami' Allahu Liman Hamida say, 'Rabbana lakal-hamd', and prostrate when he prostrates." [Bukhari]

If something happens in prayer during congregation

Abu Huraira (ra) reported: The Messenger of Allah (saws) said: Glorification of Allah (Subhan Allah) is for men and clapping of hands is meant for women (if something happens in prayer). Harmala added in his narration that Ibn Shihab told him: I saw some of the scholars glorifying Allah and making a gesture. [Muslim]

The command to keep close together in row

Jabir bin Samura (ra) reported: The Messenger of Allah (saws) came to us and said: "How is it that I see you lifting your hands like the tails of headstrong horses? Be calm in prayer." He (the narrator) said: He then again came to us and saw us (sitting) in circles. He (saws) said: "How is it that I see you in separate groups?" He (the narrator) said: He (saws) again came to us and said: "Why don't you draw yourselves up in rows as angels do in the presence of their Lord?" We said: Messenger of Allah (saws), how do the angels draw themselves up in rows in the presence of their Lord? He (saws) said: "They make the first rows complete and keep close together in the row." [Muslim]

The imam to make the prayer brief but complete

It was narrated that Abu Mas'ud Al-Ansari (ra) said: "A person came to the Messenger of Allah (saws) and said: I keep away from the morning prayer on account of such and such (a man), because; he keeps us so long. I never saw Allah's Messenger (saws) angrier when giving an exhortation than he was that day. He (saws) said: "O people, some of you are scaring people away. So whoever of you leads the people in prayer he must be brief, for behind him are the weak, the aged, and the people who have urgent needs." [Muslim]

Anas (ra) narrated: The Messenger of Allah (saws) would listen to the crying of a lad in the company of his mother, in prayer, and he would recite a short surah or a small surah. [Muslim] It was narrated that Anas bin Malik (ra) said: I have never prayed behind any Imam whose prayer was briefer yet more perfect that the Messenger of Allah (saws). [Muslim]

Beautiful voice when reciting the Qur'an

Abu Huraira (ra) reported this directly from the Messenger of Allah (saws): Allah has not listened to anything as He listens to a Prophet (saws) reciting the Qur'an in a sweet voice. [Muslim]

When should the people stand up to pray after Iqama

Abu Qatada (ra) reported: The Messenger of Allah (saws) said: When the Iqama is pronounced do not get up till you see me. Ibn Hatim was in doubt whether it was said:" When the Iqama is pronounced" or "When call is made". [Muslim]

Not to start a voluntary prayer if Iqamah is started

Abu Huraira (ra) reported the Messenger of Allah (saws) as saying: When the prayer commences then there is no prayer (valid), but the obligatory prayer. This hadith has been narrated by Warqa' with the same chain of transmitters. [Muslim]

The one who catches up with a rak`ah of the prayer

Narrated Abu Huraira (ra): Allah's Messenger (saws) said, "Whoever could get one rak`a of a prayer, (in its proper time) he has got the prayer." [Muslim, Bukhari]

It was narrated that Ibn 'Umar (ra) said: The Messenger of Allah (saws) said: "Whoever catches one Rak'ah of Friday prayer or other than it, then he has caught the prayer." [Sunan Ibn Majah]

Missing one rak'ah in Maghrib

Yahya related to me from Malik from Ibn Shihab that Sa'id ibn al-Musayyab said, "Which prayer is it when you remain in the sitting position in every rakah?'' Sa'id said, "It is maghrib when you miss one rakah, and that is the sunnah in all the prayers." [Muwatta Imam Malik]

Sitting in prayer place after Subh

Simak b. Harb reported: I said to Jabir bin Samura (ra): Did you sit in the company of the Messenger of Allah (saws)? He said: Yes, very often. He (saws) used to sit at the place where he observed the morning or dawn prayer till the sun rose or when it had risen; he would stand, and they (his Companions) would talk about matters (pertaining to the days) of ignorance, and they would laugh (on these matters) while (the Holy Prophet saws) only smiled. [Muslim]

Narrated Samura bin Jundub (ra): The Prophet (saws) used to face us on completion of the prayer [Bukhari]

Who is more entitled to lead the prayer

Abu Mas'ud al-Ansari (ra) reported Allah's Messenger (saws) as saying: The one who is the most versed in Allah's Book should act as Imam for the people. But If they are equally versed in reciting it, then the one who has most knowledge regarding Sunnah; if they are equal regarding the Sunnah, then the earliest one to emigrate; it they emigrated at the same time, then the earliest one to embrace Islam. No man must lead another in prayer where (the latter) has authority, or sit in his place of honour in his house, without his permission. Ashajj in his narration used the word," age" in place of" Islam". [Muslim]

Nawafil at home

Narrated Ibn 'Umar (ra): The Prophet (saws) had said, "Offer some of your prayers (Nawafil) at home, and do not take your houses as graves." [Bukhari]

Suhayb ibn al-Nu'man (ra) reported: The Messenger of Allah (saws) said, "The voluntary prayer of a man in his house is better than his prayer where people can see him, just as the prescribed prayers are better than the voluntary prayers." [al-Mu'jam al-Kabir lil-Ṭabarani]

A Visitor Being Imam

Abu 'Atiyyah, (a freed slave) said: Malik b. al-Huwairith (ra) came to this place of prayer of ours, and the iqamah for prayer was called. We said to him: Come forward and lead the prayer. He said to us: Put one of your own men forward to lead you in prayer. I heard the Messenger of Allah (saws) say: If anyone visits people, he should not lead them in prayer, but some person of them should lead the prayer. [Sunan Abu Dawud]

Women going out to the masjid

Ibn Umar (ra) reported: I heard the Messenger of Allah (saws) say: When your women seek your permission for going to the mosque, you grant them (permission). [Muslim]

Zainab (ra), the wife of Abdullah bin 'Umar (ra), reported: The Messenger of Allah (saws) said to us: When any one of you comes to the mosque, she should not apply perfume. [Muslim]

Combining the prayer

The Prophet (saws) combined prayers during travel

Ibn Umar (ra) reported: The Prophet (saws) combined sunset (Maghrib) and evening prayers (Isha) if he was undertaking a journey. And Ibn Abbas (ra) said, "The Messenger of Allah (saws) combined the noon prayers (Zuhr) and afternoon prayers (Asr) if he was on a journey, as well as combining the sunset (Maghrib) and evening prayers (Isha)." [Bukhari, Muslim]

Joining two prayers when not in fear nor due to rain

Abdullah b. Shaqiq al-'Uqaili reported: A person said to Ibn 'Abbas (as he delayed the prayer): Prayer. He kept silence. He again said: Prayer. He again kept silence, and he again cried: Prayer. He again kept silence and said: May you be deprived of your mother; do you teach us about prayer? We used to combine two prayers during the life of the Messenger of Allah (saws). [Muslim]

Ibn Abbas (ra) said: "Allah's Messenger (saws) combined the Zuhr and Asr (prayers), and the Maghrib and Isha (prayers) in Al-Madinah, without being in a state of fear, nor due to rain." [Tirmizi]

Sa'id ibn Jubair that Ibn 'Abbas (ra) said: The Messenger of Allah (saws) joined together Zuhr and Asr, and Maghrib and Isha in Madinah when there was no fear and no rain. I said to Ibn 'Abbas (ra): Why did he (saws) do that? He said: So that his Ummah would not be subjected to hardship. [Muslim]

Combining Prayer due to Istihadah

Istihadah means bleeding of women beyond menses period.

Hadith: Hamnah (ra), when she consulted the Prophet (saws) about Istihadah, and he said: "If you are able to delay Zuhr and bring Asr forward, then do Ghusl and pray Zuhr and Asr together, and then delay Maghrib and bring Isha' forward, then do Ghusl and offer the two prayers together, then do that." [Musnad Ahmad, Abu Dawud, and At-Tirmizi]

Note: Combining prayer should not be a regular or permanent practice. Allah SWT says:

$$إِنَّ ٱلصَّلَوٰةَ كَانَتْ عَلَى ٱلْمُؤْمِنِينَ كِتَٰبًا مَّوْقُوتًا$$

(Indeed, performing prayers is a duty on the believers at the appointed times. Surah an-Nisa, Ch 4:103; interpretation of meaning)

Fixed time range for each Salat is prescribed in authentic Hadith which is as follows:

Prophet (saws) said: "Jibril (peace be upon him) led me in prayer at the Ka`bah twice. He led me in praying Zuhr when the sun had passed the meridian and the shadow was the length of a sandal-strap; then he led me in praying `Asr when the (length of a thing's) shadow was equal to its height; then he led me in praying Maghrib at the time when the fasting person breaks his fast; then he led me in praying `Isha' at the time when the red afterglow had disappeared; then he led me in praying Fajr at the time when food and drink become prohibited to the one who is fasting. Then the next day he led me in praying Zuhr when the (length of a thing's) shadow was equal to its height; then he led me in praying `Asr when the (length of a thing's) shadow was equal to twice its height; then he led me in praying Maghrib at the time when the fasting person breaks his fast; then he led me in praying `Isha' when one third of the night had passed; then he led me in praying Fajr when it had grown light. Then he turned to me and said: O Muhammad (saws), these are the times at which the Prophets before you prayed, the time is between each of these two times (for each prayer)." [Abu Dawud, and At-Tirmizi]

Breaking fast means the sun has set. Time of food and drink prohibited for fasting is the dawn and is defined by Allah SWT in the Book (that means):

"and eat and drink until the white thread (light) of dawn appears to you distinct from the black thread (darkness of night), then complete your Sawm (fast) till the nightfall." [al-Baqarah, Ch 2:187]

The above time table may be summarised in the tabular form as follows:

Salat Particulars	Early start	Late finish
Fajr	Food and drink prohibited for fasting	Light has grown
Zuhr	Length of the shade= one sandal-strap (i.e altitude is slightly different from 90 degrees)	Length of the shade= height of the object (i.e altitude of the sun= 45 degrees)

Asr	Length of the shade= height of the object (i.e altitude of the sun= 45 degrees)	Length of the shade= twice the height of the object (i.e altitude of the sun= 26.6 degrees)
Maghrib	Breaking fast	Breaking fast
Isha	Red afterglow disappeared	One third night has passed

The sutrah (screen)

Sutrah is an object used by a person performing prayer that is set as a screen or barrier between himself and one passing in front of him.

The sutrah (screen) for one who is praying

Musa b. Talha reported on the authority of his father: We used to say prayer and the animals moved in front of us. We mentioned it to the Messenger of Allah (saws) and he (saws) said: If anything equal to the back of a saddle is in front of you, then what walks in front, no harm would come to him. Ibn Numair said: No harm would come whosoever walks in front. [Muslim]

Abu Juhaifa reported on the authority of his father: I saw the Messenger of Allah (saws) (in Makka at al-Abtah) in a red leather tent. And I saw Bilal (ra) take the ablution water (left by Allah's Messenger), and I saw the people racing, with one another to get that ablution water. If anyone got some of it, he rubbed himself with it, and anyone who did not get any got some of the moisture from his companion's hand. I then saw Bilal (ra) take a staff and fix it in the ground, after which the Messenger of Allah (saws) came out quickly in a red mantle and led the people in two rak'ahs facing the staff, and I saw people and animals passing in front of the staff. [Muslim]

Salat with furnace or fire or any other worship-able thing in front

Narrated 'Abdullah bin 'Abbas (ra): The sun eclipsed and Allah's Messenger (saws) offered the eclipse prayer and said, "I have been shown the Hellfire (now) and I never saw a worse and horrible sight than the sight I have seen today." [Bukhari]

Distance between the person offering Salat (prayer) and the Sutra?

Narrated Sahl (bin Sa`d): The distance between the Musalla of Allah's Messenger (saws) and the wall was just sufficient for a sheep to pass through. [Bukhari]

To offer Salat facing a pillar

Narrated Yazid bin Al `Ubaid: I used to accompany Salama bin Al-Akwa` (ra) and he used to pray behind the pillar which was near the place where the Qur'ans were kept. I said, "O Abu Muslim! I see you always seeking to pray behind this pillar." He replied, "I saw Allah's Messenger (saws) always seeking to pray near that pillar." [Bukhari]

Preventing one who wants to pass in front of a praying person

Abdullah bin Umar (ra) reported that the Messenger of Allah (saws) said: When any one of you prays, he should not allow anyone to pass before him, and if he refuses, he should be then forcibly resisted, for there is a devil with him. [Muslim]

Narrated Busr bin Sa`id: that Zaid bin Khalid sent him to Abi Juhaim (ra) to ask him what he had heard from Allah's Messenger (saws) about a person passing in front of another person who was praying. Abu Juhaim (ra) replied: Allah's Messenger (saws) said, "If the person who passes in front of another person in prayer knew the magnitude of his sin he would prefer to wait for 40 (days, months or years) rather than to pass in front of him." Abu An-Nadr said, "I do not remember exactly whether he said 40 days, months or years." [Bukhari]

Lying in front of one who is praying

It was narrated from 'Urwah, from 'Asiah (ra): "The Messenger of Allah (saws) used to pray at night, and I would be lying between him and the *Qiblah,* like he (saws) was facing a body, during Janazah." [Muslim]

Maimuna (ra), the wife of the Prophet (saws) reported: The Messenger of Allah (saws) offered prayer and I (lay) opposite to him while I was in menses. Sometimes his clothes touched me when he (saws) prostrated. [Bukhari, Muslim]

A'isha (ra) reported: The Apostle of Allah (saws) offered prayer at night and I was by his side in a state of menses and I had a sheet pulled over me, a portion of which was on his side. [Muslim]

If the clothes of a prayer person in prostration touched his wife

Narrates `Abdullah bin Shaddad: Maimuna (ra) said, "Allah's Messenger (saws) was praying while I was in my menses, sitting beside him and sometimes his clothes would touch me during his prostration." Maimuna (ra) added, "He prayed on a Khumra (a small mat sufficient just for the face and the hands while prostrating during prayers)." [Bukhari]

Narrated Abu Salama (ra): `Aisha (ra) the wife of the Prophet (saws) said, "I used to sleep in front of Allah's Messenger (saws) and my legs were opposite his Qibla and in prostration he pushed my legs and I withdrew then and when he stood, I stretched them." `Aisha (ra) added, "In those days the houses were without lights." [Bukhari, Muslim]

When a black dog, a woman, and a donkey passes in front of salat

Abu Zarr (ra) said that: Allah's Messenger (saws) said: "When a man performs Salat, and there is nothing in front of him like the post of a saddle, or a camel saddle, then his Salat is severed by (passing of) a black dog, a woman, and a donkey." It was said to Abu Zarr (ra): "What is the problem with the black dog rather than the red or white one?" He said: "O my nephew! I asked Allah's Messenger (saws) just as you have asked me. He (saws) said: 'The black dog is a Shaitan (devil)." [Tirmizi]

Activities disliked during salat

Yawning in salat: Abu Hurairah (ra) narrated that the Prophet (saws) said: "Yawning in prayer (salah) is from the Shaitan, so when one of you yawns then let him suppress (it) as much as possible." [Tirmizi]

Greet during salat: Abdullah b. Masu'd (ra) reported: We used to greet the Messenger of Allah (saws) while he was engaged in prayer and he would respond to our greeting. But when we returned from the Negus (Abyssinia) we greeted him and he did not respond to us; so we said:

"Messenger of Allah (saws), we used to greet you when you were engaged in prayer and you would respond to us." He (saws) replied: "Prayer demands whole attention." [Muslim]

To smooth the pebbles: It was narrated from Abu Salamah that Al-Mu'ayqib said: "The Prophet (saws) mentioned smoothing the pebbles in the *Masjid* and said: 'If you must do that, then do it only once." [Muslim]

To offer salat in a garment with markings: A'isha (ra) reported: The Apostle of Allah (saws) prayed in a garment which had designs over it, so he (saws) said: Take it to Abu Jahm and bring me a plain blanket from him, because its designs have distracted me. [Bukhari, Muslim]

Narrated `Aisha (ra): The Prophet (saws) said, "I was looking at its (Khamisa's) marks during the prayers and I was afraid that it may put me in trial (by taking away my attention)." [Bukhari]

To offer salat while restraining the urge to relieve oneself: .... She (Aisha ra) said: 'Sit down, traitor! I heard the Messenger of Allah (saws) say: "There is no prayer when food is ready, or when one is resisting the urge to relieve oneself." [Part of the Hadith from Muslim]

Things that have an offensive odour: It was narrated that Jabir (ra) said: The Messenger of Allah (saws) forbade eating onions and leeks, but we were overcome by need and we ate some of them. He (saws) said: "Whoever eats from these foul-smelling plants, let him not come near our Masjid, for the Angels are offended by the same things that offend humans." [Muslim]

It is forbidden to come in a hasty manner: Abu Huraira (ra) reported: I heard the Messenger of Allah (saws) saying: "When the Iqamah has been pronounced for prayer, do not go running to it, but go walking in tranquillity and pray what you are in time for, and complete what you have missed." [Muslim]

Waiting and sitting in Masjid: Abu Hurairah (ra) narrated that: Allah's Messenger (saws) said: "One of you does not cease to be in Salat as long as he is waiting for it. And the angels do not cease praying for one of you as long as he remains in the Masjid (saying): 'Allah! Forgive him. O Allah! Have mercy upon him' - as long as he does not commit hadath." A man from Hadramawt said: "And just what is hadath Abu Hurairah?" He said: "Breaking wind, or passing gas." [Tirmizi]

Sajdah as-sahw (forgetfulness) in prayer during Prophet (saws)

Due to forgetfulness, if a person adds something extra or omits something or is not sure about number of rakahs, then he he/she is not required to repeat the whole salat. His salat becomes valid by doing sajda as-sahw (two prostrations). If such mistakes are noticed while performing a prayer, sajdah as-sahw is performed at the end of prayer.

Hadith: Alqama narrated it on the authority of 'Abdullah bin Mas'ud (ra) who said: The Messenger of Allah (saws) offered the prayer; (the narrator added): He (saws) made some act of omission or commission when he (saws) pronounced salutation; it was said to him: Messenger of Allah (saws), is there something new about the prayer? He (saws) said: What is it? They said: You said prayer in such and such away. He (the narrator) said: He (saws) turned his feet and faced the Qibla and performed two prostrations and then pronounced salutations, and then turned his face towards us and said: If there is anything new about prayer (new command from the Lord) I informed you of that. But I am a human being and I forget as you forget, so when I forget, remind me, and when any one of you is in doubt about his prayer, he should aim at what is correct. And complete his prayer in that respect and then make two prostrations. [Muslim]

There were several situations of sajdah sahw during Prophet (saws). The cases are listed below:

Case 1: There are doubts about number of rak'ah: Abu Huraira (ra) reported: The Messenger of Allah (saws) said: When any one of you stands up to pray, the devil comes to him and confuses him to that he does not know how much he has prayed. If any one of you has such an experience he should perform two prostrations while sitting down. [Muslim]

Abu Sa'id al-Khudri (ra) reported: The Messenger of Allah (saws) said: When any one of you is in doubt about his prayer and he does not know how much he has prayed, three or four (rak'ahs), he should cast aside his doubt *and base his prayer on what he is sure of.* Then perform two prostrations before giving salutations. If he has prayed five rak'ahs, they will make his prayer an even number for him, and if he has prayed exactly four, they will be humiliation for the devil. [Muslim]

Summary: Complete salat, sajdah sahw, salutations

Case 2: When one stands up while not supposed to stand (omission): Abdullah bin Buhaina (ra) reported: The Messenger of Allah (saws) led us two rak'ah of prayer in one of the (obligatory) prayers and then got up and did not sit. And the people stood up along with him. When he finished the prayer and we expected him to pronounce salutation. He (saws) said: *"Allahu Akbar,"* while sitting and made two prostrations before salutation and then pronounced (the final) salutation. [Muslim]

Summary: complete salat, sajdah sahw, salutations

Case 3: When one performs a greater number of rak'ah than the stipulated: Abdullah bin Mas'ud (ra) reported: The Apostle of Allah (saws) said five rak'ahs of the noon prayer and when he completed the prayer, it was said to him: Has there been (commanded) an addition in prayer? He (saws) said: What is it? They said: You have said five rak'ahs, so he (saws) performed two prostrations. [Bukhari, Muslim]

Summary: salutations, sajdah sahw

Case 4: When one offers a lesser number of rak'ah than the stipulated as well as performs worldly things and talks: Ibn Sirin reported Abu Huraira (ra) as saying: The Messenger of Allah (saws) led us in one of the two evening prayers, Zuhr or `Asr, and gave salutations after two rak`ahs and going towards a piece of wood which was placed to the direction of the Qibla in the mosque, leaned on it looking as if he were angry. Abu Bakr (ra) and `Umar (ra) were among the people and they were too afraid to speak to him and the people came out in haste (saying): The prayer has been shortened. But among them was a man called Zul-Yadain (ra) who said: Messenger of Allah (saws), has the prayer been shortened or have you forgotten? The Apostle of Allah (saws) looked to the right and left and said: What was Zul-Yadain saying? They said: He is right. You offered but two rak`ahs. He (saws) offered two (more) rak`ahs and gave salutation, then said takbir and prostrated and lifted (his head) and then said takbir and prostrated, then said takbir and lifted (his head). He (the narrator) says: It has been reported to me by `Imran b. Husain that he said: He (then) gave salutation. [Muslim]

Summary: balance rakat, salutations, sajdah sahw, salutations

It was narrated from 'Imran bin Husain (ra) that the Messenger of Allah (saws) prayed *'Asr* and said the *Taslim* after three *Rak'ah,* then he went into his house. A man called al-Khirbaq, who had long arms, stood up and said: "O Messenger of Allah (saws)!" And he told him what he had done. He (saws) came out looking angry, dragging his *Rida',* (mantle) and when he (saws) reached the people he said: "Is this one telling the truth?" They said: "Yes." So he (saws) prayed one *Rak'ah,* then he said the *Taslim,* then he prostrated twice, then he said the *Taslim.* [Muslim] *Summary: balance rakat, salutations, sajdah sahw, salutations*

Making up a missed prayer (qada salat)

Abu Huraira (ra) reported that when the Messenger of Allah (saws) returned from the expedition to Khaibar, he travelled one night, and stopped for rest when he became sleepy. He (saws) told Bilal (ra) to remain on guard during the night and he (Bilal) prayed as much as he could, while the Messenger of Allah (saws) and his Companions slept. When the time for dawn approached, Bilal (ra) leaned against his camel facing the direction from which the dawn would appear but he was overcome by sleep while he was leaning against his camel, and neither the Messenger of Allah (saws) nor Bilal, nor anyone else among his Companions got up, till the sun shone on them. Allah's Messenger (saws) was the first of them to awake and, being startled, he called to Bilal who said: Messenger of Allah (saws), may my father and mother be offered as ransom for thee, the same thing overpowered me which overpowered you. He (saws) said: Lead the beasts on: so they led their camels to some distance. The Messenger of Allah (saws) then performed ablution and gave orders to Bilal who pronounced the Iqama and then led them in the morning prayer. When he (saws) finished the prayer he (saws) said: "When anyone forgets the prayer, he should observe it when he remembers it, for Allah has said: And observe the prayer for remembrance of Me" (Ch 20: 14). Yunus said: Ibn Shilab used to recite it like this:" (And observe the prayer) for remembrance." [Muslim]

It was narrated from Anas bin Malik (ra) that the Messenger of Allah (saws) said: "Whoever forgets a prayer, let him offer it as soon as he remembers, for there is no expiation for it other than that. [Bukhari, Muslim]

Narrated Jabir (ra): `Umar came cursing the disbelievers (of Quraish) on the day of Al-Khandaq (the battle of Trench) and said, "I could not offer the `Asr prayer till the sun had set. Then we went to Buthan and he offered the (`Asr) prayer after sunset and then he offered the Maghrib prayer. [Bukhari]

Salatul witr

Witr was a regular practice of the Prophet (saws)

It was narrated that Asim bin Damrah as-Salooli said: 'Ali (ra) said: Verily, Witr is not a must like your prescribed prayers, but the Messenger of Allah (saws) prayed Witr, then he said: "Pray Witr, O people of the Qur`an. Pray Witr, for Allah is One and loves that which is odd numbered." [Musnad Ahmad]

It was narrated that 'Ali (ra) said: Witr is not a must, but it is a Sunnah that the Messenger of Allah (saws) established, so pray Witr, O people of the Qur`an. [Musnad Ahmad]

Ali (bin Abu Talib) (ra) reported: The Witr prayer is not obligatory as the prescribed Salat (prayers), but the Messenger of Allah (saws) observed it as his regular practice (Sunnah). He (saws) said, "Allah is Witr (single, odd) and loves what is Witr. So perform Witr prayer. O followers of Qur'an, observe Witr (prayer)." [Tirmizi, Abu Dawud].

A'isha (ra) reported: The Messenger of Allah (saws) observed the Witr prayer every night and he completed Witr at the time of dawn. [Muslim]

Buraida said he heard Allah's Messenger (saws) say, "The *witr* is a duty, so he who does not observe it does not belong to us; the *witr* is a duty, so he who does not observe it does not belong to us; the *witr* is a duty, so he who does not observe it does not belong to us." [Mishkat al-Masabih]

Abu Basrah (ra) reported: The Prophet (saws) said, "Verily, Allah Almighty has added one to your prayers, so perform it between the evening and dawn prayers: the Witr prayer, the Witr prayer." [Musnad Ahmad]

Odd number of Rak'ah in witr

It was narrated from Abu Ayyub Al-Ansari (ra) that the Messenger of Allah (saws) said: "Witr is Haqq. Whoever wishes let him pray Witr with five (Rak'ah), and whoever wishes let him pray Witr with three

(Rak'ah), and whoever wishes let him pray Witr with one (Rak'ah)."
[Sunan Ibn Majah]

Narrated Ali ibn Abi Talib (ra): The Prophet (saws) said: Allah is single (witr) and loves what is single, so observe the witr, you who follow the Qur'an. [Abu Dawud]

Duwaid bin Nafi' said: Ibn Shihab informed me, saying: 'Ata bin Yazid narrated to me from Abu Ayyub (ra): That the Prophet (saws) said: 'Witr is a duty, and whoever wants to pray witr with seven (rak'ahs), let him do so; whoever wants to pray witr with five, let him do so, whoever wants to pray witr with three, let him do so; and whoever wants to pray witr with one, let him do so.' [Sunan Nasai]

It was narrated from 'Ali (ra) that the Prophet (saws) used to pray Witr with three raka'hs. [Musnad Ahmad]

Narrated Ibn `Abbas (ra): (One night) I stayed overnight in the house of my aunt Maimuna (ra), and said to myself, 'I will watch the prayer of Allah's Messenger (saws).' My aunt placed a cushion for Allah's Messenger (saws) and he slept on it in its length-wise direction and (woke-up) rubbing the traces of sleep off his face and then he recited the last ten Verses of Surat-al-`Imran till he finished it. Then he went to a hanging water skin and took it, performed the ablution and then stood up to offer the prayer. I got up and did the same as he had done, and stood beside him. He put his hand on my head and held me by the ear and twisted it. He offered two rak`at, then two rak`at, then two rak`at, then two rak`at, then two rak`at, then two rak`at, and finally the witr (i.e. one rak`a) prayer. [Bukhari]

Yahya related to me from Malik from Ibn Shihab that Sad ibn Abi Waqqas used to pray witr after Isha with one raka. Malik said, "This is not the situation with us. Rather three is the minimum for witr." [Muwatta Imam Malik]

Narrated Nafi`: Ibn `Umar (ra) said: While the Prophet (saws) was on the podium, a man asked him how to offer the night prayers. He (saws) replied: "Pray two rak`at at a time and then two and then two and so on, and if you are afraid of the dawn (the approach of the time of the Fajr prayer) pray one rak`a and that will be the witr for all the rak`at which you have offered." Ibn `Umar (ra) said: The last rak`at of the night prayer should be odd, for the Prophet (saws) ordered it to be so. [Bukhari]

Time Table of witr

It was narrated that 'Ali (ra) said: "At every part of the night the Messenger of Allah (saws) prayed Witr, at the beginning and in the middle, and finally his Witr was just before dawn." [Musnad Ahmad, Sunan Ibn Majah]

Masruq said: I asked 'Aishah (ra): When would the Messenger of Allah (saws) observe the witr prayer? She replied: Any time he observed the witr, sometimes in the early hours of the night, sometimes at midnight and sometimes towards the end of it. But he used to observe the witr just before the dawn when he died. [Muslim, Abu Dawud]

A'isha (ra) reported: The Messenger of Allah (saws) used to pray in the night and when he observed Witr, he said to me: O 'A'isha, get up and observe Witr. [Bukhari] A'isha (ra) reported that the Messenger of Allah (saws) used to observe Witr every night, and he would (at times) complete his Witr at the end of the night. [Muslim]

Ibn Umar (ra) narrated that: Allah's Messenger (saws) said: "When Fajr begins, then every Salat of the night and Al-Witr have gone, so perform Al-Witr before Fajr begins." [Tirmizi] Abu Hurairah (ra) narrated: "Allah's Messenger (saws) ordered me to perform Al-Witr before sleeping." [Tirmizi]

Jabir (ra) said: The Messenger of Allah (saws) said: "Whoever fears that he will not get up at the end of the night, let him pray Witr at the beginning. Whoever is sure that he will get up at the end of the night, let him pray witr at the end, for prayer at the end of the night is witnessed, and that is better." [Muslim].

If Witr is missed

Narrated Abu Sa'id al-Khudri (ra): The Prophet (saws) said: "If anyone oversleeps and misses the Witr, or forgets it, he should pray when he remembers." [Abu Dawud]

Supplicating after Witr (Qunut)

It was narrated from Ubayy bin Ka'b (ra) that the Messenger of Allah (saws) used to pray Witr and he would recite Qunut before Ruku. [Sunan Ibn Majah]

It was narrated that Abu Al-Jawza said: Al-Hasan (ra) said: The Messenger of Allah (saws) taught me some words to say in witr in

Qunut: *Allahumma ihdini fiman hadayta wa 'afini fiman afayta wa tawallani fiman tawallayta wa barik li fima a'tayta, wa qini sharra ma qadayta, fa innaka taqdi wa la yuqda 'alayk, wa innahu la yadhilluman walayta, tabarakta Rabbana wa at'alayt* (O Allah, guide me among those whom You have guided, pardon me among those You have pardoned, turn to me in friendship among those on whom You have turned in friendship, and bless me in what You have bestowed, and save me from the evil of what You have decreed. For verily You decree and none can influence You; and he is not humiliated whom You have befriended. Blessed are You, O Lord, and Exalted.) In Arabic:

اللَّهُمَّ اهْدِنِي فِيمَنْ هَدَيْتَ وَعَافِنِي فِيمَنْ عَافَيْتَ وَتَوَلَّنِي فِيمَنْ تَوَلَّيْتَ وَبَارِكْ لِي فِيمَا أَعْطَيْتَ وَقِنِي شَرَّ مَا قَضَيْتَ إِنَّكَ تَقْضِي وَلاَ يُقْضَى عَلَيْكَ وَإِنَّهُ لاَ يَذِلُّ مَنْ وَالَيْتَ تَبَارَكْتَ رَبَّنَا وَتَعَالَيْتَ

[Sunan an-Nasai, Sunan Ibn Majah]

It was narrated from Ibn 'Abbas (ra) that: The Prophet (saws) used to say in his supplication: *Rabbi! A'inni wa la tu'in 'alayya, wansurni wa la tansur 'alayya, wamkurli wa la tamkur 'alayya, wahdini wa yassiril-huda li, wansurni 'ala man bagha 'alayya. Rabbij'alni laka shakkaran laka dhakkaran, laka rahhaban, laka muti'an, 'ilayka mukhbitan, 'ilayka awwahan muniba. Rabbi! Taqabbal tawbati, waghsil hawbati wa ajib da'wati, wahdi qalbi, wa saddid lisani, wa thabbit hujjati, waslul sakhimata qalbi* (O Lord! Help me and do not help others against me, support me and do not support others against me, plan for me and do not plan against me, guide me and make guidance easy for me, and help me against those who wrong me. O Lord! Make me grateful to You, make me remember You much, make me fearful of You, obedient to You, humble before You and turning to You. O Lord! Accept my repentance and wash away my sins, answer my supplication, guide my heart, make my tongue speak the truth, make my proof firm and remove resentment from my heard)." (One of the narrators) Abul-Hasan At-Tanafisi said: I said to Waki': Shall I say it in the Qunut of Witr? He said: 'Yes.' In Arabic:

رَبِّ أَعِنِّي وَلاَ تُعِنْ عَلَيَّ وَانْصُرْنِي وَلاَ تَنْصُرْ عَلَيَّ وَامْكُرْ لِي وَلاَ تَمْكُرْ عَلَيَّ وَاهْدِنِي وَيَسِّرِ الْهُدَى لِي وَانْصُرْنِي عَلَى مَنْ بَغَى عَلَيَّ رَبِّ اجْعَلْنِي لَكَ شَكَّارًا لَكَ ذَكَّارًا لَكَ رَهَّابًا لَكَ مُطِيعًا إِلَيْكَ مُخْبِتًا إِلَيْكَ أَوَّاهًا مُنِيبًا رَبِّ

تَقَبَّلْ تَوْبَتِي وَاغْسِلْ حَوْبَتِي وَأَجِبْ دَعْوَتِي وَاهْدِ قَلْبِي وَسَدِّدْ لِسَانِي وَثَبِّتْ حُجَّتِي وَاسْلُلْ سَخِيمَةَ قَلْبِي

[Sunan Ibn Majah, Tirmizi, Abu Dawud]

It is narrated from `Abdullah ibn Mas`ud (ra) and collected in the Musannaf of Ibn Abi Shaybah, in Kitab as-Salah and the Chapter of the du`a in the qunut of witr: Slight variants of this du`a occur in other parts of the Musannaf as well (e.g. in the Book of Du`a and section on what to make du`a by in the qunut of Fajr.)

Allahumma inna nasta inuka wa nastaghfiruka, wa nu'minu bika wa natawakkalu 'alaika wa nuthni 'alaikal khair, wa nashkuruka wa la nakfuruka wa nakhla'u wa natruka manyyafjuruka, allahumma iyyaka na'budu , wa laka nusalli wa nasjudu wa ilaika nas'a wa nahfidu wa narju rahmataka wa nakhsha 'adhabaka inna 'adhabaka bil kaffari mulhiq.

It was narrated that 'Umar (ra) prayed Qunut with the following words:

Allahumma inna nasta inuka wa nastaghfiruka, wa nu'minu bika wa natawakkalu 'alaika wa nuthni 'alaikal khair, wa nashkuruka wa la nakfuruka wa nakhla'u wa natruka manyyafjuruka, allahumma iyyaka na'budu, wa laka nusalli wa nasjudu wa ilaika nas'a wa nahfidu wa narju rahmataka wa nakhsha 'adhabaka inna 'adhabaka bil kaffari mulhiq.

اللَّهُمَّ إِنَّا نَسْتَعِينُكَ وَنَسْتَغْفِرُكَ وَنُؤْمِنُ بِكَ وَنَتَوَكَّلُ عَلَيْكَ وَنُثْنِي عَلَيْكَ الْخَيْرَ وَنَشْكُرُكَ وَلَا نَكْفُرُكَ وَنَخْلَعُ وَنَتْرُكُ مَنْ يَفْجُرُكَ اللَّهُمَّ إِيَّاكَ نَعْبُدُ وَلَكَ نُصَلِّي وَنَسْجُدُ وَإِلَيْكَ نَسْعَى وَنَحْفِدُ نَرْجُو رَحْمَتَكَ وَنَخْشَى عَذَابَكَ إِنَّ عَذَابَكَ بِالْكُفَّارِ مُلْحَقٌ

"O' Allah! We implore You for help and beg forgiveness of You and believe in You and rely on You and extol You and we are thankful to You and are not ungrateful to You and we alienate and forsake those who disobey You. O' Allah! You alone do we worship and for You do we pray and prostrate and we betake to please You and present ourselves for the service in Your cause and we hope for Your mercy and fear Your chastisement. Undoubtedly, Your torment is going to overtake infidels" [al-Bayhaqi]

What to say after witr is finished

It was narrated from Ubayy bin Ka'b (ra) that: The Messenger of Allah (saws) used to pray witr with three rak'ahs. In the first he would recite: "Glorify the Name of Your Lord, the Most High" in the second: "Say: O you disbelievers!", and in the third: "Say: He is Allah, (the) One". And he would say the Qunut before bowing, and when he finished he would say: *Subhanal-Malikil-Quddus* سُبْحَانَ الْمَلِكِ الْقُدُّوسِ (Glory be to the Sovereign, the Most Holy) three times, elongating the words the last time. [Sunan an- Nasai]

There should not be two witrs in one night

It was narrated that Qais bin Talq said: "My father, Talq bin 'Ali (ra) visited me one day in Ramadan and stayed with us until the evening. He led us in praying Qiyam that night and prayed witr with us. Then he went down to a masjid and led his companions in prayer until only witr was left. Then he told a man to go forward and said to him: 'Lead them in praying witr, for I heard the Messenger of Allah (saws) say: There should not be two witrs in one night." [Sunan an-Nasai]

Emphasised Sunnah Salat

Emphasised Sunnah refers to those Sunnats which should be performed; e.g., two rak'ahs of Fajr, four rak'ahs and two rak'ahs of Zuhr, two rak'ahs of Maghrib and two rak'ahs of Isha. Prophet (saws) performed these salats regularly without leaving these.

Aishah (ra) narrated that Allah's Messenger (saws) said: "Whoever is regular with twelve Rak'ah of Sunnah (prayer), Allah will build a house for him in Paradise: Four Rak'ah before Zuhr, two Rak'ah after it, two Rak'ah after Maghrib, two Rak'ah after Isha, and two Rak'ah before Fajr." [Tirmizi]

Number after each Salah

It was narrated from Hafsah (ra) that: When the call for Subh prayer was given, the Messenger of Allah (saws) would pray two brief rak'ahs before going to the prayer. [Sunan an-Nasa'i]

Ibn Umar (ra) narrated: "I watched the Prophet (saws) for a month. In the two Rak'ah before Fajr he would recite: Say: "O you disbelievers *Kul ya aiyuhal-kafirun!*" and Say: "Allah is One *kul hu Allahu Ahad.*" [Tirmizi]

Sunnah salat before Asr

Ibn Umar (ra) narrated that: The Prophet (saws) said: "May Allah have mercy upon a man who prays four before Al-Asr." [Tirmizi]

Two rak'ah before Maghrib prayer

Mukhtar b. Fulful said: I asked Anas b. Malik (ra) about the voluntary prayers after the afternoon prayer, and he replied: 'Umar struck hit hands on prayer observed after the 'Asr prayer and we used to observe two rak'ahs after the sun set before the evening prayer during the time of the Messenger of Allah (saws). I said to him: Did the Messenger of Allah (saws) observe them? He said: He (saws) saw us observing them, but he (saws) neither commanded us nor forbade us to do so. [Muslim]

Narrated `Abdullah Al Muzam: The Prophet (Ssaws) said, "Perform (an optional) prayer before Maghrib prayer." (He repeated it thrice) and the third time he said, "Whoever wants to offer it can do so," lest the people should take it as a Sunna (tradition). [Bukhari]

The travellers' prayer (Qasar)

Ibn 'Abbas (ra) reported: Allah has prescribed the prayer through the word of your Prophet (saws) as four rak'ahs when resident, two when travelling, and one when danger is present. [Muslim]

Musa b. Salama Hudhali said: I asked Ibn 'Abbas (ra): How should I say prayer when I am in Makkah, and when I do not pray along with the Imam? He said: Two rak'ahs (of prayer) is the Sunnah of Abu'l-Qasim (saws). [Muslim]

It was narrated from 'Aishah (ra) that: She performed Umrah with the Messenger of Allah (saws), traveling from Al-Madinah to Makkah. Then, when she came to Makkah, she said: "O Messenger of Allah (saws), may my father and mother be ransomed for you, you shortened your prayers and I offered them in full, you did not fast and I fasted. He (saws) said: 'Well done, O 'Aisha!' and he (saws) did not criticize me." [Sunan an-Nasai]

It was narrated that 'Umar (ra) said: "The prayer while traveling is two rak'ah, and Friday is two rak'ah, and 'Eid is two rak'ah. They are complete and are not shortened, as told by Muhammad (saws)." [Sunan Ibn Majah]

Malik said, "Someone who intends to travel does not shorten the prayer until he has left the houses of the village. And he does not do it in full until he comes to the first houses of the village, or is nearby." [Muwatta Imam Malik]

Yahya related to me from Malik from Nafi that Ibn Umar (ra) stayed in Makkah for ten nights, shortening the prayer, except when he prayed it behind an imam, in which case he followed the imam's prayer. [Muwatta Imam Malik]

Offering Sunnah prayer during travel

Hafs b. 'Asim said: I accompanied Ibn 'Umar (ra) on the road to Makkah and he led us in two rak'ahs at the noon prayer, then he went forward and we too went along with him to a place where he alighted, and he sat and we sat along with him, and he cast a glance to the side where he said prayer and he saw people standing and asked: What are they doing? I said: They are engaged in glorifying Allah, offering Sunnah prayer. He said: If I had done so I would have perfected my prayer; O my nephew! I accompanied the Messenger of Allah (saws) on a journey, and he (saws) made no addition to two rak'ahs, till Allah called him. I accompanied Abu Bakr (ra) and he made no addition to two rak'ahs till Allah caused him to die. I accompanied 'Umar (ra) and he made no addition to two rak'ahs till Allah caused him to die. I accompanied 'Usman (ra) and he made no addition to two rak'ahs, till Allah caused him to die, and Allah has said:" There is a model pattern for you in the Messenger of Allah" (al-Qur'an, Ch 23: 21). [Muslim]

Yahya related to me that Malik said, "I have heard from Nafi that Abdullah ibn Umar (ra) used to see his son, Ubaydullah ibn Abdullah, doing voluntary prayers on a journey, and he would not disapprove of it." [Muwatta Imam Malik]

Up to what distance is a journey?

Yahya related to me from Malik from Ibn Shihab from Salim ibn Abdullah that his father rode to Rim and shortened the prayer on the journey. Malik said, "That was about four mile-stages." [Muwatta Imam Malik]

*This was Arabic miles. Four-mile stages (Burud) is approximated as 88.7 KM.

Yahya related to me from Malik that he had heard that Abdullah ibn Abbas (ra) used to shorten the prayer when he travelled a distance equivalent to that between *Makkah and Ta'if*, and that between *Makkah and Usfan* and that between *Makkah and Jedda*. Malik said, "That is four mile-stages, and to me that is the most preferable distance for shortening the prayer." [Muwatta Imam Malik]

Yahya b. Yazid al-Huna'i reported: I asked Anas b. Malik (ra) about shortening of prayer. He said: When the Messenger of' Allah (saws) had covered a distance of three miles or three farsakh (Shu'ba, one of the narrators, had some doubt about it) he observed two rak'ahs. [Muslim]

Jubair bin Nufair reported: I went along with Shurahbil bin al-Simt to a village which was situated at a distance of seventeen or eighteen miles, and he said only two rak'ahs of prayer. I said to him (about it) and he said: I saw 'Umar (ra) observing two rak'ahs at Zu'l-Hulaifa and I (too) said to him (about it) and he said: I am doing the same as I saw the Messenger of Allah (saws) doing. [Muslim]

Note: Distance of Zu'l-Hulaifa from Prophet's (saws) Mosque is about 8 KM. There is considerable scholarly disagreement on this matter. The conclusion from the Qur'anic verse is that any traveling which falls within the definition of the word "travel" would suffice to shorten one's salah, to combine them and to break the fast. Allah SWT did not state a specific distance for it to be permissible to shorten prayers, and neither did the Prophet (saws). Majority of the scholars are of the opinion that the minimum distance is four mile-stage.

When a traveller leaves his original place, he can shorten his Salat

Narrated Anas bin Malik (ra): We offered four rak`at of Zuhr prayer with the Prophet (saws) at Madinah and two rak`at at Zul-Hulaifa. (i.e. shortened the `Asr prayer). [Bukhari]

Three Rak'a of Maghrib prayer during the journey

Narrated 'Abdullah bin 'Umar (ra): I saw Allah's Messenger (saws) delaying the Maghrib prayer till he (saws) offered it along with the 'Isha' prayer whenever he (saws) was in a hurry during the journey. Salim narrated: Ibn 'Umar (ra) used to do the same whenever he was in a hurry during the journey. And Salim added, "Ibn 'Umar (ra) used to pray the Maghrib and 'Isha' prayers together in Al-Muzdalifa." Salim said, "Ibn 'Umar (ra) delayed the Maghrib prayer because at that time he heard the news of the death of his wife Safiya bint Abi 'Ubaid. I said to him: The prayer (is due). He said, 'Go on.' Again, I said: The prayer (is due). He said, 'Go on,' till we covered two or three miles. Then he got down, prayed and said: I saw the Prophet (saws) praying in this way, whenever he SA was in a hurry during the journey. 'Abdullah (bin 'Umar ra) added, Whenever the Prophet (saws) was in a hurry, he used to delay the Maghrib prayer and then offer three rak'at (of the Maghrib) and perform Taslim, and after waiting for a short while, Iqama used to be pronounced for the 'Isha' prayer when he (saws) would offer two rak'at and perform Taslim. He (saws) would never offer any optional prayer till the middle of the night (when he used to pray the Tahajjud)." [Bukhari]

Nawafil before and after the (compulsory) Salat during a journey

Narrated Hafs bin 'Asim: Ibn 'Umar (ra) went on a journey and said: I accompanied the Prophet (saws) and he (saws) did not offer optional prayers during the journey, and Allah says: 'Verily! In Allah's Messenger (saws) you have a good example to follow.' (Ch 33.21) [Bukhari]

Narrated Ibn 'Umar (ra): I accompanied Allah's Messenger (saws) and he (saws) never offered more than two rak'at during the journey. Abu Bakr, 'Umar and 'Usman (ra) used to do the same. [Bukhari]

It is permissible to combine two prayers when traveling

Ibn 'Umar (ra) reported: When the Messenger of Allah (saws) was in a state of hurry on a journey, he combined the Maghrib and 'Isha' prayers. [Muslim]

Anas (ra) reported: When the Messenger of Allah (saws) intended to combine two prayers on a journey, he delayed the Zuhr prayer till came the early time of the Asr prayer, and then combined the two. [Muslim]

For how many days shortening is practised

Narrated Ibn `Abbas (ra): The Prophet (saws) once stayed for nineteen days and prayed shortened prayers. So, when we travel led (and stayed) for nineteen days, we used to shorten the prayer but if we travelled (and stayed) for a longer period we used to offer the full prayer. [Bukhari]

Anas b. Malik (ra) reported: We went out from Madinah to Makkah with the Messenger of Allah (saws) and he prayed two rak'ahs at each time of prayer till we returned to Madinah. I said: For how long did he stay in Makkah? He said: (For) ten (days). [Bukhari, Muslim, Sunan an-Nasai]

According to Imam Shafii and Imam Ahmad bin Hanbal, reduction in the Prayer is not obligatory but merely optional. However, it is better to shorten it. Imam Abu Hanifah considers 'reduction in Prayer' as obligatory (Wajib) during travel. There is considerable scholarly disagreement on this matter from three days to four and to fifteen days.

A person can avail 'Traveller-status' if the intention to stay at the place of arrival is:

- Less than Fifteen (15) days [Hanafi]
- Less than Four (4) days [Hanbali, Maliki and Shafii] - (Days of arrival and departure are not included)

According to the Hanafi Fiqh, it's permissible for a Muslim to pray shortened prayer if he plans to stay less than 15 days. If he planned on staying less than 15 days but due to some unforeseen circumstance, he should keep Qasr salat as long as conditions haven't changed and he is not able to return home.

To get down to offer compulsory Salat

Narrated Salim: At night `Abdullah bin `Umar (ra) used to offer the prayer on the back of his animal during the journey and never cared about the direction he faced. Ibn `Umar (ra) said, "Allah's Messenger (saws) used to offer the optional prayer on the back of his Mount facing any direction and also used to pray the witr on it but never offered the compulsory prayer on it. [Bukhari]

As-Salat (the prayers) at Mina (during Hajj)

Narrated `Abdullah bin `Umar (ra): I offered the prayer with the Prophet (saws), Abu Bakr and `Umar at Mina and it was of two rak`at. `Usman in the early days of his caliphate did the same, but later on he started praying the full prayer. [Bukhari]

Narrated Haritha bin Wahab: The Prophet (saws) led us in the prayer at Mina during the peace period by offering two rak`at. [Bukhari]

Islamic scholars are unanimously agreed that if the residents pray behind a traveller Imam, and the traveller Imam finishes the salat after two rak'ahs, the non-travellers (residents) must offer the prayer in full. When the imam says the salaam after praying two rak'ahs, the non-travellers should not say the salaam, because they still have to complete their prayer, and if they were to say the salaam (at this point), their prayer will be invalidated. Rather they should stand up and complete the prayer with four rak'ahs. It was narrated that 'Imraan ibn Husain (ra) said: I was present with the Messenger of Allah (saws) at the conquest [of Makkah]. He (saws) stayed in Makkah for eighteen days, praying only two rak'ahs, and he said: 'O people of the city, pray with four rak'ahs, for we are people who are travelling.' [Abu Dawud].

This is a very common situation when Imam is not a traveller (resident) and others are (which is the case during Hajj and Umra). According to the scholars, the travellers have to pray in full when following a resident imam. If one stops praying before the imam, then he would not be following the imam that is obligatory. If a traveller prays behind a resident, the extra rak'ahs which were not incumbent upon him would be considered nawafl.

Salat in congregation without al-Fatiha

The Qur'an says (interpretation of the meaning):
"So, when the Qur'an is recited, listen to it, and remain silent, that you may receive mercy" (Ch 7:204)

Hadith: Yahya related to me from Malik from Abu Nuaym Wahb ibn Kaysan that he heard Jabir ibn Abdullah (ra) say, "Someone who prays a rakah without reciting the umm al-Qur'an in it, has not done the prayer except behind an imam." [Muwatta Imam Malik]

Hadith: Yahya related to me from Malik from al-Ala ibn Abd ar-Rahman ibn Ya'qub that he heard Abu's-Sa'ib, the mawla of Hisham ibn Zuhra, say he had heard Abu Hurairah (ra) say, I heard the Messenger of Allah (saws) say, "Whoever prays a prayer without reciting the umm al-Qur'an in it, his prayer is aborted, it is aborted, it is aborted, incomplete." So I said, Abu Hurayra (ra), sometimes I am behind the imam. He pulled my forearm and said, 'Recite it to yourself, O Persian, for I heard the Messenger of Allah (saws) said, "Allah says, I have divided the prayer into two halves between Me (i.e Allah) and my slave. One half of it is for Me and one half of it is for My slave, and My slave has what he asks." The Messenger of Allah (saws) said, "Recite." The slave says, 'Praise be to Allah, the Lord of the Worlds.' Allah the Blessed, the Exalted, says, 'My slave has praised Me.' The slave says, 'The Merciful, the Compassionate.' Allah says, 'My slave has spoken well of Me.' The slave says, 'Master of the Day of the Deen.' Allah says, 'My slave has glorified Me.' The slave says, 'You alone we worship and You alone we ask for help.' Allah says,' This ayat is between Me and My slave, and for My slave is what he asks. 'The slave says, 'Guide us in the straight Path, the Path of those whom You have blessed, not of those with whom You are angry, nor those who are in error. Allah says, 'These are for My slaves, and for my slave is what he asks.' [Muslim]

Hadith: Yahya related to me from Malik from Yazid ibn Ruman that Nafi ibn Jubayr ibn Mutim used to recite behind the imam when he did not recite aloud. Malik said, "That is the most preferable to me of what I have heard about the matter." [Muwatta Imam Malik]

There are controversies regarding reciting surah Fatiha while praying behind an Imam. It holds a very important position among the various issues of prayer, and scholars have written lengthy discussions on the subject. Following are the opinions as per various school of thoughts:

- Imam Abu Hanifa, Imam Abu Yusuf and Imam Muhammad are unanimous in their opinions regarding this issue. They state that it is forbidden (though it does not nullify the prayer) for the follower to recite any portion of the Qur'an, whether it be the Fatiha or any other verse, in both the silent and audible prayers behind the Imam. The recitation of Imam is considered enough for muqtadi (follower).

- Imam Malik and Imam Ahmad Hanbal are of the view that the follower is not required to recite Surat al-Fatiha in the audible prayer, but is required to do so in the silent prayers.
- The Imam Shafi'i, as written in his book al-Umm, is of the opinion that it is not necessary for the muqtadi to recite Surat al-Fatiha in the audible prayers; however, it should be recited in the silent prayers.
- Ibn Taymiyyah is of the view that the Fatiha should not be recited in the audible prayers.

A'uzubillahi Minash Shaitanir Rajim

A'uzubillahi minash shaitanir rajim means to seek refuge in Allah from Satan the cursed. Majority of the scholars say that saying *Auzubillahi minash shaitanir rajim* is recommended but is not obligatory in salat. One may say it in first rakat only. Some scholars said that it is obligatory, quoting this "So when you recite the Qur'an, [first] seek refuge in Allah from Satan, the expelled [from His mercy]." (Surah Nahl, Verse 98) as evidence and saying that the command mentioned therein implies that it is obligatory.

Abu Hurairah (ra) said: "When the Messenger of Allah (saws) got up from the second rak'ah, he (saws) would start to recite al-Fatihah from the words *Al-hamdu Lillahi Rabb il-'Alameen,* and he did not pause beforehand." [Muslim]

Masjid

Masjid is a place of worship for Muslims. Historically, Masjids have been the centre of Islamic education. Abu Sa'eed Al-Khudri (ra) narrated that: Allah's Messenger (saws) said: "All of the earth is a Masjid except for the grave yard and the washroom." [Tirmizi]

Virtue of building a Masjid

Usman bin Affan (ra) narrated that he heard Allah's Messenger (saws) say: "Whoever builds a Masjid for (the sake of) Allah, then Allah will build a similar house for him in Paradise." [Tirmizi]

Mahmud bin Labid reported: When (Khalifa) 'Usman bin 'Affan (ra) intended to build the mosque of the Prophet (saws), people did not approve of it. They liked that it should be kept in the same state. There upon he said: I heard the Messenger of Allah (saws) say: He who built a mosque for Allah, Allah would build a house for him like it in Paradise. [Muslim]

Narrated 'Ubaidullah Al-Khaulani: I heard 'Usman bin 'Affan (ra) saying, when people argued too much about his intention to reconstruct the Masjid of Allah's Messenger (saws): You have talked too much. I heard the Prophet (saws) saying, "Whoever built a mosque, (Bukair thought that 'Asim, another sub-narrator, added, 'Intending Allah's Pleasure'), Allah would build for him a similar place in Paradise." [Bukhari]

Prohibition of taking graves as masajid

A'isha (ra) reported: Umm Habiba (ra) and Umm Salama (ra) made a mention before the Messenger of Allah (saws) of a church which they had seen in Abyssinia and which had pictures in it. The Messenger of Allah (saws) said: When a pious person amongst them (among the religious groups) dies, they build a place of worship on his grave, and then decorate it with such pictures. They would be the worst of creatures on the Day of judgment in the sight of Allah. [Muslim]

A'isha (ra) reported: The Messenger of Allah (saws) said during his illness from which he (saws) never recovered: Allah cursed the Jews and the Christians that they took the graves of their prophets as mosques. She ('A'isha) reported: Had it not been so, his (Prophet's saws) grave would have been in an open place, but it could not be due to the fear that it may not be taken as a Masjid. [Muslim]

No announcement of lost objects in Masjid

Abu Huraira (ra) reported: The Messenger of Allah (saws) said: If anyone hears a man crying out in the mosque about something he has lost, he should say: May Allah not restore it to you, for the Masjids were not built for this. [Muslim]

Every step towards Masjid is recorded

Ubayy bin Ka'b (ra) reported: There was a man, and I do not know of any other man, whose house was farther than his from the Masjid and he never missed the prayer (in congregation). It was said to him or I said to him: It you were to buy a donkey you could ride upon it in the dark nights and in the burning sand. He said: I do not like my house to be situated by the side of the Masjid, for I (eagerly) desire that my steps towards the Masjid and back from it, should be recorded when I return to my family. Upon this the Messenger of Allah (saws) said: Allah has gathered all (rewards) for you. [Muslim]

Abu Huraira (ra) reported: The Messenger of Allah (saws) said: He who purified himself in his house, and then he walked to one of the houses of Allah for the sake of performing a Fard (obligatory act) out of the Fara'id (obligatory acts) of Allah, both his steps (would be significant) as one of them would obliterate his sin and the second one would raise his status. [Muslim]

Ata' bin Yasar reported, on the authority of Abu Huraira (ra), the Messenger of Allah (saws) as saying: He who went towards the mosque in the morning or evening, Allah would arrange a feast for him morning or evening in Paradise. [Muslim]

Narrated Anas (ra): (The people of) Bani Salama intended to shift near the mosque (of the Prophet saws) but Allah's Messenger (saws) disliked to see Madinah vacated and said, "O the people of Bani Salama! Don't you think that you will be rewarded for your footsteps which you take towards the mosque?" So, they stayed at their old places. [Bukhari]

What to say when entering and exiting the masjid

Abu Usaid (ra) reported that the Messenger of Allah (saws) said: When any one of you enters the mosque, he should say: اللَّهُمَّ افْتَحْ لِي أَبْوَابَ رَحْمَتِكَ O Allah! open for me the doors of Thy mercy"; and when he steps out he should say: اللَّهُمَّ إِنِّي أَسْأَلُكَ مِنْ فَضْلِكَ O Allah! I beg of Thee Thy Grace." (Imam Muslim said: I heard Yahya saying: I transcribed this hadith from the compilation of Sulaiman b. Bilal.) [Muslim]

Offer two rak'ah nafl prayer after entering Masjid

Abu Qatada (ra) said: I entered the mosque, when the Messenger of Allah (saws) had been sitting among people, and I also sat down among them. Upon this the Messenger of Allah (saws) said: What prevented you from offering two rak'ahs (of Nafl prayer) before sitting down? I said: Messenger of Allah (saws), I saw you sitting and people sitting (around you and I, therefore, sat in your company). He (the Holy Prophet saws) then said: When anyone among you enters the mosque, he should not sit till he has observed two rak'ahs. [Muslim]

Jabir b. 'Abdullah (ra) reported: The Apostle of Allah (saws) owed me a debt; he paid me back and made an addition (of this). I entered the mosque and he (the Holy Prophet saws) said to me: Observe two rak'ahs of prayer. [Muslim]

Yahya related to me from Malik from Abu'n Nadr, the slave of Umar ibn Ubaydullah, that Abu Salama ibn Abd ar-Rahman asked him, "Didn't I see your master sit down before praying after he had entered the mosque?" Abu'n-Nadr said, "By that he meant Umar ibn Ubaydullah, and he was finding fault with him for sitting down before praying after he had come into the mosque." Yahya said that Malik said, "It is good to do that but not obligatory." [Muwatta Imam Malik]

Women going for Masjid

Narrated Ibn 'Umar (ra): One of the wives of 'Umar (ra) used to offer the Fajr and the 'Isha' prayer in congregation in the Masjid. She was asked why she had come out for the prayer as she knew that 'Umar (ra) disliked it, and he has great ghaira (self-respect). She replied, "What prevents him from stopping me from this act?" The other replied, "The statement of Allah's Messenger (saws): 'Do not stop Allah's women-slaves from going to Allah's Mosques' prevents him." [Bukhari]

Sleeping of a man in the mosque

Narrated Nafi': 'Abdullah bin 'Umar said (ra): I used to sleep in the mosque of the Prophet (saws) while I was young and unmarried. [Bukhari]

Narrated Sahl bin Sa'd: Allah's Messenger (saws) went to Fatima's (ra) house but did not find 'Ali (ra) there. So he (saws) asked, "Where is your cousin?" She replied, "There was something between us and he got angry with me and went out. He did not sleep (midday nap) in the house." Allah's Messenger (saws) asked a person to look for him. That person came and said, "O Allah's Messenger (saws)! He (Ali) is sleeping in the

Masjid." Allah's Messenger (saws) went there and `Ali (ra) was lying. His upper body cover had fallen down to one side of his body and he was covered with dust. Allah's Messenger (saws) started cleaning the dust from him saying: "Get up! O Abu Turab. Get up! O Abu Turab" (literally means: O father of dust). [Bukhari]

Al-Hadah (passing wind) in the mosque

Narrated Abu Huraira (ra): Allah's Messenger (saws) said: The angels keep on asking Allah's forgiveness for anyone of you, as long as he is at his Musalla (praying place) and he does not pass wind (Hadath). They say, "O Allah! Forgive him, O Allah! be Merciful to him." [Bukhari]

To co-operate in building a Masjid

Narrated `Ikrima: Ibn `Abbas (ra) said to me and to his son `Ali, "Go to Abu Sa`id (ra) and listen to what he narrates." So we went and found him in a garden looking after it. He picked up his Rida', wore it and sat down and started narrating till the topic of the construction of the Masjid reached. He said, "We were carrying one adobe at a time while `Ammar (ibn Yasir) (ra) was carrying two. The Prophet (saws) saw him and started removing the dust from his body and said, "May Allah be Merciful to `Ammar. He will be inviting them (i.e. his murderers, the rebellious group) to Paradise and they will invite him to Hell-fire." `Ammar said, "I seek refuge with Allah from affliction." [Bukhari]
Note: 'Ammar (ra) was killed in the battle of Siffeen, when 'Ammar (ra) was with Khalifa 'Ali's (ra) side.

Sweeping of the mosque and removing dirt and sticks from it

Narrated Abu Huraira (ra): A black man or a black woman used to sweep the mosque and he or she died. The Prophet (saws) asked about her (or him). He was told that she (or he) had died. He (saws) said, "Why did you not inform me? Show me his grave (or her grave)." So, he (saws) went to her (his) grave and offered her (his) funeral prayer. [Bukhari]

Raising the voice in the Masjid

Narrated Al-Sa'ib bin Yazid: I was standing in the mosque and somebody threw a gravel at me. I looked and found that he was `Umar bin Al-Khattab (ra). He said to me, "Fetch those two men to me." When I did, he said to them, "Who are you? (Or) where do you come from?" They replied, "We are from Ta'if." Umar (ra) said, "Were you from this city (Madinah) I would have punished you for raising your voices in the mosque of Allah's Messenger (saws)." [Bukhari]

Summary

- We should respond to Azan. Recite durood and the following du'a: *Allahumma rabba hadhihid-da'wat it-tammah was-salat il-qaimah, ati Muahmmadan al-wasilah wal-fadilah, wab'athu maqaman mahmudan alladhi wa'adtahu. In Arabic:*

اللَّهُمَّ رَبَّ هَذِهِ الدَّعْوَةِ التَّامَّةِ وَالصَّلاةِ الْقَائِمَةِ، آتِ مُحَمَّدًا الْوَسِيلَةَ وَالْفَضِيلَةَ، وَابْعَثْهُ مَقَامًا مَحْمُودًا الَّذِي وَعَدْتَهُ

- Daily five times salat is obligatory. Offer salat in congregation.
- When salat is finished, say takbir (Allahu Akbar), recite 'astaghfirullah' three times and then recite '*Allahumma Antas-Salam wa minkas-salam. Tabarakta ya Dhal-jalali wal- ikram.*'

Arabic: لَّهُمَّ أَنْتَ السَّلَامُ وَمِنْكَ السَّلَامُ تَبَارَكْتَ يَا ذَا الْجَلَالِ وَالْإِكْرَامِ

Then recite '*La ilaha illallahu wahdahu la sharika lahu lahul mulku wa lahul hamdu wa huwa ala kulli shay in qadeer*' 3 times. Arabic:

لاَ إِلَهَ إِلاَّ اللَّهُ وَحْدَهُ لاَ شَرِيكَ لَهُ، لَهُ الْمُلْكُ، وَلَهُ الْحَمْدُ، وَهُوَ عَلَى كُلِّ شَيْءٍ قَدِيرٌ

Then recite '*Subhanallah*' 33 times, '*Alhamdulillah*' 33 times, '*Allahu Akbar*' 34 times.

Ka'b bin 'Ujrah (ra) reported: The Messenger of Allah (saws) said, "There are some words, the reciters of which will never be disappointed. These are: Tasbih [saying 'Subhan-Allah' (Allah is free from imperfection)], thirty-three times, Tahmid [saying 'Al-hamdu lillah' (praise be to Allah)] thirty-three times and Takbir [saying 'Allahu Akbar' (Allah is Greatest)] thirty-four times; and these should be recited after the conclusion of every prescribed prayer." [Muslim]

Narrated Abu Huraira (ra): Some poor people came to the Prophet (saws) and said: The wealthy people will get higher grades and will have permanent enjoyment and they pray like us and fast as we do. They have more money by which they perform the Hajj, and 'Umra; fight and struggle in Allah's Cause and give in charity." The Prophet (saws) said, "Shall I not tell you a thing upon which if you acted you would catch up with those who have surpassed you? Nobody would overtake you and you would be better than the people amongst whom you live except those who would do the same. Say "Subhanallah", "Al hamdu lillah" and "Allahu Akbar" thirty-three times each after every (compulsory) prayer." We differed and some of us said that we should say, "Subhanallah" thirty-three times and "Al hamdulillah" thirty-three times and "Allahu Akbar" thirty-four times. I went to the Prophet (saws) who said, "Say, "Subhanallah" and "Al hamdulillah" and "Allahu Akbar" all together [??], thirty-three times. [Bukhari]

It was narrated from Nu'man bin Bashir (ra) that: The Messenger of Allah (saws) said: "What you mention of glory of Allah, of Tabsih (Subhan-Allah), Tahlil (Allahu-Akbar) and Tahmid (Al-Hamdu lillah), revolves around the Throne, buzzing like bees, reminding of the one who said it. Wouldn't any one of you like to have, or continue to have, something that reminds of him (in the presence of Allah)?" [Sun Ibn Majah]

- Recite '*Ayatul Kursi*' after each salat.
- After witr, recite '*Subhanal-Malikil-Quddus*' three times.
- Offer 12 rakats emphasised sunnah salat.
- Recite '*Sayyidul Astaghfar*'. The Prophet (saws) said, "The most superior way of asking for forgiveness from Allah is: *Allahumma anta Rabbi la ilaha illa anta, Khalaqtani wa ana 'Abduka, wa ana 'ala 'ahdika wa wa'dika mastata'tu, A'udhu bika min Sharri ma sana'tu, abu'u Laka bini'matika 'alaiya, wa abu'u laka bidhanbi faghfir lee fa innahu la yaghfiru adhdhunuba illa anta*." The Prophet (saws) added. "If somebody recites it during the day with firm faith in it, and dies on the same day before the evening, he will be from the people of Paradise; and if somebody recites it at night with firm faith in it, and dies before the morning, he will be from the people of Paradise." [Bukhari] In Arabic:

اللَّهُمَّ أَنْتَ رَبِّي لا إِلَهَ إِلا أَنْتَ خَلَقْتَنِي وَأَنَا عَبْدُكَ وَأَنَا عَلَى عَهْدِكَ وَوَعْدِكَمَا اسْتَطَعْتُ أَعُوذُ بِكَ مِنْ شَرِّ مَا صَنَعْتُ أَبُوءُ لَكَ بِنِعْمَتِكَ عَلَيَّ وَأَبُوءُ لَكَ بِذَنْبِي فَاغْفِرْ لِي فَإِنَّهُ لا يَغْفِرُ الذُّنُوبَ إِلا أَنْتَ

- Recite 'Subhaanallaahi wa bihamdihi Adada khalqihi wa ridhaa nafsihi, wa zinata 'arshihi wa midaada kalimaatihi" 3 times in the morning. In Arabic:

سُبْحانَ اللهِ وَبِحَمْدِهِ عَدَدَ خَلْقِهِ ، وَرِضا نَفْسِهِ ، وَزِنَةَ عَرْشِهِ ، وَمِدادَ كَلِماتِهِ

- Recite Raditu Billahi Rabban wa bil Islami dinan wa bi Muhammadin SallAllahu 'alayhi wa sallama Nabiyyan 3 times in the morning and 3 times in the evening. In Arabic:

رَضِيتُ بالله رَبَّاً، وَبِالْإِسْلَامِ دِيناً، وَبِمُحَمَّدٍ صَلَّى اللهُ عَلِيهِ وَسَلَّمَ نَبِيَّاً

- Recite *La ilaha illallahu wahdahu la sharika lahu lahul mulku wa lahul hamdu wa huwa ala kulli shayin qadeer* 100 times daily. In Arabic:

لاَ إِلَهَ إِلاَّ اللَّهُ وَحْدَهُ لاَ شَرِيكَ لَهُ، لَهُ الْمُلْكُ، وَلَهُ الْحَمْدُ، وَهُوَ عَلَى كُلِّ شَيْءٍ قَدِيرٌ

4. Friday Prayer and Other Prayers

The *Jumu'ah*, or the Friday prayer replaces the usual Zuhr prayer on Friday. The obligation for Friday Prayer is enjoined upon Muslims in the Qur'an (Ch 62:9). Friday is a special day, performing the congregational prayer on this day holds special significance in the life of a Muslim. On this day, Muslims gather together, listen to a sermon (Khutbah) to empower them with valuable knowledge about Allah SWT, and the religion of Islam. It is a blessed day that has been designated as such no other day of the week has the same virtues. Allah SWT says (interpretation of meaning):

O believers! When the call to prayer is made on Friday, then proceed diligently to the remembrance of Allah and leave off your business. That is best for you, if only you knew. (Ch 62:9)

The virtue of Friday

Abu Huraira (ra) reported the Messenger of Allah (saws) as saying: "The best day on which the sun has risen is Friday; on it Adam was created. On it, he was made to enter Paradise, on it he was expelled from it. And the last Hour will take place on no day other than Friday." [Muslim]

This Ummah has been guided to Friday

Narrated Abu Huraira (ra): Allah's Messenger (saws) said: "We are the last (to come amongst the nations) but (will be) the foremost on the Day of Resurrection. They were given the Holy Scripture before us and we were given the Quran after them. And this was the day (Friday) about which they differed and Allah gave us the guidance (for that). So tomorrow (i.e. Saturday) is the Jews' (day), and the day after tomorrow (i.e. Sunday) is the Christians." The Prophet (saws) remained silent (for a while) and then said, "It is obligatory for every Muslim that he should take a bath once in seven days, when he should wash his head and body." [Bukhari]

The virtue of going out early for Friday prayer

Abu Huraira (ra) reported that the Messenger of Allah (saws) said: "He who takes a bath on Friday, the bath which is obligatory after the sexual discharge and then goes (to the mosque), he is like one who offers a she-camel as a sacrifice, and he who comes at the second hour would be like one who offers a cow, and he who comes at the third hour is live one who offers a ram with horns, and he who comes at the fourth hour is like one who offers a hen, and he who comes at the fifth hour is like one who offers an egg. And when the Imam comes out, the angels are also present and listen to the mention of Allah (the sermon)." [Muslim]

Narrated Abu Huraira (ra): The Prophet (saws) said, "When it is a Friday, the angels stand at the gate of the mosque and keep on writing the names of the persons coming to the mosque in succession according to their arrivals. The example of the one who enters the mosque in the earliest hour is that of one offering a camel (in sacrifice). The one coming next is like one offering a cow and then a ram and then a chicken and then an egg respectively. When the Imam comes out (for Jumu'a prayer) they (i.e. angels) fold their papers and listen to the Khutba." [Bukhari, Muslim]

Stern warning against missing Friday Prayer

Abdullah b. Umar (ra) and Abu Huraira (ra) said that they heard Allah's Messenger (saws) say on the planks of his pulpit: "People must cease to neglect the Friday prayer or Allah will seal their hearts and then they will be among the negligent (gafil)." [Muslim]

If Jumu'a is missed

Abdullah ibn 'Umar (ra) said: The Messenger of Allah (saws) said: "Whoever catches up with one Rak`ah of Jumu`ah or any other prayer, let him add more Rak`ahs to it to complete his prayer." [Sunan an-Nasai]

If someone misses the Jumu'ah congregation completely, according to the scholars, he has to perform Zuhur prayer. However, the missing should not be deliberate and the reasons must be beyond his control. Allah says (interpretation of the meaning):

"And there is no sin on you concerning that in which you made a mistake, except in regard to what your hearts deliberately intend" (Al-Ahzab, Ch 33:5)

The Prophet (saws) said: "Allah has forgiven my Ummah for what they forget and what they do by mistake, and for what they are forced to do." [Sunan Ibn Majah]

To take bath for Friday prayer

Abdullah (ra) is reported to have heard Allah's Messenger (saws) as saying: "When any one of you intends to come for Jumu'a prayer, he should take a bath." [Bukhari, Muslim]

Abdullah b. 'Umar (ra) reported from his father that while he (Umar) was addressing the people on Friday (sermon), a person, one of the Companions of the Messenger of Allah (saws) entered (the mosque). Umar (ra) said to him loudly: What is this hour (for attending the prayer)? He said: I was busy today and I did not return to my house when I heard the call (to Friday prayer), and I did no more but performed ablution only. Upon this Umar (ra) said: Just ablution! You know that the Messenger of Allah (saws) commanded (us) to take a bath (on Friday). [Bukhari, Muslim]

Sa'id al-Khudri (ra) reported Allah's Messenger (saws) as saying: "Taking a bath on Friday is essential for every adult person." [Bukhari, Muslim] Aisha (ra) reported: "The people (mostly) were workers and they had no servants. Ill-smell thus emitted out of them. It was said to them: Were you to take bath on Friday." [Muslim]

To go walking unhurriedly

Narrated Abu `Abs (ra): I heard the Prophet (saws) saying, "Anyone whose feet are covered with dust in Allah's cause, shall be saved by Allah from the Hell-Fire." [Bukhari]

Perfume and siwak on Fridays

Narrated Abu Sa`id (ra): I testify that Allah's Messenger (saws) said, "The taking of a bath on Friday is compulsory for every male Muslim who has attained the age of puberty and (also) the cleaning of his teeth with Siwak, and the using of perfume if it is available." 'Amr (a sub-narrator) said, "I confirm that the taking of a bath is compulsory, but as for the Siwak and the using of perfume, Allah knows better whether it is obligatory or not, but according to the Hadith it is as above." [Bukhari]

To use (hair) oil for the Friday prayer

Narrated Salman Al-Farsi (ra): The Prophet (saws) said, "Whoever takes a bath on Friday, purifies himself as much as he can, then uses his (hair) oil or perfumes himself with the scent of his house, then proceeds (for the Jumu'ah prayer) and does not separate two persons sitting together (in the mosque), then prays as much as (Allah has) written for him and then remains silent while the Imam is delivering the Khutbah, his sins in-between the present and the last Friday would be forgiven." [Bukhari]

To wear the best clothes (for the Jumu'a prayer)

Narrated 'Abdullah bin 'Umar (ra): 'Umar bin Al-Khattab (ra) saw a silken cloak (being sold) at the gate of the Mosque and said to Allah's Apostle (saws), "I wish you would buy this to wear on Fridays and also on occasions of the arrivals of the delegations." Allah's Messenger (saws) replied, "This will be worn by a person who will have no share (reward) in the Hereafter." Later on, similar cloaks were given to Allah's Messenger (saws) and he gave one of them to 'Umar bin Al-Khattab (ra). On that 'Umar (ra) said, "O Allah's Messenger (saws)! You have given me this cloak although on the cloak of Atarid (a cloak merchant who was selling that silken cloak at the gate of the mosque) you passed such and such a remark." Allah's Messenger (saws) replied, "I have not given you this to wear." And so 'Umar bin Al-Khattab (ra) gave it to his pagan brother in Makkah to wear. [Bukhari]

Listening attentively to the Khutbah on Friday

Narrated Abu Huraira (ra): Allah's Messenger (saws) said, "When the Imam is delivering the Khutba, and you ask your companion to keep quiet and listen, then no doubt you have done an evil act." [Bukhari, Muslim]

It was reported that Abu'l-Darda' (ra) said: The Prophet (saws) sat on the minbar and addressed the people, and recited an aayat. Ubayy ibn Ka'b (ra) was beside me and I said to him, 'O Ubayy, when was this verse revealed?' He refused to answer me. I asked him again and he ignored me, and I asked him again and he still ignored me, refusing to speak to me until the Messenger of Allah (saws) had come down from the minbar. Then Ubayy said to me, 'All you got from your Jumu'ah was speaking *idle talk*.' When the Messenger of Allah (saws) left, I went to him and told him what had happened. He said, 'Ubayy spoke the truth. If you hear your Imam speaking, then listen to him until he finishes.' [Sunan Ibn Maajah, Musnad Ahmad]

The time (lucky time) that occurs on Friday

Narrated Abu Huraira (ra): Allah's Messenger (saws) talked about Friday and said, "There is an hour (opportune time) on Friday and if a Muslim gets it while praying and asks something from Allah, then Allah will definitely meet his demand." And he (the Prophet saws) pointed out the shortness of that time with his hands. [Bukhari]

The two khutbah before the prayer, and sitting briefly in between them

Jabir bin Samura (ra) said that the Messenger of Allah (saws) used to deliver the sermon while standing. He would then sit down and then stand up and address in a standing posture; and whoever informed you that he (the Holy Prophet saws) delivered the sermon while sitting told a lie. By Allah, I prayed with him more than two thousand times. [Muslim]

Jumu`a prayer is when the sun has passed its zenith

Jabir b. 'Abdullah (ra) reported: We used to observe (Jumu'a) prayer with the Messenger of Allah (saws) and then we returned and gave rest to our camels used for carrying water. Hassan (one of the narrators) said:

I asked Ja'far (ra) what time that was. He said, 'It is the time when the sun passes the meridian'. [Muslim]

Iyas b. Salama b. Akwa' reported on the authority of his father, saying: We used to observe the Friday prayer with the Messenger of Allah (saws), and when we returned we did not find the shadow of the walls in which we could take protection (from the heat of the sun). [Muslim]

Narrated Anas bin Malik (ra): The Prophet (saws) used to offer the Jumu'a prayer immediately after midday. [Bukhari]

The verse: Surah Al-Jumu'a Ch 62:11

Jabir b. Abdullah (ra) reported that the Apostle (saws) was delivering the sermon on Friday in a standing posture when a caravan from Syria arrived. The people flocked towards it till no one was left (with the Holy Prophet saws) but twelve persons, and it was on this occasion that this verse in regard to Jumu'a was revealed." And when they see merchandise or sport. they break away to it and leave thee standing." [Muslim]

Keeping the khutbah short

Jabir b. Samura (ra) reported: I used to observe prayer with the Messenger of Allah (saws) and his prayer was of moderate length and his sermon too was of moderate length. [Muslim]

Abu Wa'il reported: 'Ammar (ra) delivered to us the sermon. It was short and eloquent. When he (Ammar) descended (from the pulpit) we said to him: O Abd al-Yaqzn, you have delivered a short and eloquent sermon. Would that you had lengthened (the sermon). He said: I have heard the Messenger of Allah (saws) as saying: The lengthening of prayer by a man and the shortness of the sermon is the sign of his understanding (of faith). So, lengthen the prayer and shorten the sermon, for there is charm (in precise) expression. [Muslim]

Khutbah of the Prophet (saws)

Jabir b. Abdullah (ra) said: When Allah's Messenger (saws) delivered the sermon, his eyes became red, his voice rose, and his anger increased so that he was like one giving a warning against the enemy and saying: "The enemy has made a morning attack on you and in the evening too." He (saws) would also say: "The Last Hour and I have been sent like these two." And he would join his forefinger and middle finger; and would further say: "The best of the speech is embodied in the Book of Allah, and the best of the guidance is the guidance given by Muhammad (saws). And the most evil affairs are their innovations; and every innovation is error." He (saws) would further say: I am dearer to a Muslim even than his self; and he who left behind property that is for his family; and he who dies under debt or leaves children (in helplessness), the responsibility (of paying his debt and bringing up his children) lies on me." [Muslim]

Jabir ibn Abdullah (ra) reported: The Messenger of Allah, peace and blessings be upon him, would praise Allah in his sermon, as He deserves to be praised, and then he would say, "Whomever Allah guides, no one can lead him astray. Whomever Allah sends astray, no one can guide him. The truest word is the Book of Allah, and the best guidance is the guidance of Muhammad (saws). The evilest matters in religion are those that are newly invented, for every newly invented matter is an innovation, every innovation is misguidance, and every misguidance is in the Hellfire." [Sunan an-Nasa'i]. In Arabic script, it is as follows:

مَنْ يَهْدِهِ اللَّهُ فَلَا مُضِلَّ لَهُ وَمَنْ يُضْلِلْهُ فَلَا هَادِيَ لَهُ إِنَّ أَصْدَقَ الْحَدِيثِ كِتَابُ اللَّهِ وَأَحْسَنَ الْهَدْيِ هَدْيُ مُحَمَّدٍ وَشَرُّ الْأُمُورِ مُحْدَثَاتُهَا وَكُلُّ مُحْدَثَةٍ بِدْعَةٌ وَكُلُّ بِدْعَةٍ ضَلَالَةٌ وَكُلُّ ضَلَالَةٍ فِي النَّارِ

Tahiyyatul Masjid during Khutbah

Jabir b. 'Abdullah (ra) reported: Sulaik Ghatafani (ra) came on Friday when the Messenger of Allah (saws) was delivering the sermon. He (Sulaik) sat down. He (saws) said to him: "O Sulaik! stand and observe two rak'ahs and make them short, and then said: When any one of you comes on Friday, while the Imam delivers the sermon, he should observe two rak'ahs and should make them short." [Muslim]

Narrated Jabir bin 'Abdullah (ra): A person entered the mosque while the Prophet (saws) was delivering the Khutba on a Friday. The Prophet (saws) said to him, "Have you prayed?" The man replied in the negative.

The Prophet (saws) said, "Get up and pray two rak`at." [Bukhari, Muslim]

Hanbali and Shafi'i schools state that it is recommended for a latecomer to the Friday prayer to pray two rak'ats for greeting the mosque even if the Imam is giving the khutba. The Hanafi and Maliki schools, however consider this to be an impermissible act. All the schools of thought argue for their recommendations with proof. Allah knows the best.

A man should not make his brother get up to sit in his place

Narrated Ibn Juraij: I heard Nazi' saying, Ibn `Umar (ra) said: "The Prophet (saws) forbade that a man should make another man to get up to sit in his place". I said to Nafi`, "Is it for Jumua prayer only?" He replied, "For Jumua prayer and any other (prayer)." [Bukhari]

What is to be recited in Jumu'ah prayer

Ibn Abu Rafi' said: Marwan appointed Abu Huraira (ra) as his deputy in Madina and he himself left for Makkah. Abu Huraira (ra) led us in the Jumu'ah prayer and recited after Surah Jumu'a in the second rak'ah 'When the hypocrites came to thee' (Surah al-Munafiqun). I then met Abu Huraira (ra) as he came back and said to him: You have recited two surahs which 'Ali b. Abu Talib (ra) used to recite in Kufah. Upon this Abu Huraira (ra) said: I heard the Messenger of Allah (saws) reciting these two in the Friday (prayer). [Muslim]

Prayer after Jumu'a

Abu Huraira (ra) reported Allah's Messenger (saws) as saying: "When any one of you observe the Jumu'ah prayer (two obligatory rak'ahs in congregation), he should observe four (rak'ahs) afterwards." [Muslim]

Suhail reported on the authority of Abu Huraira (ra) that the Messenger of Allah (saws) said: "When you observe prayer after (the two obligatory rak'ahs) of Jumu'ah, you should observe four rak'ahs (and 'Amr in his narration has made this addition that Ibn Idris said this on the authority of Suhail): And if you are in a hurry on account of something, you should observe two rak'ahs in the mosque and two when you return (to your house)." [Muslim]

Not to attend the Jumu'a (prayer) if it is raining

Narrated Muhammad bin Seereen: On a rainy day Ibn `Abbas (ra) said to his Mu'azzin, "After saying, 'Ash-hadu anna Muhammadan Rasulullah' (I testify that Muhammad is Allah's Messenger (saws)), do not say 'Haiya 'Alas-Salat' (come for the prayer) but say 'Pray in your houses'." (The man did so). But the people disliked it. Ibn `Abbas (ra) said, "It was done by one who was much better than I (i.e. the Prophet saws). No doubt, the Jumu'a prayer is compulsory but I dislike to put you to task by bringing you out walking in mud and slush." [Bukhari]
[Note: Those days, floor of the Masjid of the Prophet (saws) was not made of concrete and it was not protected from rain]

The Prophet (saws) used to recite Surah Qaf

It was narrated that Umm Hisham bin Harisah bin An-Nu'man said: "Our oven and the oven of the Messenger of Allah (saws) were the same for two years, or for one year and part of a year. And I only learned " ق وَالْقُرْآنِ الْمَجِيدِ Qaf by the Glorious Quran" from the tongue of the Messenger of Allah (saws), who used to recite it every Friday from the Minbar, when he addressed the people." [Muslim]

Tahajjud

Tahajjud is an Arabic word which means to remain awake at night. Therefore, it is called the night prayer or Qiyam-ul-lail. The prayer is highly rewarding because it is mentioned in the Quran and is encouraged by the Prophet (saws). Tahajjud prayer is optional and not obligatory and missing it is not a sin. However, there is a great significance and several blessings associated with it. Believed to be the most virtuous amongst the optional prayers, Tahajjud is considered to be a part of the Sunnah of Prophet Muhammad (saws).
Those who perform Tahajjud prayer regularly are sure to earn the blessings of Allah SWT. It is also said that this prayer brings a Muslim

closer to the Almighty and his/her life is filled with peace and brightness. The Holy Quran and several Hadiths emphasize the importance of Tahajjud prayer. Allah SWT says (interpretation of meaning):

"And they who pass the night prostrating themselves before their Lord and standing." (Ch 25:64)

"And from [part of] the night, pray with it as additional [worship] for you; it is expected that your Lord will resurrect you to a praised station." (Ch 17:79)

Usefulness of optional prayers

Narrated Abu Hurairah (saws): "The Messenger of Allah (saws) as saying: The most excellent fast after Ramadan is Allah's month al-Muharram, and the most excellent prayer after the prescribed prayer is the prayer during night." [Sunan Abu Dawud]

The Prophet (saws) said: The first thing about which the people will be called to account out of their actions on the Day of Judgment is Salat. Our Lord, the Exalted, will say to the angels, though He knows better: "Look into the prayer of My servant and see whether he has offered it perfectly or imperfectly." If it is perfect, that will be recorded perfect. If it is defective, He will say: "See there are some optional prayers offered by My servant." If there are optional prayer to his credit, He will say: "Compensate the obligatory prayer by the optional prayer for My servant." Then all the actions will be considered similarly. [Sunan Abu Dawud]

Messenger of Allah (saws) said: Allah the Exalted has said: "I will declare war against him who shows hostility to a pious worshipper of Mine. And the most beloved thing with which My slave comes nearer to Me is what I have enjoined upon him; and My slave keeps on coming closer to Me through performing Nawafil (prayer or doing extra deeds besides what is Fard) till I love him. When I love him, I become his hearing with which he hears, his seeing with which he sees, his hand with which he strikes, and his leg with which he walks; and if he asks (something) from Me, I give him, and if he asks My Protection (refuge), I protect him". [Bukhari]

In the night there is an hour when supplications are answered

Jabir (ra) said he heard Allah's Messenger (saws) say: "There is an hour during the night in which no Muslim individual will ask Allah SWT for good in this world and the next without His giving it to him; and that applies to every night." [Muslim]

Abu Huraira (ra) reported Allah's Messenger (saws) as saying: Allah SWT descends every night to the lowest heaven when one-third of the first part of the night is over and says: "I am the Lord; I am the Lord: who is there to supplicate Me so that I answer him? Who is there to beg of Me so that I grant him? Who is there to beg forgiveness from Me so that I forgive him?" He continues like this till the day breaks. [Bukhari, Muslim]

To recite for a long time in the night prayers

Abdullah (ra) reported: I prayed with the Messenger of Allah (saws) and he (saws) lengthened it till I entertained an evil thought. It was said to him what that thought was. He said: I thought that I should sit down and forsake him. [Muslim]

A'isha (ra) reported that the Messenger of Allah (saws) had a mat and he (saws) used it for making an apartment during the night and observed prayer in it, and the people began to pray with him, and he spread it (the mat) during the day time. The people crowded round him one night. He (saws) then said: "O people, perform such acts as you are capable of doing, for Allah does not grow weary but you will get tired. The acts most pleasing to Allah are those which are done continuously, even if they are small. And it was the habit of the members of Muhammad's (saws) household that whenever they did an act they did it continuously." [Muslim]

Number of rak'ahs in Tahajjud

There are no fixed set number of rak'ahs one must pray. It is recommended the Salah is offered in units of two rak'ahs. One may offer 2, 4, 6, 8, or even 10 rak'ahs for tahajjud, it is encouraged that one prays as many as he would wish. The Prophet (saws) said, "Take on only as much as you can do of good deeds, for the best of deeds is that which is done consistently, even if it is little". [Sunan Ibn Majah]

Hadith: Sa'eed bin Abi Sa'eed Al-Maqburi narrated that Abu Salamah informed him that he had asked Aishah (ra): "How was the Salat of Allah's Messenger (saws) [at night] during Ramadan?" She said: "Allah's Messenger (saws) would pray - neither in Ramadan nor in any other month - more than eleven Rak'ah. He would pray four, and do not ask about their excellence or length, then he would pray four, and do not ask about their excellence or length, then he would pray three." Aishah (ra) said: "I asked: 'O Messenger of Allah (saws)! Do you sleep before having performed Witr?" He said: "O Aishah! Indeed, my eyes sleep but my heart does not sleep." [Tirmizi]]

Hadith: Narrated Masruq: I asked Aisha (ra) about the night prayer of Allah's Messenger (saws) and she said, "It was seven, nine or eleven rak`ah besides the two rak`ah of the Fajr prayer (i.e. Sunnah). [Bukhari]

Hadith: Narrated Aisha (ra): The Prophet (saws) used to offer thirteen rak'ah of the night prayer and that included the witr and two rak`at (Sunna) of the Fajr prayer. [Bukhari]

The steps to praying the Tahajjud is the same as praying any other of the daily prayers. This prayer must be read after Isha and before Fajr. The Sunnah is to offer the Witr Salat after the Tahajjud. All other conditions for salat also apply to the Tahajjud prayer.

Time for offering Tahajjud

Narrated Masruq: I asked `Aisha (ra): "What deed was the most beloved to the Prophet (saws)?" She said, "The regular constant one." I said, "At what time did he (saws) use to get up at night (for the Tahajjud night prayer)?' She said, "He (saws) used to get up on hearing (the crowing of) the cock (the last third of the night). [Bukhari]

Istisqa' prayer (prayer for rain)

Narrated `Abdullah bin Zaid (ra): The Prophet (saws) went towards the Musalla and invoked Allah for rain. He (saws) faced the Qibla and wore his cloak inside out, and offered two rak`ah. [Bukhari]

Narrated Sharik bin `Abdullah bin Abi Namir: I heard Anas bin Malik (ra) saying: On a Friday, a person entered the main Mosque through the gate facing the pulpit while Allah's Messenger (saws) was delivering the Khutba. The man stood in front of Allah's Apostle (saws) and said, "O

Allah's Messenger (saws)! The livestock are dying and the roads are cut off; so please pray to Allah for rain." Anas (ra) added: Allah's Messenger (saws) raised both his hands and said, "O Allah! Bless us with rain! O Allah! Bless us with rain! O Allah! Bless us with rain!" Anas (ra) added: By Allah, we could not see any trace of cloud in the sky and there was no building or a house between us and (the mountains of) Sila. Anas (ra) added: A heavy cloud like a shield appeared from behind it (i.e. Sila' Mountain). When it came in the middle of the sky, it spread and then rained. Anas (ra) further said: By Allah! We could not see the sun for a week. Next Friday a person entered through the same gate and at that time Allah's Messenger (saws) was delivering the Friday's Khutba. The man stood in front of him and said: "O Allah's Messenger (saws)! The livestock are dying and the roads are cut off, please pray to Allah to withhold rain." Anas (ra) added: Allah's Messenger (saws) raised both his hands and said, "O Allah! Round about us and not on us. O Allah! On the plateaus, on the mountains, on the hills, in the valleys and on the places where trees grow." So, the rain stopped and we came out walking in the sun. Sharik asked Anas (ra) whether it was the same person who had asked for the rain (the last Friday). Anas (ra) replied that he did not know. [Bukhari]

The Istisqa' prayer consists of two Rak'at

Narrated 'Abbad bin Tamim from his uncle who said: "The Prophet (saws) invoked Allah for rain and offered a two rak'at prayer and he put his cloak inside out." [Bukhari]

Invoking for rain after Prophet's (saws) lifetime

Narrated Anas (ra): Whenever drought threatened them, 'Umar bin Al-Khattab (ra) used to ask Al-Abbas bin 'Abdul Muttalib (ra) to invoke Allah for rain. He (Umar) used to say, "O Allah! We used to ask our Prophet (saws) to invoke You for rain, and You would bless us with rain, and now we ask his uncle to invoke You for rain. O Allah! Bless us with rain." And so it would rain. [Bukhari]

To invoke Allah for rain while standing

Narrated 'Abdullah bin Yazid Al-Ansari that he went out with Al-Bara' bin 'Azib, and Zaid bin Arqam and invoked for rain. He ('Abdullah bin

Yazid) stood up but not on a pulpit and invoked Allah for rain and then offered two Rak'a prayers with loud recitation without pronouncing Adhan or Iqama. Abu Ishaq said that 'Adbullah bin Yazid (ra) had seen the Prophet (saws) (doing the same). [Bukhari]

People should raise hands along with the Imam

Narrated Anas bin Malik (ra): A Bedouin came to Allah's Messenger (saws) on a Friday and said, "O Allah's Messenger (saws)! The livestock, the offspring, and the people have perished." So, Allah's Messenger (saws) raised both his hands invoking Allah (for rain) and the people too raised their hands with Allah's Messenger (saws) invoking Allah (for rain). We had not left the mosque when it started raining. It rained till the next Friday when the same man came to Allah's Messenger (saws) and said, "O Allah's Messenger (saws)! The travellers are compelled to postpone their journeys (because of excessive rain) and the roads are overflowed." [Bukhari]

What should be said (or what to say) if it rains

Narrated Aisha (ra): Whenever Allah's Messenger (saws) saw the rain, he used to say, "O Allah! Let it be a strong fruitful rain." [Bukhari]

Salat during a solar eclipse

Narrated Abu Bakra (ra): We were with Allah's Messenger (saws) when the sun eclipsed. Allah's Messenger (saws) stood up dragging his cloak till he entered the Mosque. He led us in a two-rak'at prayer till the sun (eclipse) had cleared. Then the Prophet (saws) said, "The sun and the moon do not eclipse because of someone's death. So whenever you see these eclipses pray and invoke (Allah) till the eclipse is over." [Bukhari]
Narrated Al-Mughira bin Shu'ba (ra): The sun eclipsed in the lifetime of Allah's Messenger (saws) on the day when (his son) Ibrahim (ra) died. So the people said that the sun had eclipsed because of the death of Ibrahim. Allah's Messenger (saws) said, "The sun and the moon do not eclipse because of the death or life (i.e. birth) of someone. When you see the eclipse pray and invoke Allah." [Bukhari]

Narrated `Abdullah bin `Amr (ra): "When the sun eclipsed in the lifetime of Allah's Messenger (saws) an announcement was made that a prayer was to be offered in congregation." [Bukhari]

Benefits of Salat in the light of Science

Salat involves various physical movements and positions, which have been scientifically proven to have scientific benefits. Muslims offer their daily prayers out of their religious duty; however, modern day science has shed light on the physical advantages of offering Salat. Benefits of Salat in the light of science is reproduced (abridged) from **'The Islamic prayer (Salah/Namaaz) and yoga togetherness in mental health'** by Dr Shabbir Ahmed Sayeed and Dr Anand Prakash, Indian Journal of Psychiatry, vol 55, Jan 2013.

'Before every mandatory salat or when one intends to recite the Holy Qur'an the Muslim performs Wudu and thereby maintains a high level of physical cleanliness and spiritual purity. The mind is put to rest from worldly distractions and stress as the act of ablution conditions the psyche to focus singularly on the act of obedience and submission to His will. By commencing the salat with clean body and clear intention the worshiper enters into a state of mind appropriate to communicate with Allah. This is an exclusive act performed at least five times by the Muslims and has scientifically been noted to relax the mind and reduce stress levels as the spirituality overtakes any worldly concern. The physical and physiological benefits of salah are multiple to say the least. Most of the body muscles and joints are exercised during Salah. In the most noteworthy movement of prostration besides the limb muscles, the back and perineum muscles as well are exercised repeatedly. The neck muscles, in particular, are strengthened such that it is uncommon to find a person offering regular salah prostrating at least 34 times a day to suffer from cervical spondylosis or myalgias. Sajdah is the only position in which the head is in a position lower than the heart and therefore, receives increased blood supply. This surge in blood supply has a positive effect on memory, concentration, psyche and other cognitive abilities. During Sajdah dissipation of the electromagnetic energy accumulated from the atmosphere takes place by the grounding effect at regular intervals resulting in a calming feeling. A recent study investigating the alpha brain activity during Muslim prayers has reported increased amplitude in the parietal and occipital regions suggestive of parasympathetic elevation, thus indicating a state of relaxation.

Khushu refers to a state of mind in salah when we stand in front of Allah and fully direct our minds and hearts towards Him. Anything less not only diminishes the rewards of our worship but a lost opportunity for our spiritual rejuvenation as well. In psychological terms, we can liken this state of mind to a single-minded immersion of oneself with a deep focus on the activity at hand and one that leads to maximum performance. We know that our state of mind, directly or indirectly, impacts almost everything that we do in life. Being in a good state of mind make us feel livelier and more productive, and life generally seems more fulfilling. That is the ultimate objective of prayers and of course, of any therapy as well.'

Summary

- We must perform Friday prayer otherwise Allah will seal our hearts.
- Taking a bath on Friday is virtuous.
- During Khutbah, we should be calm and quiet and listen to it.
- There is a lucky time on Friday.
- Offer four rak'ahs prayer after fard Friday prayer in Masjid.
- Tahajjud is optional but is highly rewarding.
- Prophet (saws) used to offer salat for rain and during eclipses.

5. Fasting in Ramadan

Ramadan is observed by practicing Muslims as a month of fasting and prayer. It celebrates the first revelation of the Holy Book and is one of the five pillars of Islam. The festival Eid al-Fitr marks the end of Ramadan. The Arabic word for fasting means "to refrain," not only from food and drink but also from evil actions, thoughts, or words. The physical fast takes place on a daily basis from sunrise to sunset. Before dawn, people take their pre-fast meal called the suhoor. The fast will be broken with a meal called the iftar at sunset.

In scientific terminology, fasting in Ramadan is called 'Time Restricted Feeding' (TRF). It has attracted lot of attention in Medical Science, Nutrition Science, Diabetology etc. Detail discussion of these topics is beyond the scope of this book. However, a brief summary is presented at the end of this Chapter to illustrate importance of fasting otherwise.

Seeing the crescent moon

Talhah ibn 'Ubayd (ra) reported: Whenever the Messenger of Allah (saws) saw the crescent moon, he would say:

اللَّهُمَّ أَهْلِلْهُ عَلَيْنَا بِالْيُمْنِ وَالْإِيمَانِ وَالسَّلَامَةِ وَالْإِسْلَامِ رَبِّي وَرَبُّكَ اللَّهُ

O Allah, bring it over us with blessings and faith, safety and Islam. My Lord and your Lord is Allah. [Tirmizi]

In another narration, the Prophet (saws) said:

اللَّهُمَّ أَهِلَّهُ عَلَيْنَا بِالْأَمْنِ وَالْإِيمَانِ وَالسَّلَامَةِ وَالْإِسْلَامِ وَالتَّوْفِيقِ لِمَا تُحِبُّ وَتَرْضَى رَبَّنَا وَرَبُّكَ اللَّهُ

O Allah, bring it over us with safety and faith, security and Islam, guidance to what You love and is pleasing to You. Our Lord and your Lord is Allah. [Ibn Ḥibban]

Importance of Ramadan and its description

Allah SWT says in the Qur'an (interpretation of meaning):
O believers! Fasting is prescribed for you—as it was for those before you—so perhaps you will become mindful of Allah (Ch 2:183)

Hadith: Wasila ibn al-Asqa' (ra) reported: The Messenger of Allah, (saws) said: The scriptures of Ibrahim (as) were revealed on the first night of Ramadan. The Torah was revealed after six nights of Ramadan had passed, the Inzeel was revealed after thirteen nights of Ramadan had passed, and the Quran was revealed after twenty-four nights of Ramadan had passed. [Musnad Aḥmad]

Hadith: Narrated Ibn 'Umar (ra): I heard Allah's Messenger (saws) saying, "When you see the crescent (of the month of Ramadan), start fasting, and when you see the crescent (of the month of Shawwal), stop fasting; and if the sky is overcast (and you can't see it) then regard the month of Ramadan as of 30 days." [Bukhari]

Hadith: Narrated Abu Huraira (ra): Allah's Messenger (saws) said, "When the month of Ramadan comes, the gates of Paradise are opened and the gates of the (Hell) Fire are closed, and the devils are chained." [Bukhari]

Note: The devils here are the strongest devils and 'Maradah' are such devils. 'Maradah' is mentioned in Sunan an-Nasai and Musnad Ahmad. The 'Maradah' are the most hostile towards humans. 'Marada' is also mentioned in the Qur'an (interpretation of the meaning)

$$\text{وَحِفْظًا مِّن كُلِّ شَيْطَٰنٍ مَّارِدٍ}$$

and for protection from every rebellious devil. (Ch 37:7)

There is always a question: if devils are chained, why then people do commit sin in Ramadan? Several answers have been forwarded. There are many types of Satans with varying levels of wickedness. In Ramadan, smaller Satans are not chained. Some say that it is due to the long-term effect that Satan leaves on us. Committing a sin becomes a habit and even when Satan is chained we still tend to commit some sins that have become our habit. It is like the 'inertia of motion' in Physics and simple example is that after switching off the electric fans, it remains in motion for some period of time due to inertia of motion.

Hadith: The Prophet (saws) said: "On the first night of the month of Ramadan, the devils are chained and the jinn are restrained, the gates of Hell fire are closed and none of its gates are opened, the gates of Paradise are opened and none of its gates are closed, and a heavenly caller announces: O seeker of good, come near! O seeker of evil, stop short! Allah has those He saves from the Hellfire, and that is during every night." [Tirmizi]

Hadith: Abu Huraira (ra) reported: The Messenger of Allah (saws) said: "The five prayers, Friday to Friday, and Ramadan to Ramadan will be expiation for the sins (minor sins) between them, so long as major sins are avoided." [Muslim]

Hadith: Abu Sa'id al-Khudri (ra) reported: The Messenger of Allah, (saws) said: "Verily, Allah has people He redeems in every day and night of Ramadan, and every servant among them has a supplication that will be answered." [Musnad Aḥmad]

Hadith: Abu Zarr (ra) reported: The Messenger of Allah, (saws) said: "Verily, whoever stands for prayer in Ramadan with the Imam until he is finished, it will be recorded as if he prayed the entire night." [Tirmizi]

Hadith: Ibn Abbas (ra) reported: The Messenger of Allah, (saws) said: "Verily, the Umrah pilgrimage during Ramadan is equal to Hajj." [Bukhari]

Hadith: The Messenger of Allah, (saws) was the most generous of people and he was even more generous in Ramadan when Jibril would meet him. He would meet him every night of Ramadan to study the Quran. Thus, the Prophet (saws) would be more generous than a nourishing wind. [Bukhari]

Hadith: Abu Huraira (ra) reported: The Prophet (saws) ascended the pulpit and he (saws) said, "Amin, amin, amin." It was said, "O Messenger of Allah (saws), you ascended the pulpit and said amin, amin, amin." The Prophet (saws) said, "Verily, Jibril came to me and he said: Whoever reaches the month of Ramadan and he is not forgiven, then he will enter Hellfire and Allah will cast him far away, so say amin. I said amin. Whoever sees his parents in their old age, one or both of them, and he does not honour them and he dies, then he will enter Hellfire and Allah will cast him far away, so say amin. I said amin. Whoever has your name mentioned in his presence and he does not send blessings upon you and he dies, then he will enter Hellfire and Allah will cast him far away, so say amin. I said amin." [Ṣaḥiḥ Ibn Ḥibban]

Hadith: Abu Huraira (ra) reported: The Messenger of Allah, (saws) said: "May he be humbled, who enters the month of Ramadan and it passes before he is forgiven." [Tirmizi]

Fasting

Islamic Sharia' is quite particular about which activities are allowed and which are prohibited during Ramadan. Fasting in Ramadan starts at pre-sunrise and ends at sunset. According to the Quran, dawn is the time when "the white thread of dawn appears to you distinct from its black thread." The fasting ends when "the night appears" (Surah al-Baqarah, Ch 2: 187).

Muslims have to fast during daylight hours. But in the far north of Norway, Sweden, and Canada, in many months the Sun never sinks below the horizon. There are no clear guidelines for Iftar and Suhur for these areas. Muslim community in these areas have come up with different strategies. In Tromso, (northern Norway) people follow the sunrise and sunset times of Makkah. Muslims in Iqaluit (Canada) follow the sunrise and sunset of Ottawa in Canada which is outside the Arctic circle.

Fasting in Ramadan reminds our dependence on Almighty for sustenance, to feel compassion for the poor, and to focus on our relationship with Allah SWT. During Ramadan, Muslims abstain from eating any food, drinking any liquids, smoking cigarettes, and engaging in any sexual activity. Muslims try to control jealousy, anger, slandering and malicious gossiping.

Hadith: Narrated `Aisha (ra): Bilal (ra) used to pronounce the Azan at night, so Allah's Messenger (saws) said, "Carry on taking your meals (eat and drink) till Ibn Um Maktum (ra) pronounces the Azan, for he does not pronounce it till it is dawn." [Bukhari]

Hadith: Narrated Adi bin Hatim (ra): When the above verses were revealed: 'Until the white thread appears to you, distinct from the black thread,' I took two (hair) strings, one black and the other white, and kept them under my pillow and went on looking at them throughout the night but could not make anything out of it. So, the next morning I went to Allah's Messenger (saws) and told him the whole story. He explained to me, "That verse means the darkness of the night and the whiteness of the dawn." [Bukhari]

Hadith: Sahl ibn Sa'd (ra) reported: The Messenger of Allah (saws) said: "People will continue in goodness as long as they hasten to break their fast." [Bukhari]

Virtues and reward of fasting

Narrated Abu Huraira (ra): The Prophet (saws) said: Allah said: "The Fast is for Me and I will give the reward for it, as he (the one who observes the fast) leaves his sexual desire, food and drink for My Sake. Fasting is a screen (from Hell) and there are two pleasures for a fasting person, one at the time of breaking his fast, and the other at the time when he will meet his Lord. And the smell of the mouth of a fasting person is better in Allah's Sight than the smell of musk." [Bukhari]

Narrated Sahl (ra): The Prophet (saws) said: There is a gate in Paradise called Ar-Raiyan, and those who observe fasts will enter through it on the Day of Resurrection and none except them will enter through it. It will be said, "Where are those who used to observe fasts? They will get up, and none except them will enter through it. After their entry the gate will be closed and nobody will enter through it." [Bukhari]

Amr ibn Murrah (ra) reported: A man came to the Messenger of Allah (saws) and he said, "O Messenger of Allah (saws), what do you think if I testify there is no God but Allah and you are the Messenger of Allah, I perform the five prayers, I pay the obligatory alms, I fast the month of Ramadan and stand for prayer in it. Among whom will I be?" The Prophet (saws) said: "Among the truthful and the martyrs." [Ṣaḥiḥ Ibn Ḥibban]

Abu Huraira (ra) reported: There were two men from the tribe of Quda'ah who embraced Islam with the Messenger of Allah (saws). One of them was martyred and the other lived for another year. Talha (ra) said, "I had a dream of Paradise and I saw the one who lived longer enter Paradise before the martyr. I was amazed by that and when I woke up, I mentioned it to the Prophet (saws)." The Prophet (saws) said: "Did he not fast the month of Ramadan after him? And he performed six thousand or so bowings in prayer throughout the year?" [Musnad Aḥmad]

Abu Umamah (ra) reported: The Messenger of Allah (saws) said in his farewell sermon: "Fear Allah your Lord, pray your five prayers, fast your month of Ramadan, give charity from your wealth, and obey those in authority over you. You will enter the Paradise of your Lord." [Tirmizi]

Prohibitions in fasting

Allah SWT says (interpretation of meaning):
It has been made permissible for you to be intimate with your wives during the nights preceding the fast. Your spouses are a garment for you as you are for them. Allah knows that you were deceiving yourselves. So He has accepted your repentance and pardoned you. So now you may be intimate with them and seek what Allah has prescribed for you. You may eat and drink until you see the light of dawn breaking the darkness of night, then complete the fast until nightfall. Do not be intimate with your spouses while you are meditating in the mosques. These are the limits set by Allah, so do not exceed them. This is how Allah makes His revelations clear to people, so they may become mindful of Him . (Ch 2:187)

Hadith: Narrated Abu Huraira (ra): Allah's Messenger (saws) said, "Fasting is a shield (or a screen or a shelter). So, the person observing fasting should avoid sexual relation with his wife and should not behave foolishly and impudently, and if somebody fights with him or abuses him, he should tell him twice: I am fasting." The Prophet (saws) added, "By Him in Whose Hands my soul is, the smell coming out from the mouth of a fasting person is better in the sight of Allah than the smell of musk. (Allah says about the fasting person): He has left his food, drink and desires for My sake. The fast is for Me. So, I will reward (the fasting person) for it and the reward of good deeds is multiplied ten times." [Bukhari]

Hadith: Narrated Abu Huraira (ra): The Prophet (saws) said, "Whoever does not give up forged speech and evil actions, Allah is not in need of his leaving his food and drink (i.e. Allah will not accept his fasting.)" [Bukhari]

Hadith: Narrated Abu Huraira (ra): While we were sitting with the Prophet (saws) a man came and said, "O Allah's Messenger (saws)! I have been ruined." Allah's Messenger (saws) asked what was the matter with him. He replied, "I had sexual intercourse with my wife while I was fasting." Allah's Messenger (saws) asked him, "Can you afford to manumit a slave?" He replied in the negative. Allah's Messenger (saws) asked him, "Can you fast for two successive months?" He replied in the negative. The Prophet (saws) asked him, "Can you afford to feed sixty poor persons?" He replied in the negative. The Prophet (saws) kept silent and while we were in that state, a big basket full of dates was brought to the Prophet (saws). He (saws) asked, "Where is the questioner?" He replied, "I (am here)." The Prophet (saws) said (to him), "Take this (basket of dates) and give it in charity." The man said, "Should I give it to a person poorer than I? By Allah; there is no family between its (i.e. Madinah's) two mountains who are poorer than I." The Prophet (saws) smiled till his pre-molar teeth became visible and then said, "Feed your family with it." [Bukhari]

Hadith: The Prophet (saws) said: "When one of you wake up in the morning for fasting, then he should not use obscene language or behave foolishly. If anyone abuses him or fights with him, he should say twice: Indeed, I am fasting." [Muslim]

Suhur

Narrated Anas (ra): Zaid bin Thabit (ra) said: We took the Suhur with the Prophet (saws). Then he (saws) stood for the prayer. I asked, "What was the interval between the Suhur and the Azan?" He replied, "The interval was sufficient to recite fifty verses of the Qur'an." [Bukhari]

Narrated Anas bin Malik (ra): The Prophet (saws) said, "Take Suhur as there is a blessing in it." [Bukhari]

Al 'Irbad ibn Sariyah (ra) reported: The Messenger of Allah (saws) invited me to the pre-fasting meal during Ramadan and he (saws) said: "Onward to the blessed meal!" [Abu Dawud]

Concerning when fasting is not invalid

Narrated `Aisha (ra) and Um Salama (ra): At times Allah's Messenger (saws) used to get up in the morning in the state of Janaba after having sexual relations with his wives, he (saws) would then take a bath and fast. [Bukhari]

Narrated `Aisha (ra): The Prophet (saws) used to kiss and embrace (his wives) while he (saws) was fasting, and he (saws) had more power to control his desires than any of you. [Bukhari]

Said Jabir (ra), "The person who gets discharge after casting a look (on his wife) should complete his fast." [Bukhari]

Narrated Abu Huraira (ra): The Prophet (saws) said, "If somebody eats or drinks forgetfully then he should complete his fast, for what he has eaten or drunk, has been given to him by Allah." [Bukhari]

Narrated 'Amir bin Rabi`a (ra): I saw the Prophet (saws) cleaning his teeth with Siwak while he was fasting so many times as I can't count. And narrated Abu Huraira (ra): The Prophet (saws) said: "But for my fear that it would be hard for my followers, I would have ordered them to clean their teeth with Siwak on every performance of ablution." The same is narrated by Jabir and Zaid bin Khalid (ra) from the Prophet (saws) who did not differentiate between a fasting and a non-fasting person in this respect (using Siwak). Aisha (ra) said: The Prophet (saws) said: "It (i.e. Siwak) is a purification for the mouth and it is a way of seeking Allah's pleasures." Ata' and Qatada said, "There is no harm in swallowing the resultant saliva." [Bukhari]

Narrated Ibn `Abbas (ra): The Prophet (saws) was cupped while he was in the state of Ihram, and also while he was observing a fast. [Bukhari]

The Prophet (saws) said: "Whoever breaks his fast forgetfully in the month of Ramadan, there is no compensation or expiation for it." [Sahih Ibn Hibban]

Fasting during travel

Allah SWT says in the Quran (that means):

Ramaḍan is the month in which the Quran was revealed as a guide for humanity with clear proofs of guidance and the decisive authority. So whoever is present this month, let them fast. But whoever is ill or on a journey, then let them fast an equal number of days after Ramaḍan . Allah intends ease for you, not hardship, so that you may complete the prescribed period and proclaim the greatness of Allah for guiding you, and perhaps you will be grateful. (Ch 2:185)

Hadith: Narrated Abu Ad-Darda (ra): We set out with Allah's Messenger (saws) on one of his journeys on a very hot day, and it was so hot that one had to put his hand over his head because of the severity of heat. None of us was fasting except the Prophet (saws) and Ibn Rawaha (ra). [Bukhari]

Hadith: Narrated Jabir bin ʿAbdullah (ra): Allah's Messenger (saws) was on a journey and saw a crowd of people, and a man was being shaded (by them). He (saws) asked, "What is the matter?" They said, "He (the man) is fasting." The Prophet (saws) said, "It is not righteousness that you fast on a journey." [Bukhari]

Hadith: Narrated Anas bin Malik (ra): We used to travel with the Prophet (saws) and neither did the fasting persons criticize those who were not fasting, nor did those who were not fasting criticize the fasting ones. [Bukhari]

Hadith: Narrated Tawus: Ibn ʿAbbas (ra) said, "Allah's Messenger (saws) set out from Madinah to Makkah and he (saws) fasted till he reached 'Usfan, where he asked for water and raised his hand to let the people see him, and then broke the fast, and did not fast after that till he reached Makkah, and that happened in Ramadan." Ibn ʿAbbas (ra) used to say, "Allah's Messenger (saws) (sometimes) fasted and (sometimes) did not fast during the journeys so whoever wished to fast could fast, and whoever wished not to fast, could do so." [Bukhari]

Make-up of fasting

Allah SWT says in the Qur'an (that means):

Fast a prescribed number of days. But whoever of you is ill or on a journey, then let them fast an equal number of days after Ramaḍan. For those who can only fast with extreme difficulty, compensation can be made by feeding a needy person for every day not fasted. But whoever volunteers to give more, it is better for them. And to fast is better for you, if only you knew. (Ch 2:184)

Hadith: Narrated Abu Usama from Hisham bin 'Urwa from Fatima: Asma bint Abi Bakr (ra) said, "We broke our fast during the lifetime of the Prophet (saws) on a cloudy day and then the sun appeared." Hisham was asked, "Were they ordered to fast in lieu of that day?" He replied, "It had to be made up for." Maʿmar said: I heard Hisham saying, "I don't know whether they fasted in lieu of that day or not." [Bukhari]

Hadith: Narrated ʿAisha (ra): Allah's Messenger (saws) said, "Whoever died and he ought to have fasted (the missed days of Ramadan) then his guardians must fast on his behalf." [Bukhari]

Hadith: Narrated 'Ata: That he heard Ibn `Abbas (ra) reciting the Divine Verse: "And for those who can fast they had a choice either fast, or feed a poor for every day." (Ch 2:184) Ibn `Abbas (ra) said, "This Verse is not abrogated, but it is meant for old men and old women who have no strength to fast, so they should feed one poor person for each day of fasting (instead of fasting). [Bukhari]

Itiqaf and night of Qadr

Itikaf means staying in Masjid during the month of Ramadan. Itikaf is one of the Sunnah which the Prophet (saws) did regularly. The basic goal of the itikaf of the Prophet (saws) was to seek Night of Qadr and to spend that night in worship.

Night of Qadr is otherwise known as the Night of Power and is considered to be the Holiest night. During this night, Angel Jibril revealed the Holy Qur'an's first verses to the Prophet Muhammad (saws). This night falls within Ramadan's final 10 days, and although the exact date is unidentified, it is commonly thought of as the Holy month's 27th day. The Qur'an says (that means):

1. *Indeed, it is We Who sent this Quran down on the Night of Glory.*
2. *And what will make you realize what the Night of Glory is?*
3. *The Night of Glory is better than a thousand months.*
4. *That night the angels and the holy spirit descend, by the permission of their Lord, for every decreed matter.*
5. *It is all peace until the break of dawn. (Ch 97:1-5)*

Hadith: Aisha (ra) said: When the last ten days of Ramadan arrived, the Prophet (saws) would tighten his belt (i.e. work hard), spend the night in worship, and awaken his family. [Bukhari]

Hadith: Aisha (ra) said: The Prophet (saws) would exert himself in worship during the last ten nights of Ramadan more so than any other time. [Muslim]

Hadith: Narrated Ibn `Umar (ra): Some people were shown the Night of Qadr as being in the last seven days (of the month of Ramadan). The

Prophet (saws) said, "Seek it in the last seven days (of Ramadan)." [Bukhari]

Hadith: Narrated Abu Huraira (ra): The Prophet (saws) said, "Whoever established prayers on the night of Qadr out of sincere faith and hoping for a reward from Allah, then all his previous sins will be forgiven; and whoever fasts in the month of Ramadan out of sincere faith, and hoping for a reward from Allah, then all his previous sins will be forgiven." [Bukhari]

Hadith: Anas ibn Malik (ra) reported: The Messenger of Allah (saws) said when the month of Ramadan began: "Verily, this month has presented itself to you. There is a night within it that is better than a thousand months. Whoever is deprived of it has been deprived of all good. None is deprived of its good but that he is truly deprived." [Sunan Ibn Majah]

Hadith: Abu Huraira (ra) reported: The Messenger of Allah (saws) said when the month of Ramadan arrived: "The month of Ramadan has come, a blessed month in which Allah Almighty has obligated you to fast. In it the gates of the heavens are opened, the gates of Hellfire are closed, the devils are chained, and in it is a night that is better than a thousand months. Thus, whoever is deprived of its good is truly deprived." [Musnad Aḥmad]

Hadith: Abu Huraira (ra) said: The Prophet (saws) would review the Quran once every year in Ramadan, and he reviewed it twice in the year he passed away. The Prophet (saws) would retreat (itiqaf) in the mosque for ten days every year, and he secluded himself for twenty days in the year he passed away. [Bukhari]

Hadith: 'A'isha (ra) reported that the Messenger of Allah (saws) used to observe itikif in the last ten days of Ramadan till Allah called him back (to his heavenly home). Then his wives observed i'tikaf after him. [Muslim]

Hadith: 'Ubadah ibn al-Samit (ra) reported: The Messenger of Allah, peace and blessings be upon him, came out to inform people about the Night of Decree in Ramadan, but two Muslim men were insulting each other. The Prophet (saws) said: Verily, I have come out to tell you about the Night of Decree, but two men were insulting each other. Thus, its knowledge was taken away and perhaps it is better for you. Look for it during the seventh, ninth, or fifth night of the last ten nights. [Bukhari]

Hadith: Aisha (ra) reported: I said, "O Messenger of Allah (saws)! If I know which night is the Night of Decree, what should I say during it?" The Prophet (saws) said:

اللَّهُمَّ إِنَّكَ عُفُوٌّ تُحِبُّ الْعَفْوَ فَاعْفُ عَنِّي

Say: O Allah, You are pardoning. You love to forgive, so forgive me. [Sunan at-Tirmizi]

Hadith: Narrated Safiya bint Huyay (ra): While Allah's Messenger (saws) was in itikaf, I called on him at night and having had a talk with him, I got up to depart. He got up also to accompany me to my dwelling place, which was then in the house of Usama bin Zaid (ra). Two Ansari men passed by, and when they saw the Prophet (saws) they hastened away. The Prophet (saws) said (to them). "Don't hurry! It is Safiya, the daughter of Huyay (i.e. my wife)." They said, "Glorified be Allah! O Allah's Messenger (saws)! (How dare we suspect you?)" He (saws) said, "Satan circulates in the human mind as blood circulates in it, and I was afraid that Satan might throw an evil thought (or something) into your hearts." [Bukhari]

Hadith: Aishah (ra) said: The Sunnah is for the person in itikaf is not to visit the sick or attend funerals, or to be intimate with his wife. But there is nothing wrong with his going out for essential needs. [Sunan Abu Dawud]

What to do in the night of Qadr

Abu Hurayrah (ra) that the Prophet (saws) said: "Whoever stays up during Laylat al-Qadr out of faith and in the hope of earning reward, all his previous sins will be forgiven." [Bukhari; Muslim]

A'isha (ra) reported that when the last ten nights began Allah's Messenger (saws) kept awake at night (for prayer and devotion), wakened his family, and prepared himself to observe prayer (with more vigour). [Muslim]

These hadiths indicate that it is prescribed to stay up and spend this night in prayer.

Why night of Qadr is important?

Allah SWT says in Surah al-Dukhan (Ch 44:1-6) that the Qur'an is sent on this night and that this is the 'blessed night'. On this night, the destiny of all creatures for the coming year is decreed such as who will live, who will die, who will be saved, who will be doomed, who will be honoured, who will be humiliated, who will be constricted or reduced for his provision and everything else that Allah wills in that year. "Therein (that night) is decreed every matter of ordainments" [al-Dukhaan, Ch 44:4] Many sins are forgiven and so many faults are concealed during this night. The Night of Qadr is better than a thousand months (i.e. worshipping Allah in that night is better than worshipping Him a thousand months, i.e. more than 83 years). Allah SWT has concealed this night so that we will strive to seek it, and will strive hard in worship in offering prayer, making du'a and seeking forgiveness to Allah.

Narrated Ubayy ibn Ka'b (ra) that the Prophet (saws) announced that one of its signs was that when the sun rose on the following morning, it had no (visible) rays. [Muslim]

Narrated Wasilah ibn al-Asqa' (ra) that the Prophet (saws) said: "Laylat al-Qadr is a bright night, neither hot nor cold, in which no meteors are seen." [Musnad Ahmad]

Continuous fasting

Narrated Abu Huraira (ra): The Prophet (saws) said twice, "(O you people) Be cautious! Do not practice Al-Wisal." The people said to him, "But you practice Al-Wisal?" The Prophet (saws) replied, "My Lord gives me food and drink during my sleep. Do that much of deeds which is within your ability." [Bukhari]

Narrated `Aisha (ra): Allah's Messenger (saws) used to fast (optional fast) till one would say that he would never stop fasting, and he would abandon fasting till one would say that he would never fast. I never saw Allah's Messenger (saws) fasting for a whole month except the month of Ramadan, and did not see him fasting in any month more than in the month of Sha'ban. [Bukhari]

Fasting during menses and post-natal periods

Narrated Abu Sa`id Al-Khudri (ra): Once Allah's Messenger (saws) went out to the Musalla (to offer the prayer) of `Id-al-Azha or Al-Fitr prayer. Then he (saws) passed by the women and said, "O women! Give alms, as

I have seen that the majority of the dwellers of Hell-fire were you (women)." They asked, "Why is it so, O Allah's Messenger (saws)?" He (saws) replied, "You curse frequently and are ungrateful to your husbands. I have not seen anyone more deficient in intelligence and religion than you. A cautious sensible man could be led astray by some of you." The women asked, "O Allah's Messenger (saws)! What is deficient in our intelligence and religion?" He (saws) said, "Is not the evidence of two women equal to the witness of one man?" They replied in the affirmative. He (saws) said, "This is the deficiency in her intelligence. Isn't it true that a woman can neither pray nor fast during her menses?" The women replied in the affirmative. He (saws) said, "This is the deficiency in her religion." [Bukhari]

A'isha (ra) reported: If one amongst us had to break fasts (of Ramadan due to natural reasons, i. e. menses) during the life of the Messenger of Allah (saws) she could not find it possible to complete them so long she had been in the presence of Allah's Messenger (saws) till Sha'ban commenced. [Bukhari]

It was narrated from 'Aishah (ra) that she used to comb the hair of the Messenger of Allah (saws) when she was menstruating and he (saws) was performing itikaf. He (saws) would put his head out to her while she was in her room. [Sunan an-Nasai]

It was narrated that Hafsah (ra: Umm 'Atiyah (ra) would never mention the Messenger of Allah (saws) without saying: "May my father be ransomed for him." I said: "Did you hear the Messenger of Allah (saws) say such and such?" And she said: "Yes, may my father be ransomed for him." He (saws) said: "Let the mature girls, virgins staying in seclusion, and menstruating woman go out and witness the good occasions and the supplications of the Muslims, but let the menstruating women keep away from the prayer place." [Sunan an-Nasai]

According to the scholars, including the four imams, are of the view that there is no minimum limit for nifas (post-natal bleeding). Whenever a woman becomes pure from nifas, she has to do ghusl and pray and fast. The matter should be based on experience, since nifas may vary from woman to woman.

Sadaqat-ul- fitr

Sadaqat-ul-Fitr (also called Zakat-ul-Fitr) is a charitable donation for every Muslim who possess the Nisab (a minimum amount of wealth); it must be paid before Eid-ul-Fitr. According Imam Shafai', Muslim should give on his own behalf and on behalf of those on whom he spends, such as wives and relatives, if they cannot give it on their own behalf. If there is a non-believer among those whom he is supporting, he does not have to give Zakat al-Fitr on his behalf, because he cannot be purified by zakat. If someone who is obliged to give Zakat al-Fitr dies before giving it, it must be given from his estate... even if the person who was supporting him also dies, the obligation still stands. (Al-Mughni, part 2) Concerning giving Zakat al-Fitr on behalf of an orphan, Imam Malik said: "The guardian should give Zakat al-Fitr on behalf of the orphans some of whose wealth is under his control, even if they are minors."

Hadith: Ibn 'Abbaas (ra) said: "The Messenger of Allah (sa) made Zakat al-Fitr obligatory as a means of purifying the fasting person from idle talk and foul language, and to feed the poor. Whoever pays it before the prayer (Eid prayer), it is an accepted zakah, and whoever pays it after the prayer, it is just a kind of charity (sadaqah)." [Abu Dawud]

Hadith: Ibn 'Umar (ra) reported that the Messenger of Allah (saws) ordered that the Sadaqat-ul-Fitr should be paid before the people go out for prayer. [Muslim]

Hadith: Ibn Umar (ra) said: The Messenger of Allah, peace and blessings be upon him, made it an obligation to pay charity at the end of Ramadan, a portion of dates or barely, upon the slave and the freeman, the male and female, the young and the old among the Muslims. The Prophet (saws) ordered it to be given before people go out for the Eid prayer. [Bukhari]

Hadith: Ibn 'Umar (ra) said that the Messenger of Allah (saws) prescribed the Sadaqa of Ramadan (Sadaqat-al-Fitr) one sa' of dates or one sa' of barley for every free man or a slave, male or female, and then the people equalised (one sa' of dates or barley) with half a sa' of wheat. [Muslim] *One sa' is approximately equal to 3.150 Kg.*

Hadith: Sad b. Abu Sarh heard Abu Sa'id al-Khudri (ra) as saying: We used to take out as the Zakat of Fitr one sa' of grain, or one sa' of barley or one sa' of dates, or one sa' of cheese or one sa' of raisins. [Muslim]

Hadith: Abu Sa'id al Khudri (ra) reported: We used to take out the Zakat of Fitr in three kinds: cheese, dates and barley. [Muslim]

Testimony that one has seen the crescent

It was narrated that 'Umair bin Anas bin Malik said: My paternal uncles among the Ansar who were among the Companions of the Messenger of Allah (saws) told me: "The new crescent of Shawwal was covered with clouds, so we fasted the next day. Then some riders came at the end of the day and testified to the Prophet (saws) that they had seen the new crescent the night before. The Messenger of Allah (saws) commanded them to break their fast and to go out to offer the Eid prayer the following morning." [Sunan Ibn Majah]

Taraweeh Prayer

Taraweeh Prayer is a night Prayer specially performed by Muslims in the month of Ramadan. However, it is to be remembered that the term 'taraweeh prayer' was not coined by the Prophet (saws).

Night Prayer during the lifetime of the Prophet (saws)

Hadith: Abu Huraira (ra) reported: The Messenger of Allah (saws) encouraged standing for night prayer in the month of Ramadan, without imposing it on them. The Prophet (saws) would say: Whoever stands in prayer during Ramadan due to faith and seeking reward, his previous sins will be forgiven. [Bukhari]

Hadith: Abdur Rahman ibn Awf (ra) reported: The Messenger of Allah (saws) said: "Verily, Ramadan is a month in which Allah Almighty has obligated its fasting. I have instituted for Muslims the practice of prayer at night. Thus, whoever fasts it with faith and expecting reward will be rid of sins like the day he was born from his mother." [Musnad Aḥmad]

Hadith: Narrated 'Aishah (ra), wife of Prophet (saws): That the Prophet (saws) once offered prayer in the mosque and the people also prayed along with him. He (saws) then prayed on the following night, and the people gathered in large numbers. They gathered on the third night too, but the Messenger of Allah (saws) did not come out to them. When the morning came, he (saws) said: I witnessed what you did, and nothing prevented me from coming out to you except that I feared that this (prayer) might be prescribed to you. That was in Ramadan. [Abu Dawud, similar in Muslim]

Hadith: Abu Salama b. Abd al-Rahman asked 'A'isha (ra) about the (night) prayer of the Messenger of Allah (saws) during the month of Ramadan. She said: The Messenger of Allah (saws) did not observe either in Ramadan or in other months more than eleven rak'ahs (of the night prayer). He saws (in the first instance) observed four rak'ahs. Ask not about their excellence and their length (i. e. these were matchless in perfection and length). He (saws) again observed four rak'ahs, and ask not about their excellence and their length. He (saws) would then observe three rak'ahs (of the Witr prayer). 'A'isha (ra) again said: I said: "Messenger of Allah (saws), do you sleep before observing the Witr prayer?" He (saws) said: "O 'A'isha, my eyes sleep but my heart does not sleep." [Muslim]

Hadith: It was narrated that Abu Dharr (ra) said: "We fasted with the Messenger of Allah (saws) in Ramadan and he (saws) did not lead us in praying Qiyam until there were seven days left in the month, when he (saws) led us in praying Qiyam until one-third of the night had passed. Then he (saws) did not lead us in praying Qiyam when there were six days left. Then he (saws) led us praying Qiyam when there were five days left until one-half of the night had passed. I said: "O Messenger of Allah (saws)! What if we spend the rest of this night praying Nawafil?" He (saws) said: "Whoever prays Qiyam with the Imam until he finishes, Allah (SWT) will record for him the Qiyam of a (whole) night." Then he (saws) did not lead us in prayer or pray Qiyam until there were three days of the month left. Then he (saws) led us in praying Qiyam when there were three days left. He (saws) gathered his family and wives (and led us in prayer) until we feared that we would miss Al-Falah. I (one of the narrators) said: "What is Al-Falah?" He said: "The suhur". [Sunan an-Nasai, Sunan Ibn Majah]

Hadith: Narrated Zaid bin Sabit (ra): Allah's Messenger (saws) made a small room (with a palm leaf mat). Allah's Messenger (saws) came out (of his house) and prayed in it. Some men came and joined him in his prayer. Then again, the next night they came for the prayer, but Allah's Messenger (saws) delayed and did not come out to them. So they raised their voices and knocked the door with small stones (to draw his attention). He (saws) came out to them in a state of anger, saying, "You are still insisting (on your deed i.e. prayer in the mosque) that I thought that this prayer might become obligatory on you. So you people, offer this prayer at your homes, for the best prayer of a person is the one which he offers at home, except the compulsory (congregational) prayer." [Bukhari]

Hadith: Abu Salama is reported to have said: I came to A'isha (ra). I said: "O mother, inform me about the prayer of the Messenger of Allah (saws)". She said: "His (night prayer) in Ramadan and (during other months) was thirteen rak'ahs at night including two rak'ahs of fajr." [Muslim]

Hadith: Narrated Ibn `Abbas (ra) that the Prophet (blessings and peace of Allah be upon him) would pray thirteen Rak`ahs at night, and two Rak`ahs after dawn, the Sunnah prayer of Fajr. [Bukhari and Muslim]

Qiyamul lail during Khilafat of Abu Bakr (ra)

When Abu Bakr (ra) was Khalifa, things were same as during the time of the Prophet (saws). People used to perform night prayer in Ramadan in their houses. It is narrated by Abu Huraira (ra) that he said: "Allah's Messenger (saws) said, "Whoever prayed at night the whole month of Ramadan out of sincere Faith and hoping for a reward from Allah, then all his previous sins will be forgiven." Ibn Shihab (a sub-narrator) said, "Allah's Messenger (saws) died and the people continued observing that (i.e. Nawafil offered individually, not in congregation), and it remained as it was during the Caliphate of Abu Bakr (ra) and in the early days of 'Umar's Caliphate." [Bukhari, Tirmizi]

Hadith: Yahya related to me from Malik from Ibn Shihab from Abu Salama ibn Abdur-Rahman ibn Awf from Abu Hurayra (ra) that the Messenger of Allah (saws) used to exhort people to watch the night in prayer in Ramadan but never ordered it definitely. He used to say, "Whoever watches the night in prayer in Ramadan with trust and expectancy, will be forgiven all his previous wrong actions."

Ibn Shihab said, "The Messenger of Allah (saws) died while that was still the custom, and it continued to be the custom in the caliphate of Abu

Bakr (ra) and at the beginning of the caliphate of Umar ibn al-Khattab (ra)." [Muwatta Imam Malik]

Qiyamul lail during Khilafat of Umar (ra)

It was narrated that Abdur Rahman bin Abdul Qari said: I went out in the company of 'Umar bin Al-Khattab (ra) one night in Ramadan to the mosque and found the people praying in different groups. A man praying alone or a man praying with a little group behind him. So, 'Umar (ra) said, "In my opinion, I would better collect these (people) under the leadership of one Qari (Reciter) (i.e. let them pray in congregation!)." So, he made up his mind to congregate them behind Ubai bin Ka'b (ra). Then on another night I went again in his company and the people were praying behind their reciter. On that, 'Umar (ra) remarked, "What an excellent Bid'at (i.e. innovation in religion) this is, but the prayer which they do not perform, but sleep at its time is better than the one they are offering." He meant the prayer in the last part of the night. (In those days) people used to pray in the early part of the night." [Bukhari]

Hadith: Yahya related to me from Malik from Muhammad ibn Yusuf that as- Sa'ib ibn Yazid said, "Umar ibn al-Khattab (ra) ordered Ubayy ibn Kab (ra) and Tamim ad-Dari (ra) to watch the night in prayer with the people for eleven rak'as. The reciter of the Qur'an would recite the Mi'in (a group of medium-sized suras) until we would be leaning on our staffs from having stood so long in prayer. And we would not leave until the approach of dawn." [Muwatta Imam Malik]

Qiyamul lail during Khilafat of Usman (ra) and Ali (ra)

During the Khilafat of Usman (ra) and Ali (ra), practice of performing Qiyamul lail continued as it was there during time of Umar (ra).

It is to be noted that there is no particular number with regard to Qiyamul layl in Ramadan. The Prophet (saws) did not specify any number for that. However, the Prophet (saws) used to stand for a long time, as it is proven from an authentic narration, in the Hadith of Huzayfah (ra), that the Prophet (saws) used to recite in one Rak`ah Al-Baqarah, An-Nisa' and Al-Imran.

The number of rak'ahs offered by the Companions of the Prophet (saws) also varied. And the companions were the persons who were more adherent to the Sunnah than anybody else and who had the more comprehensive knowledge of the Sunnah of the Prophet (saws). One may offer more or fewer Rak`ahs and the subject is not a matter of dispute.

Reciting the Qur'an in Ramadan

It is sunnah for the Muslim to read the Qur'an during Ramadan and to attempt to complete it, but that is not obligatory, i.e., if he does not complete the Qur'an he is not sinning, but he has missed out a great deal of reward. Allah SWT says (that means):

"(It is) the month of Ramadan in which the Qur'an was revealed as a guidance for mankind, clear proofs giving guidance, and the Criterion (for distinguishing right and wrong). So, whoever of you witnesses this month, let him fast it." (Ch 2:185)

Hadith: Ibn Abbas (ra) said: Fatimah (ra) reported: The Messenger of Allah (saws) said: "Jibril would come to me to revise the Quran once every year. This year he revised with me twice. I do not think it means anything but that my term will come to an end." [Bukhari]

Hadith: Aisha (ra) said: I have not known the Messenger of Allah (saws) to read the entire Quran in a single night, nor to spend the whole night in prayer until the morning, nor to spend an entire month in fasting, except during the month of Ramadan. [Sunan an-Nasai]

Fasting in other months

Narrated `Aisha (ra): (The tribe of) Quraish used to fast on the Day of Ashura' in the Pre-Islamic period, and then Allah's Apostle (saws) ordered (Muslims) to fast on it till the fasting in the month of Ramadan was prescribed; whereupon the Prophet (saws) said, "He who wants to fast (on 'Ashura') may fast, and he who does not want to fast may not fast." [Bukhari]

Narrated Abu Huraira (ra): I heard the Prophet (saws) saying, "None of you should fast on Friday unless he fasts a day before or after it." [Bukhari]

Narrated Abu Huraira (ra): My friend (i.e. the Prophet saws) advised me to observe three things: (1) to fast three days a month; (2) to pray two rak`at of Duha prayer (forenoon prayer); and (3) to pray witr before sleeping. [Bukhari]

Abu Ayyub (ra) reported: The Messenger of Allah (saws) said: Whoever fasts the month of Ramadan and then follows it with six days of fasting in the month of Shawwal, it will be as if he fasted for the entire year. [Bukhari]

Abu Huraira (ra) reported: The Messenger of Allah (saws) said: Fasting the month of patience, Ramadan, and three days from every month is like fasting a lifetime. [Sunan an-Nasai]

Abu Huraira (ra) reported: The Messenger of Allah (saws) said: The best fast after the month of Ramadan is fasting in the month of Allah, al-Muharram. [Muslim]

Narrated Um Al-Fadl bint Al-Haris (ra): "While the people were with me on the day of `Arafat, they differed as to whether the Prophet (saws) was fasting or not; some said that he was fasting while others said that he was not fasting. So, I sent to him a bowl full of milk while he was riding over his camel and he drank it." [Bukhari]

A'isha (ra) said: "The Messenger (saws) used to fast until we thought he would never break his fast, and not fast until we thought he would never fast. I never saw the Messenger of Allah (saws) fasting for an entire month except in Ramadan, and I never saw him fast more than he did in Sha'ban." [Bukhari, Muslim]

Usamah ibn Zayd (ra) said: I said: "O Messenger of Allah (saws), I do not see you fasting in any other month like you fast in Sha'ban." He (saws) said: "That is a month to which people do not pay attention, between Rajab and Ramadan, and it is a month in which deeds are lifted up to the Lord of the worlds. I like for my deeds to be lifted up when I am fasting." [Sunan an-Nasai]

Narrated Aisha (ra) said: "The most beloved of months for the Messenger of Allah (saws) to fast in was Sha'ban, and his fasting in Sha'ban was continuous with his fasting in Ramadan." [Sunan Abu Dawud]

Imran b. Husain (ra) reported Allah's Messenger (saws) having said to him or to someone else: Did you fast in the middle of sha'ban? He said: No. Thereupon he (saws) said: If you did not observe fast, then you should observe fast for two days. [Muslim]

Eid-al-fitr

Eid al-fitr is one of the two major festivals in Islam after the month of Ramadan. Muslims gather on a field and offer prayer together.

Fasting on days of Eid prohibited

Narrated Abu `Ubaid: (the slave of Ibn Azhar) I witnessed the `Eid with `Umar bin Al-Khattab (ra) who said, "Allah's Messenger (saws) has forbidden people to fast on the day on which you break fasting (the fasts of Ramadan) and the day on which you eat the meat of your sacrifices (the first day of Id ul Fitr and Id ul-Azha)." [Bukhari]

Eating on the day of Fitr before Eid-al-Fitr

Narrated Anas bin Malik (ra): Allah's Messenger (saws) never proceeded (for the prayer) on the Day of `Eid-ul-Fitr unless he had eaten some dates. Anas (ra) also narrated: The Prophet (saws) used to eat odd number of dates. [Bukhari]

To proceed to a masjid without a pulpit

Narrated Abu Sa`id Al-Khudri (ra): The Prophet (saws) used to proceed to the Musalla on the days of Eid-ul-Fitr and Eid-ul-Azha; the first thing to begin with was the prayer and after that he (saws) would stand in front of the people and the people would keep sitting in their rows. Then he (saws) would preach to them, advise them and give them orders, (i.e. Khutba). And after that if he (saws) wished to send an army for an expedition, he (saws) would do so; or if he (saws) wanted to give and order, he (saws) would do so, and then depart. The people followed this tradition till I went out with Marwan, the Governor of Madina, for the prayer of Eid-ul-Azha or Eid-ul-Fitr. When we reached the Musalla, there was a pulpit made by Kathir bin As-Salt. Marwan wanted to get up on that pulpit before the prayer. I got hold of his clothes but he pulled them and ascended the pulpit and delivered the Khutbah before the prayer. I said to him, "By Allah, you have changed (the Prophet's saws tradition)." He replied, "O Abu Sa`id! Gone is that which you know." I said, "By Allah! What I know is better than what I do not know." Marwan said, "People do not sit to listen to our Khutbah after the prayer, so I delivered the Khutbah before the prayer. [Bukhari]

Eid prayer before the Khutba and no Azhan or Iqama for it

Narrated `Abdullah bin `Umar (ra): Allah's Messenger (saws) used to offer the prayer of Eid-ul-Azha and Eid-ul-Fitr and then deliver the Khutbah after the prayer. [Bukhari]

Narrated Ibn `Abbas (ra): I offered the Eid prayer with Allah's Messenger (saws), Abu Bakr, `Umar and `Usman (ra) and all of them offered the prayer before delivering the Khutba. [Bukhari]

It was narrated that 'Abdullah bin Sa'ib said (ra): I attended the 'Eid prayer with the Messenger of Allah (saws). He (saws) led us in offering the 'Eid prayer, then he said: 'I have finished the prayer. Whoever wants to sit (and listen to) the khutba (sermon), then let him sit, and whoever wants to leave, then let him leave.' [Sunan Ibn Majah]

To and fro routes are different

Narrated Jabir bin `Abdullah (ra): On the Day of Eid, the Prophet (saws) used to return (after offering the Eid prayer) through a way different from that by which he (saws) went. [Bukhari]

Ghusl before Eid prayer

One of the good etiquettes of Eid is to take a bath before going out to Eid prayer. It is reported in *al-Muwatta'* that 'Abdullah ibn 'Umar (ra) used to take a bath on the day of al-Fitr before coming to the prayer-place. [Muwatta Imam Malik]

Best clothes on Eid

Abdullah ibn 'Umar (ra) said: Umar (ra) picked up a jubbah (long outer garment) made of silk that was for sale in the market, brought it to the Messenger of Allah (saws) and said, "O Messenger of Allah (saws), buy this and wear it for Eid and when the delegations come." The Messenger of Allah (saws) said, "This is the clothing of the one who has no share of the Hereafter…" [Bukhari]

Note: Prophet (saws) rejected it because it was made of silk.

Jabir (ra) said: "The Prophet (saws) had a jubbah that he would wear on Eid and on Fridays." [Saheeh Ibn Khuzaymah]

Extra Takbirs in Eid Prayers

It was narrated from 'Aishah (ra) that the Messenger of Allah (saws) said the Takbir seven and five times in (the prayer for 'Eid) Fitr and Azha, apart from the Takbir for Ruku' (bowing). [Sunan Ibn Majah]

Kasir bin 'Abdullah bin 'Amr bin 'Awf narrated, from his father, from his grandfather, that the Messenger of Allah (saws) said the Takbir in the 'Eid prayers, seven times in the first Rak'ah and five times in the second. [Sunan Ibn Majah]

Abdur-Rahman bin Sa'd bin 'Ammar bin Sa'd, the Mu'azzin of the Messenger of Allah (saws), narrated from his father, from his father, from his grandfather, that the Messenger of Allah (saws) used to say the Takbir in the 'Eid prayer, seven times in the first (Rak'ah) before reciting Qur'an, and five times in the second before reciting Qur'an. [Sunan Ibn Majah]

As evident from the above hadiths, number of Takbirs and the places where these are to be recited varies. Thus, there are differences of opinions on the number of extra takbirs in the Eid Salat. These are as follows:

- According to Imam Malik, there will be 6 extra takbirs in the first rakaat and 5 in the second rakat. These extra takbirs will be done at the beginning of each rakat.
- Imam Ahmad bin Hanbal and Imam Shafi' are of the opinion that there will be 7 takbirs in the first rakat and 5 in the second. The extra takbirs are to be recited at the beginning of each rakat.
- According to Imam Abu Hanifa, there will be 3 extra takbirs at the beginning of the first rakat and 3 takbirs at the end of the second rakat before bowing.

Allah knows the best.

Eid ul Azha

Eid ul Azha is the feast of sacrifice which is the tenth day of the month of Zul-Hijjah. The Prophet (saws) said: "The day of 'Arafah, the day of Sacrifice, and the days of Tashriq (The days of Tashriq are the 11th, 12th and 13th of Jul-Hijjah) are our festival, us Muslims, and they are days of eating and drinking." [Tirmizi]

When the Prophet (saws) came to Madinah, he (saws) found that they had two days on which they used to play. He (saws) said, "Allah has given you two days better than these, the day of al-Fitr and the day of al-Azha." [Abu Dawud]

Prophet (saws) said: "The greatest of days before Allah is the Day of Sacrifice." [Abu Dawud]

Ibn 'Umar (ra) said: The Prophet (saws) stood between the Jamarat on the Day of Sacrifice during his Hajj and said, "This is the greatest day of Hajj." [Bukhari]

The legal way of the celebrations of Eid-ul-Azha

Narrated Al-Bara (ra): I heard the Prophet (saws) delivering a Khutba saying, "The first thing to be done on this day (first day of Eid ul Azha) is to pray; and after returning from the prayer we slaughter our sacrifices (in the name of Allah) and whoever does so, he acted according to our Sunnah (traditions)." [Bukhari]

It was narrated from Anas bin Malik (ra) that a man slaughtered on the Day of Sacrifice, (meaning) before the Eid prayer, and the Prophet (saws) ordered him to do it again. [Sunan Ibn Majah]

Days of Tashriq

The days of Tashriq are the 11th, 12th and 13th of Jul-Hijjah. There are several verses and hadiths which speak of their virtue. The Prophet (saws) said concerning the days of Tashriq: "Do not fast on these days, for they are the days of eating, drinking and remembering Allah." [Musnad Ahmad]

Cutting hair and nails in Jul Hijjah

Umm Salama (ra) reported (these words) directly from Allah's Messenger (saws): If anyone has in his possession a sacrificial animal to offer as a sacrifice (on Eid al-Azha), he should not get his hair cut and nails trimmed after he has entered the first days of Jul Hijja. [Muslim]

It was narrated from Umm Salama (ra) that the Messenger of Allah (saws) said: "When the (first) ten (days of Jul-Hijjah) begin, and one of you wants to offer a sacrifice, let him not remove anything from his hair or skin." [Sunan an-Nasai]

The one who cannot find a sacrifice

It was narrated from 'Abdullah bin 'Amr bin al-As (ra) that the Messenger of Allah (saws) said to a man: "I have been instructed to take the Day of Sacrifice as an Eid which Allah, the Might and Sublime, has ordained for this Ummah." The man said: "What do you think if I cannot find anything but a female sheep that has been loaned to me so that I may benefit from its milk - should I sacrifice it?" He (saws) said: "No. Rather cut something from your hair and your nails, trim your moustache and shave your pubic hairs, and you will have a complete reward with Allah, the Might and Sublime, as if you had offered the sacrifice." [Sunan an-Nasai]

To offer sacrifice at the prayer place

It was narrated from Nafi that: Abdullah (ra) told him that the Messenger of Allah (saws) used to offer the sacrifice at the prayer place. [Sunan an-Nasai]

It was narrated from 'Abdullah bin 'Umar (ra) that the Messenger of Allah (saws) offered the sacrifice on the Day of Sacrifice in Al-Madinah. He said: "If he did not offer the Nahr (sacrifice a camel) he would have offered Jabihah (Sacrificed a sheep) at the prayer place." [Sunan an-Nasai]

Aspects of animals for sacrifice

Jabir (ra) reported the Messenger (saws) as saying, "Sacrifice only a full-grown animal unless it is difficult for you, in which case sacrifice a she-lamb." [Muslim]

Ali (ra) said: "The Messenger of Allah (saws) commanded us to examine the eyes and ears (of animals for sacrifice)." [Sunan an-Nasai]

It was narrated from 'Ali bin Abi Talib (ra) that the messenger of Allah (saws) said: "Do not sacrifice and animal with its ears slit from the front, and animal with its ears slit from the back, an animal with its ears slit lengthwise, and animal with a round hole in its ears, or an animal with one bad eye." [Sunan an-Nasai]

It was narrated that 'Ali bin Abi Talib, (ra) said: "The Messenger of Allah (saws) forbade sacrificing an animal with its ears slit form the front, and animals with its ears slit form the back, and animal with its ears slit lengthwise, an animal with a round hole in tits ear, or an animals with its nose cut off." [Sunan an-Nasai]

Ubaid bin Fairuz said: "I said to Al-Bara bin Azib: Tell me of the sacrificial animals that the Messenger of Allah (saws) disliked or forbade. He said: "The Messenger of Allah (saws) gestured like this with his hand, and my hands are shorter than the hand of the Messenger of Allah (saws), (and he said): "There are four that will not do as sacrifices: The animal that clearly has one bad eye: the sick animals that is obviously sick; the lame animal with an obvious lamp; and the animal that is so emaciated that it is as if there is no marrow in its bones." He (saws) said: "And I dislike that the animal should have some fault in its horns or ears." He (saws) said: "What you dislike, forget about it, and do not make it forbidden to anyone." [Sunan an-Nasai]

Ali (ra) said: "Messenger of Allah (saws) forbade us from sacrificing an animal with a broken horn." I (the narrator) mentioned that to Sa'eed bin Al_Musayyab and he said: "Yes, unless half or more of the horn is missing." [Sunan an-Nasai]

It was narrated from 'Uqbah bin 'Amir (ra) that the Messenger of Allah (saws) divided some sacrificial animals among his Companions, and I got a Jadh'ah sheep. I said: "O Messenger of Allah (saws), I got a Jadh'ah sheep." He (saws) said: "Sacrifice it." [Sunan an-Nasai]

It was narrated that Ibn 'Abbas (ra) said: "We were with the Messenger of Allah on a journey, when the Day of Sacrifice came, so we shared a camel among ten men, and a cow among seven." [Sunan an-Nasai]

It was narrated that Jabir (ra) said: "We would make Tamattu' when the Prophet (saws) was with us, and we would sacrifice a cow on behalf of seven people, sharing it among ourselves." [Sunan an-Nasai]

Slaughter in the name of Allah

It was narrated from Rafi bin Khadij (ra) that the Messenger of Allah (saws) said: "If the blood is shed and the name of Allah is mentioned, then eat, unless (it is slaughtered) with teeth or nails." [Sunan an-Nasai]

It was narrated that Shaddad bin Aws (ra): There are two things that I memorized from the Messenger of Allah (saws), who said: "Allah has decreed proficiency in all things, so when you kill, kill well, and when you slaughter, slaughter well. Let one of you sharpen his blade and spare suffering to the animal he slaughters." [Sunan an-Nasai]

Anas (ra) said: "The Messenger of Allah (saws) sacrificed two horned, Amlah rams, saying: *'Allahu Akbar* and pronouncing the Name of Allah. I saw him slaughtering them with his own hand, and placing his foot on their sides." I said: "You heard it from Him?" He said: "Yes." [Sunan an-Nasai]

It was narrated that 'Amir bin Wasilah said: A man asked 'Ali (ra): "Did the Messenger of Allah (saws) used to tell you anything in secret that he (saws) did not tell the people?" Ali (ra) got so angry that his face turned red, and he said: "He (saws) used not to tell me anything in secret that he (saws) did not tell the people except that he (saws) told me four things when he (saws) and I were alone in the house." He (saws) said: "(i) Allah curses the alone who curses his father, (ii) Allah curses the one who offers a sacrifice to anyone other than Allah, (iii) Allah curse the one who gives refuge to an offender and (iv) Allah curses the one who changes boundary markers." [Sunan an-Nasai]

Abu Tufail 'Amir b. Wisila reported: I was in the company of 'Ali b. Abi Talib (ra), when a person came to him, and said: What was it that Allah's Apostle (saws) told you in secret? Thereupon he (Ali) was enraged and said: Allah's Apostle (saws) did not tell me anything in secret that he hid from people, except that he told me four things. He said: Commander of Faithful, what are these? He said: Allah cursed him who cursed his father; Allah cursed him who sacrificed for anyone besides Allah; and Allah cursed him who accommodates an innovator (in religion); and Allah cursed him who changed the minarets (the boundary lines) of the land. [Muslim]

Animals sacrificed on An-Nusub and for the idols

Narrated 'Abdullah (ra): Allah's Messenger (saws) said that he met Zaid bin 'Amr Nufail at a place near Baldah and this had happened before Allah's Messenger (saws) received the Divine Inspiration. Allah's Messenger (saws) presented a dish of meat (that had been offered to him by the pagans) to Zaid bin 'Amr, but Zaid refused to eat of it and then said (to the pagans), "I do not eat of what you slaughter on your stone altars (Ansabs) nor do I eat except that on which Allah's Name has been mentioned on slaughtering." [Bukhari]

Slaughtering by a lady

Narrated Ka`b bin Malik (ra): A lady slaughtered a sheep with a stone and then the Prophet (saws) was asked about it and he permitted it to be eaten. [Bukhari]

Slaughtering by unknown persons

Narrated `Aisha (ra): A group of people said to the Prophet (saws), "Some people bring us meat and we do not know whether they have mentioned Allah's Name or not on slaughtering the animal." He (saws) said, "Mention Allah's Name on it and eat." Those people had embraced Islam recently. [Bukhari]

Slaughtering of horse and chicken

Narrated Asma' bint Abu Bakr (ra): We slaughtered a horse (by Nahr) during the lifetime of Allah's Messenger (saws) and ate it. [Bukhari] Narrated Abu Musa Al-Ash`ari (ra): I saw the Prophet (saws) eating chicken. [Bukhari]

Slaughtering of donkey and animal with fang

Narrated Jabir bin `Abdullah (ra): On the Day of the battle of Khaibar, Allah's Messenger (saws) made donkey's meat unlawful and allowed the eating of horse flesh. [Bukhari] Narrated Abu Tha`laba (ra): Allah's Messenger (saws) forbade the eating of the meat of beasts having fangs (pointed teeth). [Bukhari]

Use of skin of animals

Narrated `Abdullah bin `Abbas (ra): Once Allah's Messenger (saws) passed by a dead sheep and said (to the people), "Why don't you use its hide?" They said, "But it is dead," He (saws) said, "Only eating it is prohibited." [Bukhari]

Eating rabbits

Once we provoked a rabbit at Marr-az-Zahran. The people chased it till they got tired. Then I caught It and brought it to Abu Talha (ra), who slaughtered it and then sent both its pelvic pieces (or legs) to the Prophet (saws), and the Prophet (saws) accepted the present. [Bukhari]

The one who kills a small bird for no reason
It was narrated from 'Abdullah bin 'Amr (ra), who attributed it to the Messenger of Allah (saws): "There is no person who kills a small bird or anything larger, for no just reason, but Allah will ask him about it." It was said: "O Messenger of Allah (saws), what does 'just reason' mean?" He (saws) said: "That you slaughter it and eat it, and not cut off its head and throw it aside." [Sunan an-Nasai]

The skins of Al-Hadi are to be given in charity
Narrated `Ali (ra): The Prophet (saws) ordered me to supervise the (slaughtering) of Budn (Hadi camel) and to distribute their meat, skins and covering sheets in charity and not to give anything (of their bodies) to the butcher as wages for slaughtering. [Bukhari]

Scientific explanation of fasting

'A study carried out by Yoshinori Ohsumi, a Japanese Doctor who won the noble prize in 2016, discovered the principle of fasting, which helps us to stay young and healthy. He argued that when we starve for some time, the cells recycle everything which is unwanted and become young, a process known as '**autophagy**'. Intermittent fasting contributes to restoring homeostasis. The cells respond to intermittent fasting by engaging in the coordinated adaptive stress response that leads to increased expression of antioxidant defense, DNA repair, protein quality control, mitochondrial biogenesis and autophagy, and downregulation of inflammation.

Studies reported that total cholesterol (TC), low-density lipoprotein (LDL), high density lipoprotein (HDL) and blood glucose have been improved after Ramadan compared to before Ramadan among athletes. Conducted studies have assessed the impact of Ramadan fasting on a different aspect of human metabolic and healthy such as an immune system, hormones secretion and gestation. The good effect of Ramadan on diseases (e.g., gastrointestinal diseases) has been also examined. Medical, nutritional and physical activity consulting is necessary for individuals with diabetes who want to fast during Ramadan.'

(Reference: Rouhani M H, Azadbakht L. *Is Ramadan fasting related to health outcomes? A review on the related evidence?* Journal of Research in Medical Science, 2014; 19: 987-92.)

For more details, readers may go through a book titled 'Medical Miracles of the Qur'an', written by Dr Sharif Kaf Al-Ghazal, Published by The Islamic Foundation, Markfield, Leicestershire, UK. The book covers many aspects such as embryology, skin, eye, Ramadan, wudu, breast feeding etc.

Summary

- Fasting in Ramadan is obligatory.
- Evil action and forged speeches are prohibited during fasting.
- Prophet (saws) advised for Suhur as there is a blessing in it.
- Physical relation with wives is prohibited during fasting.
- Fasting during journey may be avoided but it is to be made up later.
- Fasting during menses and post-natal period is exempted and is to be made up later.
- It is recommended to spend the night of Qadr in worship.
- Sadaka-ul-Fitr must be paid before Eid prayer.
- Qiyamul lail is highly virtuous.
- It is a Sunnah for Muslim to recite the Qur'an during Ramadan.
- Fasting on the days of Eid is prohibited.
- Animals sacrificed without Allah's name is not allowed to eat.
- Animals sacrificed on stone altars of dis-believers and for the idols are prohibited to eat.
- Skins of sacrificed animals are to be given in charity.

6. Sadaqa and Zakat

Zakat is one of the five pillars of Islam and thus is an obligatory act. Sadaqa is a voluntary charity and is optional. Sadaqa is not limited to money alone. Any good behaviour like smiling towards a person can be a Sadaqa. It is narrated by Jabir bin Abdullah (ra) that the Prophet (saws) said: "Every good is charity. Indeed, among the good is to meet your brother with a smiling face, and to pour what is left in your bucket into the vessel of your brother." [Tirmizi].

Sadaqa

Sadaqa is mentioned in the Qur'an in several places and some of these verses are as follows (interpretation of meaning):
- *And spend [in the way of Allah] from what We have provided you before death approaches one of you and he says, "My Lord, if only You would delay me for a brief term so I would give charity and be of the righteous." (Ch 63:10)*
- *If you disclose your charitable expenditures, they are good; but if you conceal them and give them to the poor, it is better for you, and He will remove from you some of your misdeeds [thereby]. And Allah, of what you do, is [fully] Aware. (Ch 2:271)*
- *Indeed, the men who practice charity and the women who practice charity and [they who] have loaned Allah a goodly loan – it will be multiplied for them, and they will have a noble reward. (Ch 57:18)*
- *If only they had attempted the challenging path of goodness instead ! And what will make you realize what attempting the challenging path is? It is to free a slave, or to give food in times of famine to an orphaned relative or to a poor person in distress, (Ch 90: 11-16)*
- *Say, "Indeed, my Lord extends provision for whom He wills of His servants and restricts [it] for him. But whatever thing you*

spend [in His cause] – He will compensate it; and He is the best of providers." (Ch 34:39)

- o *You will never achieve righteousness until you donate some of what you cherish. And whatever you give is certainly well known to Allah. (Ch 3:92)*
- o *The example of those who spend their wealth in the cause of Allah is that of a grain that sprouts into seven ears, each bearing one hundred grains. And Allah multiplies the reward even more to whoever He wills. For Allah is All-Bountiful, All-Knowing. (Ch 2:261)*
- o *Those who spend their wealth in charity day and night, secretly and openly—their reward is with their Lord, and there will be no fear for them, nor will they grieve. (Ch 2:274)*
- o *Do not be so tight-fisted, for you will be blameworthy; nor so open-handed, for you will end up in poverty. (Ch 17:29)*

Wealth is from Allah and we have to donate from it

Words *'We have provided'* in Ch 63:10, Ch 2:254 etc are to be noted. Allah SWT is reminding us that whatever wealth we have, are actually from Allah SWT. It is purely Allah's favour and grace that He favours a person with wealth. However, whoever has wealth, must then fulfil the rights of wealth. One such right is spending in Allah's cause and helping those who are less fortunate. Remember, we are not spending our wealth, we are spending Allah's wealth to Allah's needy creation. Allah SWT instructed that it is a duty of a person 'mindful of Allah.' Allah Says (that means):

الٓمٓ

ذَٰلِكَ ٱلْكِتَٰبُ لَا رَيْبَ فِيهِ هُدًى لِّلْمُتَّقِينَ

(This is the Book! There is no doubt about it—a guide for those mindful of Allah)

ٱلَّذِينَ يُؤْمِنُونَ بِٱلْغَيْبِ وَيُقِيمُونَ ٱلصَّلَوٰةَ وَمِمَّا رَزَقْنَٰهُمْ يُنفِقُونَ

(who believe in the unseen, establish prayer, and donate from what We have provided for them,)

وَٱلَّذِينَ يُؤْمِنُونَ بِمَآ أُنزِلَ إِلَيْكَ وَمَآ أُنزِلَ مِن قَبْلِكَ وَبِٱلْءَاخِرَةِ هُمْ يُوقِنُونَ

(and who believe in what has been revealed to you O Prophet and what was revealed before you, and have sure faith in the Hereafter.)

أُوْلَـٰئِكَ عَلَىٰ هُدًى مِّن رَّبِّهِمْ ۖ وَأُوْلَـٰئِكَ هُمُ ٱلْمُفْلِحُونَ

(Those are upon [right] guidance from their Lord, and it is those who are the successful.) (Surah Baqarah, Ch 2)

Hadith: Abu Waqid (ra) reported: The Messenger of Allah (saws) said: Allah said: "Verily, We have sent down wealth for the performance of prayer and offering charity. If the son of Adam owned a valley, he would like to have a second. If he had two valleys, he would like to add a third. Nothing satisfies the belly of the son of Adam but the dust of the grave, yet Allah will sympathize to whoever repents." [Bayhaqi]

Hadith: Malik (ra) narrated: The Messenger of Allah (saws) said, "The hands are three types: The Hand of Allah is the highest, the hand of the giver is next to it, and the hand of the beggar is the lowest. Give from your surplus wealth and do not be weakened by your ego." [Sunan Abu Dawud]

Hadith: Narrated Haritha bin Wahb (ra): I heard Allah's Messenger (saws) saying, "Give in charity because there will come a time on the people when a person will go out with his alms from place to place but will not find anybody to accept it." [Bukhari]

Virtues of charity Here

The prophet (saws) said: "To give something to a poor man brings one reward, while giving the same to a needy relation brings two: one for charity and the other for respecting the family ties." [Tirmizi]

Anas (ra) reported Allah's Messenger (saws) saying, "Sadaqa appeases the Lord's anger and averts an evil death." [Mishkat al- Masabih]

Abdullah ibn Mu'awiya (ra) reported: The Prophet (saws) said, "Whoever does three deeds will taste the sweetness of faith: one who worships Allah alone, who declares there is no God but Allah, and who gives charity from his wealth each year with a cheerful and earnest soul." [Sunan Abu Dawud]

Abu Huraira (ra) reported: The Prophet (saws) said, "Allah continues to fulfil the needs of the servant as long as he fulfils the needs of his brother." [Ṭabarani]

Abu Huraira (ra) reported: The Messenger of Allah (saws) said, "A man intended to give charity, so he went out with his charity and placed it in the hands of a thief. In the morning, people were saying: Charity was given to a thief! The man said: O Allah, praise be to you! The man again intended to give charity, so he went out with his charity and placed it in the hands of an adulteress. In the morning, people were saying: Charity was given to an adulteress in the night! The man said: O Allah, praise be to you for the adulteress! The man again intended to give charity, so he went out with his charity and placed it in the hands of a wealthy person. In the morning, people were saying: Charity was given to a wealthy person! The man said: O Allah, praise be to you for the thief, the adulteress, and the wealthy person! Then, it came to him in a dream and it was said: As for your charity to the thief, perhaps it will cause him to give up stealing. As for the adulteress, perhaps it will cause her to give up adultery. As for the wealthy person, perhaps he will learn a lesson and spend in charity from what Allah has given him." [Bukhari, Muslim]

Al-Bara' ibn 'Azib (ra) reported: The Messenger of Allah (saws) said, "Whoever donates a gift of milk, or a piece of silver, or who guides others through a passage, he will be rewarded as if he has freed a slave." [Tirmizi]

Virtues of charity Hereafter

Allah SWT says (interpretation of meaning):

O believers! Donate from what We have provided for you before the arrival of a Day when there will be no bargaining, friendship, or intercession. Those who disbelieve are truly the wrongdoers. (Ch 2:254)

Those who spend their wealth in the cause of Allah and do not follow their charity with reminders of their generosity or hurtful words—they will get their reward from their Lord, and there will be no fear for them, nor will they grieve. (Ch 2:262)

Narrated Abu Huraira (ra): Allah's Messenger (saws) said, "If somebody gives in charity something equal to a date from his honestly earned money-for nothing ascends to Allah except good-then Allah will take it in His Right (Hand) and bring it up for its owner as anyone of you brings up a baby horse, till it becomes like a mountain." Abu Huraira (ra) said:

The Prophet (saws) said, "Nothing ascends to Allah except good." [Bukhari]

Abu Huraira (ra) reported: The Messenger of Allah (saws) said, "Allah Almighty will say on the Day of Resurrection: O son of Adam, I was sick but you did not visit Me. He will say: My Lord, how can I visit You when You are the Lord of the worlds? Allah will say: Did you not know that My servant was sick and you did not visit him, and had you visited him you would have found Me with him? O son of Adam, I asked you for food but you did not feed Me. He will say: My Lord, how can I feed You when You are the Lord of the worlds? Allah will say: Did you not know that My servant asked you for food but you did not feed him, and had you fed him you would have found Me with him? O son of Adam, I asked you for drink but you did not provide for Me. He will say: My Lord, how can I give You drink when You are the Lord of the worlds? Allah will say: My servant asked you for a drink but you did not provide for him, and had you given it to him you would have found Me with him." [Muslim]

Narrated Abu Huraira (ra): I heard the Prophet (saws) saying, "Whoever spends a couple (of objects) in Allah's cause, will be called by the Gatekeepers of Paradise who will say, "O so-and-so, come on!" Abu Bakr (ra) said, "Such a person will never perish or be miserable' The Prophet (saws) said, "I hope you will be among such person." [Bukhari]

Abu Huraira (ra) reported: The Messenger of Allah (saws) said, "The servant says: My wealth, my wealth! Verily, he only gets three from his wealth: he eats and it perishes, or he wears clothes and they degrade, or he gives in charity and it is stored for him. Whatever is beyond this will depart him and be left behind for people." [Muslim]

Narrated Abu Huraira (ra): Allah's Messenger (saws) said: "We (Muslims) are the last (to come) but will be the foremost on the Day of Resurrection. The narrators of this Hadith said: Allah said (to man), 'Spend (in charity), for then I will compensate you (generously)." [Bukhari]

Narrated `Ali (ra): While the Prophet (saws) was in a funeral procession, he took a stick and started scraping the earth with it and said, "There is none of you but has his place assigned either in Hell or in Paradise." They (the people) said, "Shall we not depend upon that (and give up doing any deeds)?' He (saws) said, "Carry on doing (good deeds) for everybody will find it easy to do such deeds as will lead him to his destined place for which he has been created." (And then the Prophet saws recited the Verse): 'As for him who gives (in charity) and keeps his duty to Allah...' (Ch 92: 5) [Bukhari]

Uqbah ibn 'Amir (ra) reported: The Messenger of Allah (saws) said, "Everyone will be in the shade of their charity until judgment is carried out between the people." [Ibn Ḥibban]

Khuraym ibn Fatik (ra) reported: The Messenger of Allah (saws) said, "Whoever donates charity in the way of Allah, it will be multiplied up to seven hundred times in his record." [Sunan at-Tirmizi]

Marsad ibn Abdullah (ra) reported: The Prophet (saws) said, "The shade of the believer on the Day of Resurrection is his charity." [Musnad Aḥmad]

Ibn Mas'ud (ra) reported: The Prophet (saws) said, "Which of you love the wealth of his heirs more than his own wealth?" They said, "O Messenger of Allah (saws), there are none of us but his own wealth is more beloved to him." The Prophet (saws) said, "Verily, his true wealth is what he puts forward, and the wealth of his heirs is what is left behind." [Bukhari]

Aisha (ra) reported: The Messenger of Allah (saws) said, "Verily, Allah will raise up a date or a morsel in charity, just as one of you raises his mare or his young, until it becomes like the mountain of Uhud." [Ibn Ḥibban]

'Uqbah ibn 'Amir (ra) reported: The Messenger of Allah (saws) said, "Verily, charity will extinguish the heat of the graves for their people. Only the believer can seek shade on the Day of Resurrection in the shade of his charity." [Al-Iman lil-Bayhaqi]

Narrated 'Aisha (ra): Some of the wives of the Prophet (saws) asked him, "Who amongst us will be the first to follow you (i.e. die after you)?" He (saws) said, "Whoever has the longest hand." So, they started measuring their hands with a stick and Sauda's (ra) hand turned out to be the longest. (When Zainab bint Jahsh (ra) died first of all in the caliphate of 'Umar (ra)), we came to know that the long hand was a symbol of practicing charity, so she was the first to follow the Prophet (saws) and she used to love to practice charity. (Sauda died later). [Bukhari]

We should not remind people that we have donated

Reminding people for sadaqa hurts the people and is prohibited. Sadaqa must be to please the Almighty. Allah SWT says (interpretation of meaning):

O you who believe, do not nullify your acts of charity by boasting about (doing people a) favour and by causing (them) hurt, like the one who spends his wealth to show off before peopleand does not believe in Allah and in the Last Day. So, his example is like a rock on which there is dust, then a heavy rain came over it and left it barren. They have no ability to gain anything out of what they have done, and Allah does not give guidance to the people who disbelieve. (Ch 2:264)

The example of those who spend their wealth to seek the pleasure of Allah and to make firm (their faith) from (the depths of) their souls is like a garden on a foothill on which came a heavy rain, and it yielded its produce twofold. Even if a heavy rain does not come to it, a light drizzle is enough, and Allah is watchful of what you do. (Ch 2:265)

Abu Zarr (ra) said that the Messenger of Allah (saws) said, "Three persons whom Allah shall neither speak to on the Day of Resurrection nor look at nor purify, and they shall receive a painful torment: he who reminds (the people) of what he gives away, he who lengthens his clothes below the ankles and he who swears an oath while lying, to sell his merchandise." [Muslim]

Warning if charity not done by a wealthy person

Allah SWT says in the Qur'an (interpretation of meaning):

Those who withhold in miserliness what Allah has given them out of His grace should not take it as good for them. Instead, it is bad for them. They shall be forced, on the Doomsday, to put on what they withheld, as iron-collars round their necks. To Allah belongs the inheritance of the heavens and the earth. Allah is All-Aware of what you do. (Ch 3:180)

Narrated Abu Hurayrah (ra) that the Messenger of Allah (saws) said, "Whoever Allah makes wealthy and he does not pay the Zakat due on his wealth, then (on the Day of Resurrection) his wealth will be made in the likeness of a bald-headed poisonous male snake with two black spots over the eyes. The snake will encircle his neck and bite his cheeks and proclaim, `I am your wealth, I am your treasure." The Prophet (saws) then recited the Ayah, '*Those who withhold in miserliness what Allah*

*has given them out of His grace should not take it as good for them.
Instead, it is bad for them'* until the end. [Bukhari]

Hadith: Asma (ra) reported: The Messenger of Allah (saws) said, "Spend in charity and do not count it, lest Allah count it against you. Do not hoard (accumulate) it, lest Allah withhold from you." [Bukhari, Muslim]

Hadith: Narrated Asma' bint Abu Bakr (ra) that she had gone to the Prophet (saws) and he (saws) said, "Do not shut your money bag; otherwise Allah too will withhold His blessings from you. Spend (in Allah's Cause) as much as you can afford." [Bukhari]

Hadith: Narrated Abu Huraira (ra): The Prophet (saws) said: Every day two angels come down from Heaven and one of them says, "O Allah! Compensate every person who spends in Your Cause," and the other (angel) says, "O Allah! Destroy every miser." [Bukhari]

Sadaqa is not for show off

Abu Mas'ud (ra) reported: When the verses of charity were revealed, we were employed to transport it. A man came and gave many things in charity. They said, "He is showing off." Another man came and he gave a small amount in charity. They said, "Indeed, Allah does not need this small amount!" Then, the verse was revealed, "Those who disparage willing givers of charity among the believers and who find nothing to spend but their effort, so they mock them, Allah will mock them and they will have an agonizing punishment." (Ch 9:79) [Bukhari, Muslim]

Narrated Abu Huraira (ra): The Prophet (saws) said, "Seven people will be shaded by Allah under His shade on the day when there will be no shade except His. They are: (1) a just ruler; (2) a young man who has been brought up in the worship of Allah, (i.e. worship Allah (Alone) sincerely from his childhood), (3) a man whose heart is attached to the mosque (who offers the five compulsory congregational prayers in the mosque); (4) two persons who love each other only for Allah's sake and they meet and part in Allah's cause only; (5) a man who refuses the call of a charming woman of noble birth for an illegal sexual intercourse with her and says: I am afraid of Allah; (6) a person who practices charity so secretly that his left hand does not know what his right hand has given (i.e. nobody knows how much he has given in charity). (7) a person who remembers Allah in seclusion and his eyes get flooded with tears." [Bukhari]

Whom to donate?

Allah SWT says (that means):

Alms are meant only for the poor, the needy, those who administer them, those whose hearts need winning over, to free slaves and help those in debt, for Allah's cause, and for travellers in need. This is ordained by Allah; Allah is all knowing and wise." (Ch 9:60)

Hadith: Hakim ibn Hizam (ra) reported: A man asked the Messenger of Allah (saws), "What act of charity is the best?" The Prophet (saws) said, "One given to a separated relative." [Musnad Aḥmad]

Hadith: Thawban (ra) reported: The Messenger of Allah (saws) said, "The best coin for a man to spend is the coin spent on his dependents, and the coin spent by a man on his mount in the way of Allah, and the coin spent by a man on his companions in the way of Allah." [Muslim]

Hadith: Al-Miqdam ibn Ma'di (ra) reported: The Messenger of Allah (saws) said, "What you feed yourself is your charity, what you feed your children is your charity, what you feed your wife is your charity, and what you feed your servant is your charity." [Bukhari]

Hadith: Aisha (ra) reported: I said, "O Messenger of Allah (saws), I have two neighbours; to whom should I send my gifts?" The Prophet, peace and blessings be upon him, said, "To the neighbour who is closest to your door." [Bukhari]

Hadith: Narrated Anas bin Malik (ra): Out of all the Ansar, living in Madinah, Abu Talha (ra) had the largest number of (date palm trees) gardens, and the most beloved of his property to him was Bairuha garden which was standing opposite the Mosque (of the Prophet saws). Allah's Messenger (saws) used to enter it and drink of its good water. When the Verse: "By no means shall you attain righteousness unless you spend (in charity) of that which you love." (Ch 3: 92) Abu Talha (ra) got up and said: O Allah's Messenger (saws), Allah says: "By no means shall you attain righteousness unless you spend (in charity) of that which you love." (Ch 3.92) and the most beloved of my property to me is the Bairuha garden, so I give it (as a charitable gift) in Allah's Cause and hope to receive good out of it, and to have it stored for me with Allah. So, O Allah's Messenger (saws)! Dispose it of (i.e. utilize it) in the way

Allah orders you (to dispose it of). Allah's Messenger (saws) said, "Bravo! That is a fruitful property! That is a fruitful property! I have heard what you have said and I think that you should distribute that (garden) amongst your relatives." Then Abu Talha (ra) distributed that garden amongst his relatives and his cousins. [Bukhari]

Are children and women included under the term of relatives (concerning wills)?

Narrated Abu Huraira (ra): When Allah revealed the Verse: "Warn your nearest kinsmen," Allah's Messenger (saws) got up and said, "O people of Quraish (or said similar words)! Buy (i.e. save) yourselves (from the Hellfire) as I cannot save you from Allah's Punishment; O Bani 'Abd Manaf! I cannot save you from Allah's Punishment, O Safiya, the Aunt of Allah's Messenger (saws)! I cannot save you from Allah's Punishment; O Fatima (ra) bint Muhammad (saws)! Ask me anything from my wealth, but I cannot save you from Allah's Punishment." [Bukhari]

Note: Fathima (ra) is the leader of women in the Heaven. The sayings of the prophet (saws) are warnings to us.

Abu Huraira (ra) reported Allah's Messenger (saws) as saying: "Of the dinar you spend as a contribution in Allah's path, or to set free a slave, or as a sadaqa given to a needy, or to support your family, the one yielding the greatest reward is that which you spent on your family." [Muslim]

Sauban (ra) reported Allah's Messenger (saws) as saying: The most excellent dinar is one that a person spends on his family, and the dinar which he spends on his animal in Allah's path, and the dinar he spends on his companions in Allah's path. Abu Qilaba (one of the narrators) said: He (the narrator) started with family, and then Abu Qilaba said: Who is the person with greater reward than a person who spends on young members of his family (and thus) preserves (saves them from want) (and by virtue of which) Allah brings profit for them and makes them rich. [Muslim]

Jabir (ra) reported: A person from the Banu 'Uzra set a slave free after his death. This news reached the Messenger of Allah (saws). Upon this, he (saws) said: "Have you any property besides it?" He said: "No." Upon this he (saws) said: "Who would buy (this slave) from me?" Nulaim b. Abdullah bought it for eight hundred dirhams and (this amount was) brought to the Messenger of Allah (saws) who returned it to him (the owner), and then said: "Start with your own self and spend it on yourself, and if anything is left, it should be spent on your family, and if anything is left (after meeting the needs of the family) it should be spent on relatives, and if anything is left from the family, it should be spent like this, like this." And he (saws) was saying: In front of you, on your right and on your left. [Muslim]

How much to donate?

There is no prescribed quantity of sadaqa unlike zakat. However, it is advised to donate more and more.

Hadith: Abu Huraira (ra) reported: The Messenger of Allah (saws) said, "One silver coin is ahead of one hundred thousand others." They said, "O Messenger of Allah (saws), how is it so?" The Prophet (saws) said, "A man has only two coins, so he takes one and gives it in charity. Another man has abundant wealth, so he takes one hundred thousand coins from a mere portion of it and gives it in charity." [Sunan al-Nasa'i]

Hadith: Aisha (ra) reported: The Messenger of Allah (saws) said to her, "O Aisha, set up a barrier from the Hellfire, even with half of a date in charity, for it settles the hungry in place of the full." [Musnad Aḥmad]

Hadith: Umm Bujayd (ra) reported: She said, "O Messenger of Allah (saws), the poor come to my door and I cannot find anything to give them." The Messenger of Allah (saws) said, "If you can find nothing but a burnt trotter, hand it over to them." [Sunan at-Tirmizi]

Hadith: Abu Huraira (ra) reported: He said, "O Messenger of Allah (saws), which charity is the best?" The Messenger of Allah (saws) said, "One with little property to give. Begin with your dependents." [Sunan Abu Dawud]

Hadith: Adi ibn Hatim Tai (ra) reported: The Prophet (saws) said, "Guard yourself against the Hellfire, even with half of a date in charity. If one cannot find it, then with a kind word." [Bukhari, Muslim]

Hadith: Narrated Ka`b bin Malik (ra): I said, "O Allah's Messenger (saws)! For the acceptance of my repentance I wish to give all my property in charity for Allah's sake through His Apostle (saws)." He (saws) said, "It is better for you to keep some of the property for yourself." I said, "Then I will keep my share in Khaibar." [Bukhari]

One has to donate quality goods

While donating, we must spend from the good things we have earned. Satan may threaten us not to donate from good things or else we will become poor. Remember, Allah is Rich and He shall reward him for his charity and multiply it many times. Allah SWT says (that means):

O you who believe, spend of the good things you have earned, and of what We have brought forth for you from the earth, and do not opt for a bad thing, spending only from it, while you are not going to accept it (if such a thing is offered to you), unless you close your eyes to it, and know well that Allah is All-Independent, Ever-Praised. (Ch 2:267)

Satan frightens you with poverty, and bids you to commit indecency, and Allah promises you forgiveness from Him, and grace as well. And Allah is All-Embracing, All-Knowing. (Ch 2:268)

Hadith: Awf ibn Malik (ra) reported: The Messenger of Allah (saws) came to us in the mosque and he (saws) had a staff in his hand. A man among us had hung a bundle of brittle dates, so the Prophet (saws) started striking that bundle with his staff and said, "If he wished he could have given better charity than this. Verily, the one who gave this in charity will eat brittle dates on the Day of Resurrection." [Sunan Abu Dawud]

What acts are considered charity

Abu Hurairah (ra) reported: Messenger of Allah (saws) said, "Every day the sun rises charity (Sadaqah) is due on every joint of a person: you administer justice between two men is a charity; and assisting a man to mount his beast, or helping him load his luggage on it is a charity; and a good word is a charity; and every step that you take (towards the mosque) for Salat (prayer) is a charity and removing harmful things from the road is a charity". [Bukhari and Muslim]

It is reported on the authority of 'Aisha (ra) that Messenger of Allah (saws) said, "Every one of the children of Adam has been created with three hundred and sixty joints; so he who declares the Glory of Allah (i.e., saying Allahu Akbar), praises Allah (i.e., Al-hamdu lillah), declares Allah to be One (i.e., La ilaha illallah), glorifies Allah, and seeks forgiveness from Allah (i.e., Astaghfirullah), and removes stone, or thorn, or bone from people's path, and enjoins good and forbids evil, to the number of those three hundred and sixty, will walk that day having rescued himself from Hell." [Muslim]

Abu Jurayy (ra) reported: I came to the Messenger of Allah (saws) and I said, "O Messenger of Allah (saws), we are people of the desert. Teach us something with which Allah will benefit us." The Prophet (saws) said, "Do not belittle any good deed, even pouring your leftovers into another's cistern, even speaking to your brother while smiling at him. Beware of trailing your garment; it is a form of vanity that Allah does not approve. If a man insults you with what he knows about you, do not insult him with what you know about him. Verily, you will have a reward, and the penalty is upon the one who spoke it." [Ṣaḥiḥ Ibn Ḥibban]

Abu Zarr (ra) reported: The Messenger of Allah, peace and blessings be upon him, said, "Smiling in the face of your brother is your charity. Enjoining good and forbidding evil is charity. Guiding a lost man through the land is your charity. Lending your eyesight to a man who cannot see well is your charity. Removing rocks, thorns, and bones from the road is your charity. Pouring your leftovers into the vessel of your brother is your charity." [Sunan at-Tirmizi]

Anas bin Malik (ra) reported: The Messenger of Allah (saws) said, "No Muslim plants a tree or sows a seed and then a bird, or a human, or an animal eats from it but that it is charity for him." [Bukhari, Muslim]

Narrated Abu Huraira (ra): Allah's Messenger (SA) said, "While a man was on the way, he found a thorny branch of a tree there on the way and removed it. Allah thanked him for that deed and forgave him." [Bukhari]

Donation from unlawful wealth

Abu Huraira (ra) reported: The Messenger of Allah (saws) said, "Whoever accumulates unlawful wealth and then gives it in charity, he will never be rewarded and the burden of sin will be upon him." [Ṣaḥiḥ Ibn Ḥibban]

Narrated Abu Huraira (ra): Allah's Messenger (saws) said: "If one gives in charity what equals one date-fruit from the honestly earned money and Allah accepts only the honestly earned money, Allah takes it in His right (hand) and then enlarges its reward for that person (who has given it), as anyone of you brings up his baby horse, so much so that it becomes as big as a mountain." [Bukhari]

Charity on behalf of deceased

Aisha (ra) reported: A man came to the Prophet (saws) and he said, "O Messenger of Allah (saws), my mother died suddenly without writing a will. I think if she could speak, she would give in charity. Will she have a reward if I give charity on her behalf?" The Prophet (saws) said, "Yes." [Bukhari]

Sa'd ibn 'Ubadah (ra) reported: I said, "O Messenger of Allah (saws), my mother has died. Shall I give charity on her behalf?" The Prophet (saws) said, "Yes." I said, "Which charity is the best?" The Prophet (saws) said, "A drink of water." [Sunan an-Nasai]

Narrated Ibn `Abbas (ra): The mother of Sa`d bin 'Ubada (ra) died in his absence. He said, "O Allah's Messenger (saws)! My mother died in my absence; will it be of any benefit for her if I give Sadaqa on her behalf?" The Prophet (saws) said, "Yes." Sa`d (ra) said, "I make you a witness that I gave my garden called Al- Makhraf in charity on her behalf." [Bukhari]

To encourage for charity

Narrated Abu Huraira (ra): The Prophet (saws) said, "If I had gold equal to the mountain of Uhud, I would love that, before three days had passed, not a single Dinar thereof remained with me if I found somebody to accept it excluding some amount that I would keep for the payment of my debts.'' [Bukhari]

Abu Huraira (ra) reported Allah's Messenger (saws) as saying that Allah said to him: "Spend, I will bestow upon you." And the Messenger of Allah (saws) said: "The right hand of Allah is full and spending (the riches) liberally during day and night will not diminish (the resources of Allah). Don't you see what (an enormous amount of resources) He has spent since He created the heaven and the earth, and what is in His right hand has not decreased? His Throne is upon the water. And in His other hand is death, and He elevates and degrades (whom He likes)." [Muslim]

What kind of charity is the best?

Narrated Abu Huraira (ra): A man asked the Prophet (saws): "O Allah's Messenger (saws)! What kind of charity is the best?" He (saws) replied: "To give in charity when you are healthy and greedy hoping to be wealthy and afraid of becoming poor. Don't delay giving in charity till the time when you are on the death bed when you say, 'Give so much to so and so and so much to so and so,' and at that time the property is not yours but it belongs to so-and-so (i.e. your inheritors)." [Bukhari]

Charity of a convert while he/she was Mushrik

Narrated Hakim bin Hizam (ra): I said to Allah's Messenger (saws), "Before embracing Islam I used to do good deeds like giving in charity, slave-manumitting, and the keeping of good relations with kith and kin. Shall I be rewarded for those deeds?" The Prophet (saws) replied, "You became Muslim with all those good deeds (Without losing their reward)." [Bukhari]

The servant gets a reward for giving charity

Narrated `Aisha (ra): Allah's Messenger (saws) said, "When a woman gives in charity from her husband's meals without wasting the property of her husband, she will get a reward for it, and her husband too will get a reward for what he earned and the storekeeper will have the reward likewise." [Bukhari]

Sadaqah Jariyah or ongoing sadaqa

Sadaqah Jariyah is a powerful concept in Islam that encourages Muslims to engage in acts of charity that continue to benefit others long after the initial donation has been made. Ongoing charity (sadaqa jariyah) is a charity the reward of which continues after a person dies.

Hadith: Abu Qatadah (ra) reported: The Messenger of Allah (saws) said, "The best of what a man leaves behind are three: a righteous child who supplicates for him, ongoing charity the reward of which reaches him, and knowledge that is acted upon after him." [Sunan Ibn Majah]

Hadith: The Prophet (saws) said: "Verily, among the good deeds that will join a believer after his death are these: knowledge which he taught and spread, a righteous child he leaves behind, a copy of the Quran he leaves for inheritance, a mosque he has built, a house he built for travellers, a well he has dug, and charity distributed from his wealth while he was alive and well. These deeds will join him after his death." [Sunan Ibn Majah]

Virtue of plantation

Jabir (Allah be pleased with him) reported Allah's Messenger (saws) as saying: "Never does a Muslim plant a tree except that he has the reward of charity for him, for what is eaten out of that is charity; what is stolen out of that, what the beasts eat out of that, what the birds eat out of that is charity for him. (In short) none incurs a loss to him but it becomes a charity on his part." [Muslim]

Zakat

One of the Five Pillars of Islam, Zakat is a fundamental part of being a Muslim. Zakat is the act of giving a defined percentage of one's total wealth to charity each lunar year and is required of every Muslim whose accumulated wealth exceeds the current Zakat nisab value. The importance of Zakat in the Quran is mentioned in 32 verses. It is a highly significant factor in maintaining social order and removing beggary.

The minimum amount of an individual's wealth at which they are eligible to pay Zakat is called 'nisab'. The different sources of income and wealth have different calculations for the total nisab.

Who should pay zakat?

Narrated Abu Sa`id (ra): Allah's Messenger (saws) said, "No Zakat is due on property mounting to less than five Uqiyas (of silver), and no Zakat is due on less than five camels, and there is no Zakat on less than five Wasqs." (5 wasqs=900 Kg approximately) [Bukhari]

Narrated Abu Sa`id Al-Khudri (ra): Allah's Messenger (saws) said, "There is no Zakat on less than five camels and also there is no Zakat on less than five Awaq (of silver). (5 Awaq = 22 Fransa Riyals of Yemen or 200 Dirhams.) And there is no Zakat on less than five Awsuq. (A special measure of food-grains, and one Wasq equals 60 Sa's.) (For gold, 20 Dinars i.e. equal to 12 Guinea English. No Zakat for less than 12 Guinea (English) of gold or for silver less than 22 Fransa Riyals of Yemen.)

Narrated Abi Sa`id Al-Khudri (ra): I heard the Prophet (saws) saying (as above). [Bukhari]

The hadith reported by Ali (ra) quotes the Prophet (saws) as saying: "In the case of gold, you have nothing to pay until you own 20 dinars. If you have 20 dinars and you have had it for a year, the duty is to pay half a dinar." [Abu Dawud]

[Note: After conversion, the threshold for gold is estimated to be equivalent to 87.479 grams (Seven and a Half Tola). The threshold for silver is 200 dirhams which is equivalent now to 607.350 grams (Fifty-Two and a Half Tola of Silver.]

Narrated Salim bin `Abdullah from his father: The Prophet (saws) said, "On a land irrigated by rain water or by natural water channels or if the land is wet due to a nearby water channel, Ushr (i.e. one-tenth) is compulsory (as Zakat); and on the land irrigated by the well, half of an Ushr (i.e. one-twentieth) is compulsory (as Zakat on the yield of the land)." [Bukhari]

It was narrated that 'Ali (ra) said: "No zakat is due on wealth until one year has passed." [Musnad Ahmad]

Rate of zakat is 2.5% or one fortieth

The authentic Sunnah states that the zakat on gold and silver is one quarter of one tenth, i.e., 2.5%. A similar rate applies to trade goods and currency nowadays.

Hadith: Narrated Anas (ra) that Abu Bakr (ra) wrote to him this document when he sent him to Bahrain: "This is the obligatory charity that the Messenger of Allah (saws) enjoined upon the Muslims and that Allah enjoined upon His Messenger (saws):… for silver, one quarter of one tenth." [Bukhari]

Hadith: Narrated Ali Ibn Abu Talib (ra): that the Prophet (blessings and peace of Allah be upon him) said: "If you have two hundred dirhams and one full year has passed, then five dirhams are due on them. You do not have to pay anything - i.e. on gold -- unless you have twenty dinars; if you have twenty dinars and one full year has passed, then half a dinar is due on them, and if the number increases then work it out on this basis." [Abu Dawud]

Hadith: Narrated Ibn 'Umar and `Aishah (ra) that the Prophet (saws) used to take from every twenty dinars or more, half a dinar, and from forty dinars, one dinar. [Sunan Ibn Majah]

Hadith: Narrated Ali (ra): "Nothing is due on anything less than twenty dinars; for twenty dinars, half a dinar is due; for forty dinars, one dinar is due. For anything more than that, it is to be worked out." [Musnad Ibn Abi Shaybah]

Virtues of zakat

Narrated Abu Aiyub (ra): A man said to the Prophet (saws), "Tell me of such a deed as will make me enter Paradise." The people said, "What is the matter with him? What is the matter with him?" The Prophet (saws) said, "He has something to ask. (What he needs greatly) The Prophet (saws) said: (In order to enter Paradise) you should worship Allah and do not ascribe any partners to Him, offer prayer perfectly, pay the Zakat and keep good relations with your Kith and kin." [Bukhari]

Narrated Khalid bin Aslam: We went out with 'Abdullah bin 'Umar (ra) and a bedouin said (to 'Abdullah): Tell me about Allah's saying: "And those who hoard up gold and silver (Al-Kanz - money, gold, silver etc., the Zakat of which has not been paid) and spend it not in the Way of Allah (Ch 9:34)." Ibn 'Umar (ra) said, "Whoever hoarded them and did not pay the Zakat thereof, then woe to him. But these holy Verses were revealed before the Verses of Zakat. So when the Verses of Zakat were revealed, Allah made Zakat a purifier of the property." [Bukhari]

Whom to pay zakat

Narrated Hakim bin Hizam (ra): The Prophet (saws) said, "The upper hand is better than the lower hand (i.e. he who gives in charity is better than him who takes it). One should start giving first to his dependents. And the best object of charity is that which is given by a wealthy person (from the money which is left after his expenses). And whoever abstains from asking others for some financial help, Allah will give him and save him from asking others, Allah will make him self-sufficient." [Bukhari and Muslim]

If zakat is not paid

Narrated Abu Huraira (ra): Allah's Messenger (saws) said, "Anyone whom Allah has given wealth but he does not pay its Zakat, then, on the Day of Resurrection, his wealth will be presented to him in the shape of a bald-headed poisonous male snake with two poisonous glands in its mouth and it will encircle itself round his neck and bite him over his cheeks and say, "I am your wealth; I am your treasure." Then the Prophet (saws) recited this Divine Verse: "And let not those who covetously withhold of that which Allah has bestowed upon them of His Bounty." (Ch 3:180) [Bukhari]

Narrated Abu Huraira (ra): The Prophet (saws) said, "(On the Day of Resurrection) camels will come to their owner in the best state of health they have ever had (in the world), and if he had not paid their Zakat (in the world) then they would tread him with their feet; and similarly, sheep will come to their owner in the best state of health they have ever had in the world, and if he had not paid their Zakat, then they would tread him with their hooves and would butt him with their horns." The Prophet (saws) added, "One of their rights is that they should be milked while water is kept in front of them." The Prophet (saws) added, "I do not want anyone of you to come to me on the Day of Resurrection, carrying over his neck a sheep that will be bleating. Such a person will (then) say, 'O Muhammad (saws)! (please intercede for me) I will say to him. 'I can't help you, for I conveyed Allah's Message to you.' Similarly, I do not want anyone of you to come to me carrying over his neck a camel that will be grunting. Such a person (then) will say "O Muhammad (saws)! (please intercede for me)." I will say to him, "I can't help you for I conveyed Allah's message to you." [Bukhari]

To practise charity before such time when nobody would accept it

Narrated Haritha bin Wahab (ra): I heard the Prophet (saws) saying: O people! Give in charity as a time will come upon you when a person will wander about with his object of charity and will not find anybody to accept it, and one (who will be requested to take it) will say, "If you had brought it yesterday, would have taken it, but today I am not in need of it." [Bukhari]

Narrated Abu Huraira (ra): The Prophet (saws) said: The Hour (Day of Judgment) will not be established till your wealth increases so much so that one will be worried, for no one will accept his Zakat and the person to whom he will give it will reply, 'I am not in need of it.' [Bukhari]

The prophet (saws) accepted gifts but refused Charity

Abu Huraira (ra) reported: Whenever the Messenger of Allah (saws) was presented with food, he (saws) asked about it, if he (saws) was told that it was a gift, he (saws) ate out of that, and if he (saws) was told that it was a sadaqa, he (saws) did not eat out of that. [Muslim]

Pleasing the Zakat Collector unless he asks for something unlawful

Jarir b. 'Abdullah (ra) said: 'When the collector of sadaqat (Zakat) comes to you, (you should see) that he goes away pleased with you.' [Muslim]

Beggars versus poor man (miskin)

Warning against begging

Hamza, son of 'Abdullah (ra) reported on the authority of his father that the Messenger of Allah (sa) said: When a man is always begging from people, he would meet Allah (in a state) that there would be no flesh on his face. [Muslim]

Who is a miskin?

Abu Huraira (ra) reported Allah's Messenger (saws) as saying: The poor man (miskin) is not the one who goes around to the people and is dismissed with one or two morsels and one or two dates. They (the Companions) said: Messenger of Allah (saws), then who is miskin? He (saws) said: He who does not get enough to satisfy him, and he is not considered so (as to elicit the attention of the benevolent people), so that charity way be given to him and he does not beg anything from people. [Muslim]

When is begging permissible?

Qabisa b. Mukhariq al-Hilali (ra) said: I was under debt and I came to the Messenger of Allah (saws) and begged from him regarding it. He (saws) said: Wait till we receive Sadaqa, so that we order that to be given to you. He (saws) again said: Qabisa, begging is not permissible but for one of the three (classes) of persons: one who has incurred debt, for him begging is permissible till he pays that off, after which he must stop it; a man whose property has been destroyed by a calamity which has smitten him, for him begging is permissible till he gets what will support life, or will provide him reasonable subsistence; and a person who has been smitten by poverty, the genuineness of which is confirmed by three intelligent members of this people for him begging is permissible till he gets what will support him, or will provide him subsistence. Qabisa, besides these three, (every other reason) begging is forbidden, and one who engages in such, consumes that what is forbidden. [Muslim]

It is disliked to be eager to acquire worldly gains
Abu Huraira (ra) reported from the Messenger of Allah (saws) as having said this: The heart of an old person feels young for the love of two things: love for long life and wealth. [Muslim]
Anas (ra) reported Allah's Messenger (saws) as saying: If the son of Adam were to possess two valleys of riches, he would long for the third one. And the stomach of the son of Adam is not filled but with dust. And Allah returns to him who repents. [Muslim]

Sufficient provision and contentment
Amr b. al-'As (ra) reported Allah's Messenger (saws) as saying: He is successful who has accepted Islam, who has been provided with sufficient for his want and been made contented by Allah with what He has given him. [Muslim]

Orphans (Yatim)

In the Quran, the topic on orphans has been mentioned by Allah SWT for over 23 times and is also emphasized by the Prophet (saws) countlessly. The Prophet (saws) himself was an orphan. In the Qur'an, maximum verses are on general good treatment and financial generosity upon orphans, with the largest number of verses on warning against the severe crime of usurping their general or financial rights and strictly rebuking those that do so. Allah SWT says (that means):
"and give food—despite their desire for it—to the poor, the orphan, and the captive (Ch 76:8)
Those who consume the wealth of orphans unjustly, they are only filling their bellies with fire.' (Ch 4: 10)
Sahl ibn Sa'd (ra) reported: The Prophet, peace and blessings be upon him, said, "Myself and the caretaker of an orphan will be in Paradise like this," and he held his two fingers together." [Bukhari]

The Prophet (saws) has stated: Whomsoever passes his hand over the head of an orphan to please Allah Almighty gets a virtue in return for every hair that his hand passes over. Moreover, whosoever does good to an orphan boy or girl, I and he will be like this in Paradise (he saws said this after having joined his two fingers). [Musnad Ahmad]

It is a blessed saying of the Holy Prophet (saws), "Best homes among the homes of Muslims are those in which orphans are treated kindly, and the worst homes among the homes of Muslims are those in which orphans are mistreated." [Sunan Ibn Majah]

The Prophet (saws) said: "Four types of people are such that Allah Almighty will neither make them enter Paradise nor make them experience its blessings. One among them is also he who unjustly usurps the wealth of an orphan." [Al-Mustadrak Hakim]

Summary

- Zakat is obligatory. If it is not paid, Prophet (saws) will not intercede on the Day of Judgement.
- Sadaqa is voluntary charity.
- Wealth is from Allah and we have to donate from it.
- Charity is to be given first to the nearest relatives.
- Even a kind word and a smiling face are charity.
- Donation from unlawful wealth is rejected.
- Charity on behalf of deceased person is allowed.
- Sadaqa Jariyya continues after death.

7. Hajj and Umrah

Hajj is one of the Five pillars of Islam. Allah SWT says (interpretation of meaning):

"Complete the pilgrimage and minor pilgrimage for Allah. But if prevented from proceeding , then offer whatever sacrificial animals you can afford. And do not shave your heads until the sacrificial animal reaches its destination. But if any of you is ill or has a scalp ailment requiring shaving , then compensate either by fasting, charity, or a sacrificial offering. In times of peace, you may combine the pilgrimage and minor pilgrimage then make the sacrificial offering you can afford. Whoever cannot afford that offering , let them fast three days during pilgrimage and seven after returning home —completing ten. These offerings are for those who do not live near the Sacred House. And be mindful of Allah, and know that Allah is severe in punishment." (Ch 2:196)

Umrah (minor pilgrimage) is an Islamic pilgrimage to Makkah that can be made any time in a year. Hajj, the Arabic word for pilgrimage, occurs once a year and lasts for five or six days during the last month of the Islamic calendar. Umrah is optional but highly virtuous.

Hajj is obligatory once in a lifetime

Narrated Aisha: (ra) I said, "O Allah's Messenger (saws)! We consider Jihad as the best deed." The Prophet (saws) said, "The best Jihad (for women) is Hajj Mabrur." [Bukhari]

Abu Huraira (ra) reported: Allah's Messenger (saws) addressed us and said: "O people, Allah has made Hajj obligatory for you; so, perform Hajj." Thereupon a person said: "Messenger of Allah (saws), (is it to be performed) every year? He (the Holy Prophet saws) kept quiet, and he (saws) repeated (these words) thrice, whereupon Allah's Messenger (saws) said: "If I were to say Yes, it would become obligatory (for you to perform it every year) and you would not be able to do it." Then he (saws) said: "Leave me with what I have left to you, for those who were before you were destroyed because of excessive questioning, and their opposition to their apostles. So, when I command you to do anything, do it as much as it lies in your power and when I forbid you to do anything, then abandon it." [Muslim]

Substitute Hajj

Narrated Abdullah bin Abbas (ra): Al-Fadl (ra) (his brother) was riding behind Allah's Messenger (saws) and a woman from the tribe of Khatham came and Al-Fadl (ra) started looking at her and she started looking at him. The Prophet (saws) turned Al-Fadls face to the other side. The woman said, "O Allah's Messenger (saws)! The obligation of Hajj enjoined by Allah on His devotees has become due on my father and he is old and weak, and he cannot sit firm on the Mount; may I perform Hajj on his behalf?" The Prophet (saws) replied, "Yes, you may." That happened during the Hajj-al-Wida (of the Prophet (saws). [Bukhari]

Being prevented from completing Hajj

Al-Hajjaj bin Amr Al-Ansari (ra) reported the Apostle of Allah (saws) as saying: "If anyone breaks (a bone or leg) or becomes lame, he has come out of the sacred state and must perform Hajj the following year." Ikrimah said, I asked Ibn Abbas (ra) and Abu Hurairah (ra) about this. They replied, "He spoke the truth". [Abu Dawud]

When setting out for Hajj or any other purpose

Ibn Umar (ra) reported that whenever Allah's Messenger (saws) mounted his camel while setting out on a journey, he glorified Allah (uttered Allahu-Akbar) thrice, and then said:

سُبْحَانَ الَّذِي سَخَّرَ لَنَا هَذَا وَمَا كُنَّا لَهُ مُقْرِنِينَ وَإِنَّا إِلَى رَبِّنَا لَمُنْقَلِبُونَ

اللَّهُمَّ إِنَّا نَسْأَلُكَ فِي سَفَرِنَا هَذَا الْبِرَّ وَالتَّقْوَى وَمِنَ الْعَمَلِ مَا تَرْضَى اللَّهُمَّ

هَوِّنْ عَلَيْنَا سَفَرَنَا هَذَا وَاطْوِ عَنَّا بُعْدَهُ اللَّهُمَّ أَنْتَ الصَّاحِبُ فِي السَّفَرِ وَالْخَلِيفَةُ فِي الْأَهْلِ اللَّهُمَّ إِنِّي أَعُوذُ بِكَ مِنْ وَعْثَاءِ السَّفَرِ وَكَآبَةِ الْمَنْظَرِ وَسُوءِ الْمُنْقَلَبِ فِي الْمَالِ وَالْأَهْلِ

(Hallowed is He Who subdued for us this (ride) and we were not ourselves powerful enough to use it as a ride, and we are going to return to our Lord. O Allah, we seek virtue and piety from Thee in this journey of ours and the act which pleaseth Thee. O Allah, lighten this journey of ours, and make its distance easy for us. O Allah, Thou art (our) companion during the journey, and guardian of (our) family. O Allah, I seek refuge with Thee from hardships of the journey, gloominess of the sights, and finding of evil changes in property and family on return.) And he (saws) uttered (these words), and made this addition to them: We are returning, repentant, worshipping our Lord. and praising Him. [Muslim]

What should be said when returning from Hajj and other journeys

Abdullah bin Umar (ra) reported that whenever Allah's Messenger (saws) came back from the battle or from expeditions or from Hajj or Umrah and as he reached the top of the hillock or upon the elevated hard ground, he uttered Allahu- Akbar thrice, and then said:

لاَ إِلَهَ إِلاَّ اللَّهُ وَحْدَهُ لاَ شَرِيكَ لَهُ لَهُ الْمُلْكُ وَلَهُ الْحَمْدُ وَهُوَ عَلَى كُلِّ شَيْءٍ قَدِيرٌ آيِبُونَ تَائِبُونَ عَابِدُونَ سَاجِدُونَ لِرَبِّنَا حَامِدُونَ صَدَقَ اللَّهُ وَعْدَهُ وَنَصَرَ عَبْدَهُ وَهَزَمَ الْأَحْزَابَ وَحْدَهُ

(There is no god but Allah. He is One, there is no partner with Him, His is the sovereignty and His is the praise and He is Potent over everything. (We are) returning, repenting, worshipping, prostrating before our Lord, and we praise Him Allah fulfilled His promise and helped His servant, and routed the confederates alone.) [Muslim]

Virtues of Hajj

Narrated Abu Huraira (ra): The Prophet (saws) said, "Whoever performs Hajj for Allah's pleasure and does not have sexual relations with his wife, and does not do evil or sins then he will return (after Hajj free from all sins) as if he were born a new." [Bukhari]

Abu Huraira (ra) reported Allah's Messenger (saws) as saying: "An Umra is an expiation for the sins committed between it and the next, and Hajj which is accepted will receive no other reward than Paradise." [Muslim]

Abu Huraira (ra) reported Allah's Messenger (saws) as saying: "He who came to this House (Kaba) (with the intention of performing Pilgrimage), and neither spoke indecently nor did he act wickedly would return (free from sin) as on the (very first day) his mother bore him." [Muslim]

Types of Hajj

There are three types of Hajj:
1. Ifrad: Ifrad means Hajj-only mode. This is performed by those who live within the Miqat boundaries and the Haram of Makkah.
2. Qiran: Qiran means Umrah merged with Hajj. Irham is maintained throughout during the same journey and the people are required to stay within the Haram boundaries.
3. Tamattu: Tamattu is the Umrah followed with Hajj. Suppose a person is going for Hajj for the first time in his life from a very long distance and he will be the therein Makkah for many days. Then he can choose Tamattu. He will perform Umrah and enjoy staying in Makkah for remaining days until Hajj rituals comes. Then he will do all rituals of Hajj, resume Irham on 8th Zul-Hijja.

Pilgrims performing Tamattu or Qiran are required to slaughter an animal as a token of gratitude for the concessions granted to them by Allah.

Hadith: Narrated Anas bin Malik (ra): "Allah's Messenger (saws) offered four rakat of Zuhr prayer at Madina and we were in his company, and two rakat of the Asr prayer at Zul-Hulaifa and then passed the night there till it was dawn; then he (saws) rode, and when he (saws) reached Al-Baida, he (saws) praised and glorified Allah and said Takbir (i.e. Al hamdu-lillah and Subhanallah and Allahu-Akbar). Then he (saws) and the people along with him recited Talbiya with the intention of performing Hajj and Umra. When we reached (Makkah) he (saws) ordered us to finish the Irham (after performing the Umrah) (only those who had no Hadi (animal for sacrifice) with them were asked to do so) till the day of Tarwiya that is 8th Dhul-Hijja when they assumed Ihram for Hajj. The Prophet (saws) sacrificed many camels (slaughtering them) with his own hands while standing. While Allah's Apostle (saws) was in Madinah, he (saws) sacrificed two horned rams black and white in colour in the Name of Allah." [Bukhari]

Hadith: Narrated Anas bin Malik (ra): Ali (ra) came to the Prophet (saws) from Yemen (to Makkah). The Prophet (saws) asked Ali (ra), "With what intention have you assumed Ihram?" Ali (ra) replied, "I have assumed Ihram with the same intention as that of the Prophet (saws)." The Prophet (saws) said, "If I had not the Hadi with me I would have finished the Ihram." Muhammad bin Bakr narrated extra from Ibn Juraij: The Prophet (saws) said to Ali, "With what intention have you assumed the Ihram, O Ali?" He replied, "With the same (intention) as that of the Prophet (saws)." The Prophet (saws) said, "Have a Hadi and keep your Ihram as it is." [Bukhari]

Hadith: Narrated Abu Musa (ra): The Prophet (saws) sent me to some people in Yemen and when I returned, I found him at Al-Batha. He (saws) asked me, "With what intention have you assumed Ihram (i.e. for Hajj or for Umrah or for both?") I replied, "I have assumed Ihram with an intention like that of the Prophet (saws)." He (saws) asked, "Have you a Hadi with you?" I replied in the negative. He (saws) ordered me to perform Tawaf round the Kaba and between Safa and Marwa and then to finish my Ihram. I did so and went to a woman from my tribe who combed my hair or washed my head. Then, when Umar (ra) came (i.e. became Caliph) he said, "If we follow Allah's Book, it orders us to complete Hajj and Umrah; as Allah says: "Perform the Hajj and Umrah for Allah." (Ch 2:196). And if we follow the tradition of the Prophet (saws) who did not finish his Ihram till he sacrificed his Hadi." [Bukhari]

Hajj-at-Tamattu, Hajj-al-Qiran, and Hajj-al-Ifrad

Narrated Aisha (ra): We set out with Allah's Messenger (saws) in the year of the Prophets (saws) Last Hajj. Some of us had assumed Ihram for Umrah only, some for both Hajj and Umrah, and others for Hajj only. Allah's Apostle (saws) assumed Ihram for Hajj. So, whoever had assumed Ihram for Hajj or for both Hajj and Umrah did not finish the Ihram till the day of sacrifice. [Bukhari]

Narrated Abu Musa (ra): Ali (ra) came to the Prophet (saws) (from Yemen and was assuming Ihram for Hajj) and he ordered me to finish the Ihram (after performing the Umrah). [Bukhari]

Narrated Ibn Umar (ra): Hafsa (ra), the wife of the Prophet (saws) said, "O Allah's Messenger (saws)! Why have the people finished their Ihram after performing Umrah but you have not finished your Ihram after performing Umrah?" He (saws) replied, "I have matted my hair and garlanded my Hadi. So, I will not finish my Ihram till I have slaughtered (my Hadi)." [Bukhari]

Narrated Abu Shihab: I left for Makkah for Hajj-at-Tamattu assuming Ihram for Umrah. I reached Makkah three days before the day of Tarwiya (8th Zul-Hijja). Some people of Makkah said to me: Your Hajj will be like the Hajj performed by the people of Makkah (i.e. you will lose the superiority of assuming Ihram from the Miqat). So I went to Ata asking him his view about it. He said: Jabir bin Abdullah (ra) narrated to me: "I performed Hajj with Allah's Messenger (saws) on the day when he drove camels with him. The people had assumed Ihram for Hajj-al-Ifrad. The Prophet (saws) ordered them to finish their Ihram after Tawaf round the Kaba, and between Safa and Marwa and to cut short their hair and then to stay there (in Makkah) as non-Muhrims till the day of Tarwiya (i.e. 8th of Zul-Hijja) when they would assume Ihram for Hajj and they were ordered to make the Ihram with which they had come as for Umrah only. They asked: How can we make it Umrah (Tamattu) as we have intended to perform Hajj? The Prophet (saws) said: Do what I have ordered you. Had I not brought the Hadi with me, I would have done the same, but I cannot finish my Ihram till the Hadi reaches its destination (i.e. is slaughtered). So, they did (what he saws ordered them to do)." [Bukhari]

Ibn Abbas (ra) said that he has been asked regarding Hajj-at-Tamattu on which he said: The Muhajirin and the Ansar and the wives of the Prophet (saws) and we did the same. When we reached Makkah, Allah's Messenger (saws) said, "Give up your intention of doing the Hajj (at this moment) and perform Umrah, except the one who had garlanded the Hadi." So, we performed Tawaf round the Kaba and [Sai] between As-safa and Al-Marwa, slept with our wives and wore ordinary (stitched) clothes. The Prophet (saws) added, "Whoever has garlanded his Hadi is not allowed to finish the Ihram till the Hadi has reached its destination (has been sacrificed)". Then on the night of Tarwiya (8th Zul Hijjah, in the afternoon) he ordered us to assume Ihram for Hajj and when we have performed all the ceremonies of Hajj, we came and performed Tawaf round the Kaba and (Sai) between As-Safa and Al-Marwa, and then our Hajj was complete, and we had to sacrifice a Hadi according to the statement of Allah: ... "... He must slaughter a Hadi such as he can afford, but if he cannot afford it, he should observer Saum (fasts) three days during the Hajj and seven days after his return (to his home)" (Ch 2:196). And the sacrifice of the sheep is sufficient. So, the Prophet (saws) and his Companions joined the two religious deeds, (i.e. Hajj and Umrah) in one year, for Allah revealed (the permissibility) of such practice in His book and in the Sunnah (legal ways) of His Prophet (saws) and rendered it permissible for all the people except those living in Makkah. Allah says: "This is for him whose family is not present at the Al-Masjid-Al-Haram, (i.e. non- resident of Makkah)." The months of Hajj which Allah mentioned in His book are: Shawwal, Zul-Qada and Zul-Hijjah. Whoever performed Hajj-at-Tamattu in those months, then slaughtering or fasting is compulsory for him. [Bukhari]

Narrated Urwa: Aisha (ra) said, "The first thing the Prophet (saws) did on reaching Makkah, was the ablution and then he performed Tawaf of the Kaba and that was not Umrah (alone), (but Hajj-al-Qiran). Urwa added: Later Abu Bakr (ra) and Umar (ra) did the same in their Hajj." And I performed the Hajj with my father Az- Zubair, and the first thing he did was Tawaf of the Kaba. Later I saw the Muhajirin (Emigrants) and the Ansar doing the same. My mother (Asma) told me that she, her sister (Aisha), Az-Zubair (ra) and such and such persons assumed Ihram for Umrah, and after they passed their hands over the Black Stone Corner (of the Kaba) they finished the Ihram. (i.e. After doing Tawaf of the Kaba and Sai between Safa-Marwa. [Bukhari]

Narrated Aisha (ra): We set out with Allah's Messenger (saws) in the year of his Last Hajj and we mended (the Ihram) for Umrah. Then the Prophet (saws) said, "Whoever has a Hadi with him should assume Ihram for both Hajj and Umrah, and should not finish it till he performs both of the them (Hajj and Umrah)." When we reached Makkah, I had my menses. When we had performed our Hajj, the Prophet (saws) sent me with Abdur-Rahman (her brother) to Tanim and I performed the Umrah. The Prophet (saws) said, "This is in lieu of your missed Umrah."

Those who had assumed Ihram for Umrah performed Tawaf (between Safa and Marwa) and then finished their Ihram. And then they performed another Tawaf (between Safa and Marwa) after returning from Mina. And those who had assumed Irham for Hajj and Umrah to get her (Hajj-Qiran) performed only one Tawaf (between Safa and Marwa). [Bukhari] Narrated Nafi: Ibn Umar (ra) intended to perform Hajj in the year when Al-Hajjaj attacked Ibn Az-Zubair. Somebody said to Ibn Umar (ra), "There is a danger of an impending war between them." Ibn Umar (ra) said, "Verily, in Allah's Messenger (saws) you have a good example. (And if it happened as you say) then I would do the same as Allah's Messenger (saws) had done. I make you witness that I have decided to perform Umrah." Then he set out and when he reached Al-Baida, he said, "The ceremonies of both Hajj and Umrah are similar. I make you witness that I have made Hajj compulsory for me along with Umrah." He drove (to Makkah) a Hadi which he had bought from (a place called) Qudaid and did not do more than that. He did not slaughter the Hadi or finish his Ihram, or shave or cut short his hair till the day of slaughtering the sacrifices (10th Zul-Hijja). Then he slaughtered his Hadi and shaved his head and considered the first Tawaf (of Safa and Marwa) as sufficient for Hajj and Umrah. Ibn Umar (ra) said, "Allah's Messenger (saws) did the same." [Bukhari]

Irham

The word Ihram is derived from the Arabic verb harama (حرم), which means "to be forbidden". It refers to a state of purity the pilgrim is required to be in order to perform Hajj, Umrah or both before entering the perimeter of Makkah. After having made the intention for Ihram, the pilgrim must abide by its prohibitions. In the state of Irham, one has to put on prescribed clothes, and sometimes the clothes are called Irhams. Ihram for men consists of two pieces of white, unsewn cloth, one of the pieces (*izar*) is wrapped around the midriff to cover his body from just above his navel to his ankles, and the other (Rida) is draped around his shoulders to cover the upper body. During Tawaf, mens right shoulder should be open while other parts are wrapped as before. This is called Idtiba. Sandals may be stitched or unstitched, but must not cover the heel and ankle bones.

After wearing Ihram clothes, one has to perform two Rakahs of Salat al-Ihram before making the intention to enter into the state of Ihram, by consensus of scholars. Talbiya is then recited. This should be performed before the Miqat is crossed.

Performing ghusl to initiate Ihrams

It was narrated from Abu Bakr (ra): That he went out for Hajj with the Messenger of Allah (saws) on the Farewell Pilgrimage, and his wife Asma bint Umais Al-Khathamiyyah (ra) was with him. When they were at Zul-Hulaifah, Asma (ra) gave birth to Muhammad bin Abu Bakr (ra). Abu Bakr (ra) came to the Prophet (saws) and told him, and the Messenger of Allah (saws) told him to tell her to perform Ghusl, then begin the Talbiyah for Hajj, and to do everything that the people do, except that she should not do tawaf the House. [Sunan Ibn Majah]

Ghusl of the Muhrim in Irham

It was narrated from Abdullah bin Abbas (ra) and Al-Miswar bin Makhramah that they had a difference of opinion in al-Abwa. Ibn Abbas (ra) said: "The Muhrim (Pilgrim in Ihram) may wash his head." Al-Miswar said: "He should not wash his head." Ibn Abbas (ra) sent me (the narrator) to Abu Ayyub Al-Ansari (ra) to ask him about that. I found him performing Ghusl in front of the well, screened with a cloth. I greeted him with Salam and said: "Abdullah bin Abbas (ra) has sent me to you to ask you how the Messenger of Allah (saws) used to wash his head when he was in Ihram." Abu Ayyub (ra) put his hand on the cloth and lowered it, until his head appeared, then he told someone to pour water on his head. Then he rubbed his head with his hands, back and forth, and said: "This is what I saw the Messenger of Allah (saws) do." [Sunan Ibn Majah]

Irham of women

Women are not required to conform to a specific dress code and are free to wear what they please. Clothing should be normal, modest Islamic dress with a head covering of any colour. Socks may be worn but the hands and faces must be uncovered. Women in a state of menstruation should not perform the Salah, rather they should make their intention for Hajj or Umrah and recite the Talbiyah.

Hadith: Ibn Umar (ra) reported that the Prophet (saws) as saying: A woman in the sacred state (wearing ihram) must not be veiled or wear gloves. [Abu Dawud]

Hadith: Abdullah bin Umar (ra) said that he heard the Apostle of Allah (saws) prohibiting women in the sacred state (wearing ihram) to wear gloves, veil (their faces) and to wear clothes with dye of waras or saffron on them. But afterwards they can wear any kind of clothing they like dyed yellow or silk or jewellery or trousers or shirts or shoes. Abu Dawud said Abdah and Muhammad bin Ishaq narrated this tradition from Muhammad bin Ishaq up to the words "And to wear clothes with dye of waras or saffron on them". They did not mention the words after them. [Abu Dawud]

Hadith: Narrated Aisha (ra), Ummul Muminin: Salim ibn Abdullah said: Abdullah ibn Umar (ra) used to do so, that is to say, he would cut the shoes of a woman who put on ihram; then Safiyyah, daughter of Abu Ubayd, reported to him that Aisha (ra) narrated to her that the Messenger of Allah (saws) gave licence to women in respect of the shoes (i.e. women are not required to cut the shoes). He, therefore, abandoned it. [Abu Dawud]

The prohibition of women covering their faces in Ihram

It was narrated that Ibn Umar (ra) said: A man stood up and said: "O Messenger of Allah (saws)! What garments do you command us to wear in Ihram?" The Messenger of Allah (saws) said: "Do not wear shirts or pants, or Imamahs, or burnouses, or Khuffs except if someone does not have sandals, in which case let him wear Khuffs that come below the ankles. And do not wear any garment that has been touched by (dyed with) saffron or Wars. And women should not cover their faces when in Ihram, or wear gloves." [Sunan Ibn Majah]

Uncovering the right shoulder during tawaf

Narrated Yala (ra): The Messenger of Allah (saws) went round the House (the Kaba) wearing a green Yamani mantle under his right armpit with the end over his left shoulder. [Abu Dawud]

Perfumes after assuming Irham

Narrated Safwan bin Yala: Yala said to Umar (ra): Show me the Prophet (saws) when he is being inspired Divinely. While the Prophet (saws) was at Jirana (in the company of some of his Companions) a person came and asked, "O Allah's Messenger (saws)! What is your verdict regarding that person who assumes Ihram for Umra and is scented with perfume?" The Prophet (saws) kept quiet for a while and he was Divinely inspired (then). Umar (ra) signalled Yala. So he came, and the Allah's Messenger (saws) was shaded with sheet. Yala put his head in and saw that the face of Allah's Messenger (saws) was red and he was snoring. When the state of the Prophet (saws) was over, he (saws) asked, "Where is the person who asked about Umrah?" Then that person was brought and the Prophet (saws) said, "Wash the perfume off your body thrice and take off the cloak and do the same in Umrah as you do in Hajj." [Bukhari]

Perfume before assuming Irham

Narrated Aisha (ra): I used to scent Allah's Messenger (saws) when he wanted to assume Ihram and also on finishing Ihram before the Tawaf round the Kaba (Tawaf-al-ifada). [Bukhari]

Marriage not allowed for Muhrim

It was narrated from Aban bin Uthamn, from his father that the Prophet (saws) forbade the Muhrim to get married, arrange a marriage for anyone else, or propose marriage. [Sunan Ibn Majah]

Clothes of Irham

Narrated Abdullah bin Umar (ra): A man asked, "O Allah's Messenger (saws)! What kind of clothes should a Muhrim wear?" Allah's Messenger (saws) replied, "He should not wear a shirt, a turban, trousers, a head cloak or leather socks except if he can find no slippers, he then may wear leather socks after cutting off what might cover the ankles. And he should not wear clothes which are scented with saffron or Waras (kinds of Perfumes)." [Bukhari]

Narrated Abdullah bin Abbas (ra): The Prophet (saws) with his companions started from Madina after combing and oiling his hair and putting on two sheets of Irham (upper body cover and waist cover). He did not forbid anyone to wear any kind of sheets except the ones coloured with saffron because they may leave the scent on the skin. And so in the early morning, the Prophet (saws) mounted his Mount while in Zul-Hulaifa and set out till they reached Baida, where he and his companions recited Talbiya, and then they did the ceremony of Taqlid (which means to put the coloured garlands around the necks of the Budn (camels for sacrifice). And all that happened on the 25th of Zul-Qada. And when he reached Makkah on the 4th of Zul-Hijja he performed the Tawaf round the Kaba and performed the Tawaf between Safa and Marwa. And as he had a Badana and had garlanded it, he did not finish his Ihram. He proceeded towards the highest places of Makkah near Al-Hujun and he was assuming the Ihram for Hajj and did not go near the Kaba after he performed Tawaf (round it) till he returned from Arafat. Then he ordered his companions to perform the Tawaf round the Kaba and then the Tawaf of Safa and Marwa, and to cut short the hair of their heads and to finish their Ihram. And that was only for those people who had not garlanded Budn. Those who had their wives with them were permitted to contact them (have sexual intercourse), and similarly perfume and (ordinary) clothes were permissible for them. [Bukhari]

Narrated Nafi: Whenever Ibn Umar (ra) intended to go to Makkah, he used to oil himself with a sort of oil that had no pleasant smell, then he would go to the Mosque of Al-Hulaita and offer the prayer, and then ride. When he mounted well on his Mount and the Mount stood up straight, he would proclaim the intention of assuming Ihram, and he used to say that he had seen the Prophet (saws) doing the same. [Bukhari]

How should a menstruating woman assume Ihram?

Narrated Aisha (ra): We set out with the Prophet (saws) in his last Hajj and we assumed Ihram for Umra. The Prophet (saws) then said, "Whoever has the Hadi (animal for sacrifice) with him should assume Ihram for Hajj along with Umra and should not finish the Ihram till he finishes both." I was menstruating when I reached Makkah, and so I neither did Tawaf round the Kaba nor Tawaf between Safa and Marwa. I complained about that to the Prophet (saws) on which he replied, "Undo and comb your head hair, and assume Ihram for Hajj (only) and leave the Umra." So, I did so. When we had performed the Hajj, the Prophet (saws) sent me with my brother Abdur-Rahman bin Abu Bakr (ra) to Tanim. So I performed the Umra. The Prophet (saws) said to me, "This

Umra is instead of your missed one." Those who had assumed Ihram for Umra (Hajj-atTamattu) performed Tawaf round the Kaba and between Safa and Marwa and then finished their Ihram. After returning from Mina, they performed another Tawaf (between Safa and Marwa). Those who had assumed Ihram for Hajj and Umra together (Hajj-al-Qiran) performed only one Tawaf (between Safa and Marwa). [Bukhari]

Narrated Al-Qasim bin Muhammad: Aisha (ra) said: We set out with Allah's Messenger (saws) in the months of Hajj, and (in) the nights of Hajj, and at the time and places of Hajj and in a state of Hajj. We dismounted at Sarif (a village six miles from Makkah). The Prophet (saws) then addressed his companions and said, "Anyone who has not got the Hadi and likes to do Umra instead of Hajj may do so (i.e. Hajj-al-Tamattu) and anyone who has got the Hadi should not finish the Ihram after performing Umra). (i.e. Hajj-al-Qiran)." Aisha (ra) added, "The companions of the Prophet (saws) obeyed the above (order) and some of them (i.e. who did not have Hadi) finished their Ihram after Umra." Allah's Messenger (saws) and some of his companions were resourceful and had the Hadi with them, they could not perform Umra (alone) (but had to perform both Hajj and Umra with one Ihram). Aisha (ra) added: Allah's Messenger (saws) came to me and saw me weeping and said, "What makes you weep, O Hantah?" I replied, "I have heard your conversation with your companions and I cannot perform the Umra." He asked, "What is wrong with you? I replied, "I do not offer the prayers (i.e. I have my menses)." He said, "It will not harm you for you are one of the daughters of Adam, and Allah has written for you (this state) as He has written it for them. Keep on with your intentions for Hajj and Allah may reward you that." Aisha (ra) further added, "Then we proceeded for Hajj till we reached Mina and I became clean from my menses. Then I went out from Mina and performed Tawaf round the Kaba." Aisha (ra) added, "I went along with the Prophet (saws) in his final departure (from Hajj) till he dismounted at Al-Muhassab (a valley outside Makkah), and we too, dismounted with him." He (saws) called Abdur-Rahman bin Abu Bakr (ra) and said to him: "Take your sister outside the sanctuary of Makkah and let her assume Ihram for Umra, and when you had finished Umra, return to this place and I will wait for you both till you both return to me." Aisha (ra) added, "So we went out of the sanctuary of Makkah and after finishing from the Umra and the Tawaf we returned to the

Prophet (saws) at dawn. He said, "Have you performed the Umra?" We replied in the affirmative. So, he (saws) announced the departure amongst his companions and the people set out for the journey, and the Prophet (saws) too left for Madina." [Bukhari]

What is not prohibited to kill during Irham

Narrated Abdullah bin Umar (ra): Allah's Messenger (saws) said, "It is not sinful of a person in the state of Ihram to kill any of these five animals: The scorpion, the rat, the rabid dog, the crow and the kite." [Bukhari]

Miqat

Miqat is the boundary wherefrom pilgrims put on the Ihram garments; it is not permissible to pass the boundary except in the state of Ihram. Those who cross the boundary, they have to perform an animal sacrifice as expiation, called Damm.

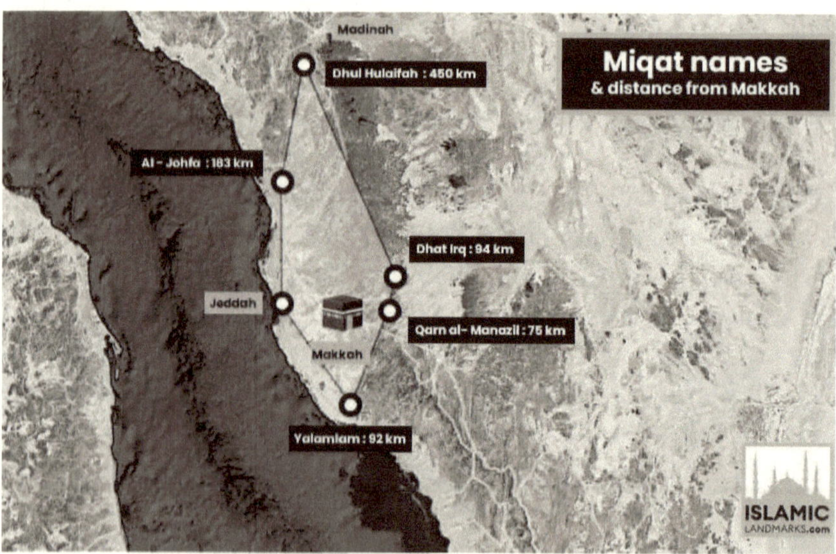

Photo: The Miqat Boundary (courtesy: www.islamiclandmarks.com) and

Narrated Ibn Abbas (ra): Allah's Messenger (saws) made Zul-Hulaifa as the Miqat for the people of Madinah; Al-Juhfa for the people of Sham; Qarn-al-Manazil for the people of Najd; and Yalamlam for the people of

Yemen; and these Mawaqit are for the people at those very places, and besides them for those who come thorough those places with the intention of performing Hajj and Umra; and whoever is living within these boundaries can assume Irham from the place he starts, and the people of Makkah can assume Ihram from Makkah. [Bukhari]

It is recommended to stop in Batha of Zul-Hulaifah and pray there when departing from Hajj and Umrah, or any time one passes through it. Abdullah b. Umar (ra) reported that Allah's Messenger (saws) made (his camel) kneel down (i.e. halt at the stony ground of Zul-Hulaifa) and prayed there, and so did Abdullah bin Umar (ra). [Muslim]

Masjid-al-Haram Makkah

Al-Masjid al-Haram (the Sacred Mosque) is situated in Makkah. It is the Masjid surrounding the Kaaba. The open space around the Kaaba for tawaf is known as Mataf. The history of the mosque goes back to its founding at the time of Ibrahim and his son Ismail, peace be upon them both. This is the first mosque that was built for people on earth. Allah says in the Quran (that means):

"Verily, the first House (of worship) appointed for mankind was that at Bakkah (Makkah), full of blessing, and a guidance for al-a'lamin (mankind and jinns)." (Ch 3:96).

Allah has forbidden entry of Mushriks in Masjid al-Haram because they are impure. Apart from physical impurity, they are spiritually impure; and shirk is the worst impurity. Allah SWT says (interpretation of meaning):

"O you who believe, the Mushriks are impure indeed, so let them not approach Al-Masjid-ul-Haram after this year. And if you apprehend poverty, then, Allah shall, if He wills, make you self-sufficient with His grace. Surely, Allah is All-Knowing, All-Wise." (At- Tawbah, Ch 9:28).

In the above verse (Ch 9:28), this year means 9th Hijri when Muslims performed Hajj under the leadership of Abu Bakr (ra). Disbelievers also gathered for Hajj in the same year and Makkah was already conquered.

Hadith: Narrated Abu Zar (ra): I said, "O Allah's Messenger (saws)! Which mosque was first built on the surface of the earth?" He (saws) said, "Al- Masjid-ul-Haram (in Makkah)." I said, "Which was built next?" He (saws) replied "The mosque of Al-Aqsa (in Jerusalem)." I said, "What was the period of construction between the two?" He (saws) said, "Forty years." He (saws) added, "Wherever (you may be, and) the prayer time becomes due, perform the prayer there, for the best thing is to do so (i.e. to offer the prayers in time). [Bukhari]

The Ka'ba – which is the Qibla for Muslims throughout the world, is situated roughly in the middle of al-Masjid al-Haram. It is a stone structure more or less in the shape of a cube. It was built by Ibrahim (peace be upon him) on the command of Allah.

"And (remember) when We showed Ibrahim the site of the (Sacred) House (the Kaba at Makkah) (saying): Associate not anything (in worship) with Me, and sanctify My House for those who circum-ambulate it, and those who bow and make prostration." (Ch 22:26)

"And (remember) when Ibrahim and (his son) Ismail were raising the foundations of the House (the Kaba at Makkah)…" (Ch 2:127)

Hadith: Narrated Abida bin Humaid: Abdul Aziz bin Rufai said: I saw Abdullah bin Az-Zubair performing Tawaf of the Kaba after the morning prayer then offering the two rakat prayer. Abdul Aziz added, "I saw Abdullah bin Az-Zubair offering a two rakat prayer after the Asr prayer." He informed me that Aisha (ra) told him that the Prophet (saws) used to offer those two rakat whenever he entered the House." [Bukhari]

Hadith: Aisha (ra) said: "I asked the Messenger of Allah (saws) about al-Jadr [the wall] and whether it was part of the House [the Kaba]." He (sa) said, "Yes." I asked, "So why is it not incorporated into the House?" He (saws) said, "Your people ran out of money." I asked, "What about the door? Why is it high up?" He (saws) said, "Your people did that so they could let in whomever they wanted and keep out whomever they wanted. If it were not for the fact that your people are still new [in Islam] and too close to their Jahiliyyah, and I am afraid that they would resent it, I would think of incorporating al-Jadr into the House and bringing the door down to ground level." [Muslim]

Hadith: Narrated Abu Wail: (One day) I sat along with Shaiba on the chair inside the Kaba. He (Shaiba) said: No doubt, Umar (ra) sat at this place and said, "I intended not to leave any yellow (i.e. gold) or white (i.e. silver) (inside the Kaba) undistributed." I said (to Umar), "But your two companions (i.e. The Prophet (saws) and Abu Bakr (ra) did not do so." Umar (ra) said, "They are the two persons whom I always follow." [Bukhari]

The multiplication of reward for prayer in al-Masjid al-Haram is proven in the report narrated from Jabir (ra), that the Messenger of Allah (saws) said: "One prayer in my mosque is better than one thousand prayers elsewhere, except al-Masjid al-Haram, and one prayer in al-Masjid al-Haram is better than one hundred thousand prayers elsewhere (i.e one lakh prayers)." [Musnad Ahmad, Sunan Ibn Majah]

Maqam Ibrahim is the rock on which Ibrahim (peace be upon him) stood whilst he was building the Kaba. After the construction of Kaba was completed, the sacred stone was left at the eastern side of the Holy Kaba. During his Khilafat, Umer (ra) ordered the Muslims to move the stone from the eastern side to the front of the Kaba. This change was done so that pilgrims do not face any difficulties while performing Tawaf. However, today, the stone is located at the spot where Prophet Ibrahim (as) offered two Rakah payers after Holy Kaba was constructed. Thousands of years later, the impressions of Prophet Ibrahim (as) feet are still on the miraculous rock.

There is also the Well of Zamzam, which is a spring of water brought forth by Allah for Haajar (as) and her child Ismail (peace be upon him) when he got thirsty. Nowadays it is covered and not visible.

There are Black Stone and al-Rukn al-Yameni, which are two of the precious stones of Paradise. This corner of the Kaba is called the Rukan Yamani because it is situated on the side of the Kaba which faces the land of Yemen. It is on the wall opposite to that of the Black stone. Hajar al-Aswad is a sacred rock encased with silver that has been placed in the south-eastern corner of Kaba, believed to have descended from heaven. It was originally white in colour but eventually turned black by absorbing the sins of people.

Hadith: Abdullah Ibn Amr (ra) said: "I heard the Messenger of Allah (saws) saying that the Rukn and the Maqam are two of the precious stones of Paradise, whose light has been extinguished by Allah. If He had not extinguished their light, it would illuminate everything between the East and the West." [Tirmizi]

Hadith: Narrated Abis bin Rabia: Umar (ra) came near the Black Stone and kissed it and said "No doubt, I know that you are a stone and can neither benefit anyone nor harm anyone. Had I not seen Allah's Messenger (saws) kissing you I would not have kissed you." [Bukhari]

Near the Mosque are the two hills of al-Safa and al-Marwah. Walking between Safa and Marwah seven times is called Sai. Allah says (interpretation of the meaning):

"Verily! Al-Safa and al-Marwah are of the Symbols of Allah. So it is not a sin on him who performs Hajj or Umrah (pilgrimage) of the House to perform the going (tawaf) between them. And whoever does good voluntarily, then verily, Allah is All-Recognizer, All-Knower." [al-Baqarah Ch 2:158]

Virtue of Makkah

Narrated Abdullah bin Adi bin Hamra [Az-Zuhri]: I saw the Messenger of Allah (saws) standing at Al-Hazwarah, and he (saws) said: "By Allah! You are the best of Allah's earth, and the most beloved of Allah's earth to Allah, and if it were not that I was expelled from you I would not have left." [Tirmizi]

Narrated Ibn Abbas (ra) that the Messenger of Allah (saws) said about Makkah: "How sweet of a land you are and how dear you are to me, and if it were not that my people expelled me from you, I would not have lived in other than you." [Tirmizi]

History of Zamzam and Sa'i

Sa'i (Arabic: السعي) is one of the essential rituals of Hajj and Umrah. It refers to walking back and forth seven times between the two small hills of Safa and Marwa, located adjacent to the Kaba in Masjid al-Haram. Between Safa and Marwa, one will encounter two sets of green fluorescent lights approximately 50 metres apart, which indicate the distance that Hajar (as) ran in order to get to higher ground. Between these two lights, it is sunnah for men to run at a medium pace while women should continue normally. Sa'i starts from Safa and ends at Marwa.

Hadith: Narrated Ibn Abbas (ra): The first lady to use a cummerbund was the mother of Ishmael (as). She used a girdle so that she might hide her tracks from Sarah. Ibrahim (as) brought her and her son Ishmael while she was suckling him, to a place near the Kaba under a tree on the spot of Zamzam, at the highest place in the mosque. During those days there was nobody in Makkah, nor was there any water So he made them sit over there and placed near them a leather bag containing some dates, and a small water-skin containing some water, and set out homeward. Ishmaels mother followed him saying, "O Ibrahim! Where are you going, leaving us in this valley where there is no person whose company we may enjoy, nor is there anything (to enjoy)?" She repeated that to him many times, but he did not look back at her Then she asked him, "Has Allah ordered you to do so?" He said, "Yes." She said, "Then He will not neglect us," and returned while Ibrahim proceeded onwards, and on reaching the Thaniya where they could not see him, he faced the Kaba, and raising both hands, invoked Allah saying the following prayers: O our Lord! I have made some of my offspring dwell in a valley without cultivation, by Your Sacred House (Kaba at Makkah) in order, O our Lord, that they may offer prayer perfectly. So, fill some hearts among men with love towards them, and (O Allah) provide them with fruits, so that they may give thanks. (Ch 14:37) Ishmaels mother went on suckling Ishmael and drinking from the water (she had). When the water in the water-skin had all been used up, she became thirsty and her child also became thirsty. She started looking at him (i.e. Ishmael) tossing in agony; she left him, for she could not endure looking at him, and found that the mountain of Safa was the nearest mountain to her on that land. She stood on it and started looking at the valley keenly so that she might see somebody, but she could not see anybody. Then she descended from Safa and when she reached the valley, she tucked up her robe and ran in the valley like a person in distress and trouble, till she crossed the valley and reached the Marwa mountain where she stood and started looking, expecting to see somebody, but she could not see anybody. She repeated that (running between Safa and Marwa) seven times." The Prophet (saws) said, "This is the source of the tradition of the walking of people between them (i.e. Safa and Marwa)." When she reached the Marwa (for the last time) she heard a voice and she asked herself to be quiet and listened attentively. She heard the voice again and said: "O, (whoever you may be)! You have made me hear your voice; have you got something to help me?" And behold! She saw an angel at the place of Zamzam, digging the earth with his heel (or his wing), till water flowed from that place. She started to make something like a basin around it, using her hand in this way, and started filling her water-skin with water with her hands, and the water was flowing out after she had scooped some of it." The Prophet (saws) added, "May Allah bestow Mercy on Ishmaels mother! Had she let the Zamzam (flow without trying to control it) (or had she not scooped from that water) (to fill her water-skin), Zamzam would have been a stream flowing on the surface of the earth." The Prophet (saws) further added, "Then she drank (water) and suckled her child. The angel said to her: Don't be afraid of being neglected, for this is the House of Allah which will be built by this boy and his father, and Allah never neglects His people. The House (i.e. Kaba) at that time was on a high place resembling a hillock, and when torrents came, they flowed to its right and left. She lived in that way till some people from the tribe of Jurhum or a family from Jurhum passed by her and her child, as they (i.e. the Jurhum people) were coming through the way of Kada. They landed in the lower part of Makkah where they saw a bird that had the habit of flying around water and not leaving it. They said: This bird must be flying around water, though we know that there is no water in this valley. They sent one or two messengers who discovered the source of water, and returned to inform them of the water. So, they all came (towards the water)." The Prophet (saws) added, "Ishmaels mother was sitting near the water. They asked her: Do you allow us to stay with you? She replied: Yes, but you will have no right to possess the water. They agreed to that." The Prophet (saws) further said, "Ishmaels mother was pleased with the whole situation as she used to love to enjoy the company of the people. So, they settled there, and later on they sent for their families who came and settled with them so that some families became permanent residents there. The child (i.e. Ishmael) grew up and learnt Arabic from them and (his virtues) caused them to love and admire him as he grew up, and when he reached the age of puberty they made him marry a woman from amongst them. After Ishmaels mother had died, Ibrahim came after Ishmaels marriage in order to see his family that he had left before, but he did not find Ishmael there. When he asked Ishmaels wife about him, she replied: He has gone in search of our livelihood. Then he asked her about their way of living and their condition, and she replied: We are living in misery; we are living in hardship and destitution, complaining to him. He said: When your husband returns, convey my salutation to him and tell him to change the threshold of the gate (of his house). When Ishmael came, he seemed to have felt something unusual, so he asked his wife: Has anyone visited you? She replied: Yes, an old man of so-and-so description came and asked me about you and I informed him, and he asked about our state of living, and I told him that we were living in a hardship and poverty. On that Ishmael said: Did he advise you anything? She replied: Yes, he told me to convey his salutation to you and to tell you to change the threshold of your gate. Ishmael said: It was my father, and he has ordered me to divorce you. Go back to your family. So, Ishmael divorced her and married another woman from amongst them (i.e. Jurhum). Then Ibrahim stayed away from them for a period as long as Allah wished and called on them again but did not find Ishmael. So, he came to Ishmaels wife and asked her about Ishmael. She said: He has gone in search of our livelihood. Ibrahim asked her: How are you getting on? asking her about their sustenance and living. She replied: We are prosperous and well-off (i.e. we have everything in abundance). Then she thanked Allah. Ibrahim said: What kind of food do you eat? She said: Meat. He said: What do you drink? She said: Water." He said, "O Allah! Bless their meat and water." The Prophet (saws) added, "At that time they did not have grain, and if they had grain, he would have also invoked Allah to bless it." The Prophet (saws) added, "If somebody has only these two things as his sustenance, his health and disposition will be badly affected, unless he lives in Makkah." The Prophet (saws) added, "Then Ibrahim said Ishmaels wife: When your husband comes, give my regards to him and tell him that he should keep firm the threshold of his gate. When Ishmael came back, he asked his wife: Did anyone call on you? She replied: Yes, a good-looking old man came to me, so she praised him and added. He asked about you, and I informed him, and he asked about our livelihood and I told him that we were in a good condition. Ishmael asked her: Did he give you any piece of advice? She said: Yes, he told me to give his regards to you and ordered that you should keep firm the threshold of your gate. On that Ishmael said: It was my father, and you are the threshold (of the gate). He has ordered me to keep you with me. Then Ibrahim stayed away from them for a period as long as Allah wished, and called on them afterwards. He saw Ishmael under a tree near Zamzam, sharpening his arrows. When he saw Ibrahim, he rose up to welcome him (and they greeted each other as a father does with his son or a son does with his father). Ibrahim said, O Ishmael! Allah has given me an order.

Ishmael said: Do what your Lord has ordered you to do. Ibrahim asked: Will you help me? Ishmael said, I will help you. Ibrahim said: Allah has ordered me to build a house here, pointing to a hillock higher than the land surrounding it." The Prophet (saws) added, "Then they raised the foundations of the House (i.e. the Kaba). Ishmael brought the stones and Ibrahim was building, and when the walls became high, Ishmael brought this stone and put it for Ibrahim who stood over it and carried on building, while Ishmael was handing him the stones, and both of them were saying, O our Lord! Accept (this service) from us, Verily, You are the All-Hearing, the All-Knowing." The Prophet (saws) added, "Then both of them went on building and going round the Kaba saying: O our Lord! Accept (this service) from us, Verily, You are the All-Hearing, the All-Knowing." (Ch 2.127) [Bukhari]

Types of tawaf

Tawaf refers to walking in circles around the Kaba in counter-clockwise direction. Seven complete rounds, with each one starting and ending at the black stone (Hajar-al-Aswad) constitute one Tawaf. At Hajar-al-Aswad, pilgrims are supposed to kiss, touch or gesture towards the stone as they pass it as part of a ritual called Istilam. Following are the types of Tawaf:

Tawaful Qudum (Tawaf of arrival): Initial Tawaf when pilgrims enter for the first time in the Masjid ul-Haram. It requires Ihram with Idtiba (Leaving right armpits uncover).

Tawaful-Wadaa (Farewell Tawaf): It is the farewell Tawaf before leaving Makkah. It is done with normal dress.

Tawaful-Nafl: Extra Tawaf that the pilgrims can perform at any time during their visit in Makkah with/without Ihram.

Tawaf al-Ifadah: It is performed by pilgrims after returning from Mina on 10th Zul Hijjah after completing Rami at Jamarat al-Aqabah.

[Note: Rami means throwing stones]

Talbiyah

The Talbiyah is a recitation invoked by the pilgrims as urging that they intend to perform the Hajj or Umrah for the glory of Allah SWT.

Talbiyah is repeatedly invoked upon putting on the Irham, so the pilgrims can purify and rid themselves of worldly concerns.

Starting of Talbiyah

Narrated Umar (ra): I saw that Allah's Messenger (saws) used to ride on his Mount at Zul Hulaifa and used to start saying, "Labbaik" when the Mount stood upright. [Bukhari]

Duration of Talbiya

Narrated Ubaidullah bin Abdullah: Ibn Abbas (ra) said: Usama (ra) rode behind Allah's Messenger (saws) from Arafat to Al-Muzdalifa; and then Al-Fadl (ra) rode behind Allah's Messenger (saws) from Al-Muzdalifa to Mina. Ibn Abbas (ra) added: Both of them said, "The Prophet (saws) kept on reciting Talbiya till he did the Rami of Jamrat-Al-Aqaba." [Bukhari]

Talbiya is to be recited aloud

Narrated Anas (ra): The Prophet (saws) offered four rakat of the Zuhr prayer in Madina and two rakat of the Asr prayer in Zul-Hulaifa and I heard them (the companions of the Prophet saws) reciting Talbiya together loudly to the extent of shouting. [Bukhari]

The Talbiya

Narrated Abdullah bin Umar (ra): The Talbiya of Allah's Messenger (saws) was : *Labbaika Allahumma labbaik, Labbaika la sharika Laka labbaik, Inna-l-hamda wan-nimata Laka walmulk, La sharika Laka* (I respond to Your call O Allah, I respond to Your call, and I am obedient to Your orders, You have no partner, I respond to Your call All the praises and blessings are for You, All the sovereignty is for You, And You have no partners with you.)

بَّيْكَ اللَّهُمَّ لَبَّيْكَ، لَبَّيْكَ لاَ شَرِيكَ لَكَ لَبَّيْكَ، إِنَّ الْحَمْدَ وَالنِّعْمَةَ لَكَ وَالْمُلْكَ، لاَ شَرِيكَ لَكَ

[Bukhari]

Note: Women are not to recite the Talbiyah loud, rather they should say it quietly. [Reported in Musannaf Ibn Abi Shaybah, Bayhaqi]

On entering Makkah

Taking a bath on entering Makkah

Narrated Nafi: On reaching the sanctuary of Makkah, Ibn Umar (ra) used to stop, reciting Talbiya and then he would pass the night at Jhi-Tuwa and then offer the Fajr prayer and take a bath. He used to say that the Prophet (saws) used to do the same. [Bukhari]

Tawaf with wudu

Narrated Muhammad bin Abdur-Rahman bin Nawfal Al-Qurashi: I asked Urwa bin Az-Zubair (regarding the Hajj of the Prophet saws). Urwa replied: Aisha (ra) narrated: "When the Prophet (saws) reached Makkah, the first thing he started with was the ablution, then he performed Tawaf of the Kaba and his intention was not Umra alone (but Hajj and Umra together). ….." [a part from Bukhari]

Makkah is a sanctuary (Haram)

Narrated Ibn Abbas (ra): On the Day of the Conquest of Makkah, Allah's Messenger (saws) said, "Allah has made this town a sanctuary. Its thorny bushes should not be cut, its game should not be chased, and its fallen things should not be picked up except by one who would announce it publicly." [Bukhari]

The Haram (Arabic: حرم) is the sacred boundary of Makkah within which certain acts are considered unlawful which may be lawful elsewhere. If a violation is carried out within the boundary of the Haram, Damm is required as expiation. The boundaries of the Haram are as follows:

1. Tan'im: Masjid Aisha (ra), located about 8 km from the Kaba in the direction of Madinah.
2. Adaat Laban: On the road to Yemen, 11 km away from Makkah.
3. Wadi Nakhla: On the road to Iraq, 11 km away from Makkah.
4. Arafat: On the road to Ta'if, close to Majid Namirah in Arafat, 11 km away from Makkah.
5. Ji'ranah: Masjid al-Ji'ranah, located about 14 km away from Makkah.
6. Hudaibiyah: Masjid al-Hudaibiyah, on the road to Jeddah, about 16 km away from Makkah.

Prayer inside the Kaba

Narrated Salim that his father said: "Allah's Messenger (saws), Usama bin Zaid (ra), Bilal (ra) and Usman bin Abu Talha (ra) entered the Kaba and then closed its door. When they opened the door, I was the first person to enter (the Kaba). I met Bilal (ra) and asked him, "Did Allah's Messenger (saws) offer a prayer inside (the Kaba)?" Bilal (ra) replied in the affirmative and said, "(The Prophet (saws) offered the prayer) in between the two right pillars." [Bukhari]

Narrated Nafi: Whenever Ibn Umar (ra) entered the Kaba he used to walk straight keeping the door at his back on entering, and used to proceed on till about three cubits from the wall in front of him, and then he would offer the prayer there aiming at the place where Allah's Messenger (saws) prayed, as Bilal (ra) had told him. There is no harm for any person to offer the prayer at any place inside the Kaba. [Bukhari]

Ramal during tawaf

Narrated Salim that his father said: I saw Allah's Messenger (saws) arriving at Makkah; he kissed the Black Stone Corner first while doing Tawaf and did Ramal (walking speedily) in the first three rounds of the seven rounds (of Tawaf). [Bukhari]

Narrated Ibn Abbas (ra): When Allah's Messenger (saws) and his companions came to Makkah, the pagans circulated the news that a group of people were coming to them and they had been weakened by the Fever of Yathrib (Madina). So, the Prophet (saws) ordered his companions to do Ramal (i.e walking fast) in the first three rounds of Tawaf of the Kaba and to walk between the two corners (The Black Stone and Yemenite corner). The Prophet (saws) did not order them to do Ramal in all the rounds of Tawaf out of pity for them. [Bukhari]

Narrated Abdullah bin Umar (ra): The Prophet (saws) did Ramal in (first) three rounds (of Tawaf), and walked in the remaining four, in Hajj and Umrah. [Bukhari]

Narrated Zaid bin Aslam from his father who said: Umar bin Al-Khattab (ra) addressed the Corner (Black Stone) saying, By Allah! I know that you are a stone and can neither benefit nor harm. Had I not seen the Prophet (saws) touching (and kissing) you, I would never have touched (and kissed) you. Then he kissed it and said: "There is no reason for us to do Ramal (in Tawaf) except that we wanted to show off before the pagans, and now Allah has destroyed them." Umar (ra) added, "(Nevertheless), the Prophet (saws) did that and we do not want to leave it (i.e. Ramal)." [Bukhari]

Note: Women do not have to walk quickly (Ramal) during tawaf or run (rakd) during sai between Safa and Marwah. [Reported in Musannaf Ibn Abi Shaybah, Bayhaqi]

Pointing by stick towards the black stone

Narrated Ibn Abbas (ra): Allah's Messenger (saws) performed Tawaf (of the Kaba) riding a camel (at that time the Prophet (saws) had a foot injury). Whenever he came to the Corner (having the Black Stone) he would point out towards it with a thing in his hand and say, "Allahu-Akbar." [Bukhari]

Touching all corners of Kaba

Abu Ash-Shatha said, "Who keeps away from some portion of the Kaba?" Muawiya (ra) used to touch the four corners of the Kaba, Ibn Abbas (ra) said to him, "These two corners (the one facing the Hijr) are not to be touched." Muawiya said, "Nothing is untouchable in the Kaba." And Ibn Az-Zubair used to touch all the corners of the Kaba. [Bukhari]

To lead others by hand during Tawaf

Narrated Ibn Abbas (ra): While the Prophet (saws) was performing Tawaf of the Kaba, he passed by a person who had tied his hands to another person with a rope or string or something like that. The Prophet (saws) cut it with his own hands and said, "Lead him by the hand." [Bukhari]

Supplications during Tawaf

Prophet (saws) recited between the Yemen corner and the Black Stone: "*Rabbana atina fid-dunya hasanah wa fil-akhirati hasanah wa qinna adhab an-nar* (Our Lord, give us in this world [that which is] good and in the Hereafter [that which is] good and protect us from the punishment of the Fire)" [Musnad Ahmad]

Tawaf and Sai for Hajj and Umrah

Ata said: The Prophet (saws) said to Aisha (ra): "Your observance of circumambulation of the Kaba and your running between Al Safa and al Marwah (only once) are sufficient for your Hajj and your Umrah." Al Shafii said: The narrator Sufyan has transmitted this tradition from Ata on the authority of Aisha (ra) and also narrated it on the authority of Ata stating that the Prophet (saws) said to Aisha (ra). [Abu Dawud]

Tawaf of woman

Ibn Juraij said: Ata informed us that when Ibn Hisham forbade women to perform Tawaf with men he said to him: How do you forbid them while the wives of the Prophet (saws) used to perform Tawaf with the men? I said: Was this before decreeing of the use of the veil or after it? Ata took an oath and said: I saw it after the order of veil. I said: How did they mix with the men? Ata said: The women never mixed with the men, and Aishah (ra) used to perform Tawaf separately and never mixed with men. Once it happened that Aishah (ra) was performing the Tawaf and woman said to her: O Mother of believers! Let us touch the Black stone. Aishah (ra) said to her: Go yourself, and she herself refused to do so. The wives of the Prophet (saws) used to come out in night, in disguise and used to perform Tawaf with men. But whenever they intended to enter the Kaba, they would stay outside till the men had gone out. I and Ubaid bin Umair used to visit Aishah (ra) while she was residing at Jauf Thabir. I asked: What was her veil? Ata said: She was wearing an old Turkish veil, and that was the only thing (veil) which was screen between us and her. I saw a pink cover on her. [Bukhari]

Prayer behind Maqam Ibrahim

Narrated Abdullah bin Umar (ra): When Allah's Messenger (saws) performed Tawaf of the Kaba for Hajj or Umrah, he used to do Ramal during the first three rounds, and in the last four rounds he used to walk;

then after the Tawaf he used to offer two rakat and then performed Tawaf between Safa and Marwa. [Bukhari]

Narrated Ibn Umar (ra): The Prophet (saws) reached Makkah, circumambulated the Kaba seven times and then offered a two rakat prayer behind Maqam Ibrahim. Then he went towards the Safa. Allah has said, "Verily, in Allah's Apostle you have a good example." [Bukhari]

Regarding salat in the Hijr

Narrated Aisha (ra): I liked to enter the House (the Kaba) and pray therein. The Messenger of Allah (saws) caught me by hand and admitted me to al-Hijr. He (saws) then said: "Pray in al-Hijr when you intend to enter the House (the Kaba), for it is a part of the House (the Kaba). Your people shortened it when they built the Kaba, and they took it out of the House." [Abu Dawud]

One should not go near his wife before Sai

Narrated Amr: We asked Ibn Umar (ra): "May a man have sexual relations with his wife during the Umrah before performing Tawaf between Safa and Marwa?" He said, "Allah's Messenger (saws) arrived (in Makkah) and circum-ambulated the Kaba seven times, then offered two rakat behind Maqam Ibrahim (the station of Ibrahim), then performed Tawaf between Safa and Marwa." Ibn Umar (ra) added, "Verily! In Allah's Apostle you have a good example." And I asked Jabir bin Abdullah (the same question), and he replied, "You should not go near your wives (have sexual relations) till you have finished Tawaf between Safa and Marwa. [Bukhari]

What is said about Zamzam (water)

Narrated Anas bin Malik (ra) that Abu Dhar (ra) said: Allah's Messenger (saws) said, "The roof of my house was made open while I was at Makkah (on the night of Miraj) and Jibril descended. He opened up my chest and washed it with the water of Zamzam. The he brought the golden tray full of Wisdom and Belief and poured it in my chest and then closed it. The he took hold of my hand and ascended to the nearest heaven. Jibril told the gatekeeper of the nearest heaven to open the gate. The gatekeeper asked, "Who is it?" Jibril replied, "I am Jibril." [Bukhari] Narrated Ibn Abbas (ra): I gave Zamzam water to Allah's Messenger (saws) and he drank it while standing. Asim (a sub-narrator) said that Ikrima took the oath that on that day the Prophet (saws) had not been standing but riding a camel. [Bukhari]

The tawaf (sai) between as-Safa and al-Marwa

Narrated Urwa: I asked Aisha (ra): "How do you interpret the statement of Allah: Verily! (the mountains) As-Safa and Al-Marwa are among the symbols of Allah, and whoever performs the Hajj to the Kaba or performs Umra, it is not harmful for him to perform Tawaf between them (Safa and Marwa.) (Ch 2:158). By Allah! (it is evident from this revelation) there is no harm if one does not perform Tawaf between Safa and Marwa." Aisha (ra) said, "O, my nephew! Your interpretation is not true. Had this interpretation of yours been correct, the statement of Allah should have been, It is not harmful for him if he does not perform Tawaf between them. But in fact, this divine inspiration was revealed concerning the Ansar who used to assume Irham for worshipping an idol called "Manat" which they used to worship at a place called Al-Mushallal before they embraced Islam, and whoever assumed Ihram (for the idol), would consider it not right to perform Tawaf between Safa and Marwa. When they embraced Islam, they asked Allah's Messenger (saws) regarding it, saying, "O Allah's Apostle (saws)! We used to refrain from Tawaf between Safa and Marwa." So, Allah revealed: Verily; (the mountains) As-Safa and Al-Marwa are among the symbols of Allah. Aisha (ra) added, "Surely, Allah's Apostle (saws) set the tradition of Tawaf between Safa and Marwa, so nobody is allowed to omit the Tawaf between them." Later on, I (Urwa) told Abu Bakr bin Abdur-Rahman (of Aisha's narration) and he said: I have not heard of such information, but I heard learned men saying that all the people, except those whom Aisha (ra) mentioned and who used to assume Irham for the sake of Manat, used to perform Tawaf between Safa and Marwa. When Allah referred to the Tawaf of the Kaba and did not mention Safa and Marwa in the Quran, the people asked, "O Allah's Messenger (saws)! We used to perform Tawaf between Safa and Marwa and Allah has revealed (the verses concerning) Tawaf of the Kaba and has not mentioned Safa and Marwa. Is there any harm if we perform Tawaf between Safa and Marwa?" So Allah revealed: "Verily As-Safa and Al-Marwa are among the symbols of Allah." Abu Bakr (ra) said, "It seems that this verse was revealed concerning the two groups, those who used to refrain from Tawaf between Safa and Marwa in the Pre- Islamic Period of ignorance and those who used to perform the Tawaf then, and after embracing Islam they refrained from the Tawaf between them as Allah had enjoined Tawaf of the Kaba and did not mention Tawaf (of Safa and Marwa) till later after mentioning the Tawaf of the Kaba." [Bukhari]

Narrated Amr bin Dinar: We asked Ibn Umar (ra) whether a man who, while performing Umra, had performed Tawaf of the Kaba; and had not yet performed Tawaf between Safa and Marwa, could have sexual relation with his wife, Ibn Umar (ra) replied "The Prophet (saws) reached Makkah and performed the seven rounds (of Tawaf) of the Kaba and then offered a two-rakat prayer behind Maqam Ibrahim and then performed the seven rounds (of Tawaf) between Safa and Marwa." He added, "Verily! In Allah's Messenger (saws) you have a good example." We asked Jabir bin Abdullah (the same question) and he said, "He (that man) should not come near (his wife) till he has completed Tawaf between Safa and Marwa." [Bukhari]

A menstruating woman can perform all the ceremonies of Hajj except Tawaf

Narrated Aisha (ra): I was menstruating when I reached Makkah. So, I neither performed Tawaf of the Kaba, nor the Tawaf between Safa and Marwa. Then I informed Allah's Messenger (saws) about it. He replied, "Perform all the ceremonies of Hajj like the other pilgrims, but do not perform Tawaf of the Kaba till you get clean (from your menses). [Bukhari]

The virtue of the Umrah performed during Ramadan

Ataa reported: I heard Ibn Abbas (ra) narrating to us that Allah's Messenger (saws) said to a woman of the Ansar (Ibn Abbas had mentioned her name but I have forgotten it): What has prevented you that you do not perform Hajj along with us? She said: We have only two camels for carrying water. One of the camels has been taken by my husband and my son for performing Hajj and one has been left for us for carrying water, whereupon he (saws) said: "So when the month of Ramadan come, perform Umra, for Umra in this (month) is equal to Hajj (in reward)." [Muslim]

Summary of procedure of Umrah

- Get purified
- Wear Irham clothes from respective Miqat
- Offer two rakah prayer
- Intention and Talbiya (Labbayka Allahumma labbayk(a), labbayka la sharika laka labbayk(a), inna l-hamda wa n-nimata, laka wa l-mulk(a), la sharika lak)
- Proceed towards the Kaba
- Perfrom seven circum-ambulation around the Kaba (Tawaf), each time kissing (or flying kiss) Hajr al-Aswad, saying bismillahi wallahu akbar.
- During Tawaf, there is no specific dua. Supplicate to the Almighty whatever is there in your mind: pray for forgetfulness and repent.
- During each round between Yemen corner and Hajr al-Aswad, recite Rabbana atina fid-dunya hasanatan wafil-akhirati hasanatan waqina azaban-nar.
- Pray two rakah prayer behind Maqam Ibrahim after seven rounds, drink zamzam
- Proceed to Safa, perform Sai (seven rounds between Safa and Marwa)
- Cut hair/shave head
- Put off Irham clothes.

It is prescribed for women is to cut the hair, not to shave the head, and there is no difference of opinion concerning that. It was narrated that Ibn 'Abbas (ra) said: The Messenger of Allah (saws) said: "Women do not have to shave their heads; rather women have to cut their hair." [Sunan Abu Dawood]

Hadith: It was narrated that 'Ali (ra) said: The Messenger of Allah (saws) told women not to shave their heads. [Tirmizi]

Hajj starts on 8ᵗʰ Zul-Hijjah in Mina

First day of Hajj is Mina. Mina is a valley about 8 KM east of Makkah. It is where Hajj pilgrims spend overnight on the 8th, 11th, 12th (and some even on the 13th) of Zul Hijjah. The Mina valley is an open space covered with more than one lakh air-conditioned tents and it can accommodate more than 2.6 million people, extending over 2.5 million square meters. Mina is known as the largest tent city in the world. Pilgrims must stay in Mina during Hajj and perform the Stoning of the Satan at the Jamarat.

The boundaries for Mina are indicated by large green signposts. One must ensure he/she remains in the specified boundary of Mina during the 10ᵗʰ, 11ᵗʰ, 12ᵗʰ and possibly 13ᵗʰ of Jhul Hijjah.

When one reaches Mina, he has to be familiar with the surroundings including roads, bridge if any, or any other milestone. The most important is the tent number. The group number on the wrist belt has no relation with the tent number. A set of tents is given a number, say 94. But 94 is huge area. The pole next to the tent will show exact location of the tent. Say the pole number is 3/94. That means one has to reach area 94 (group of tents) and then 3/94 and you are at the tent. Remember, all tents and tent areas look alike and if pole number and tent number are not noted, one may be in trouble.

The main mosque in Mina is known as Masjid al-Khayf, located near the smallest Jamarat at the base of the mountain in the south of Mina. It is reported that the Prophet (saws), as well as 70 prophets who preceded him, performed Salat here. Yazeed bin Aswad (ra) says that when he performed Hajj with the Prophet (saws), it was at Masjid Al Khayf that he performed Fajr salah with the Prophet (saws). This was also when Prophet (saws) advised the Ansar and Muhajireen to make a settlement near Masjid Al-Khayf and to rest there for a while before continuing Hajj. Abdur-Rahman bin Muaz (ra) reports that after Prophet (saws) delivered a sermon in Mina, he (saws) instructed the Muhajireen to set up camp in front of Masjid Al Khayf, and the Ansar to set up camp behind it. The rest of the Muslims were to camp behind them. [Abu Dawud]

A very important place of Mina is the Jamarat. Three stone pillars at which pilgrims pelt stones is the Jamarat and the throwing of stone is called Rami. Rami is done with the intention to observe the actions of Prophet Ibrahim (as) and fight the evils of their soul, such as greed, pride, and anger. Hajj is incomplete without performing the act of Rami.

There are three Jamarats namely: Jamarat-al-Shughra, Jamarat-al-Wusta, and Jamarat-al-Aqabah. These are the locations when Prophet Ibrahim (as) pelted stone at Satan when Satan tried to persuade against him from sacrificing his son, Prophet Ismail (as) in the way of Allah SWT. Ibrahim (as) was instructed by the Angel Jibril to throw pebbles at Satan. The stoning of Jamarat denotes complete obedience to the commands of Allah.

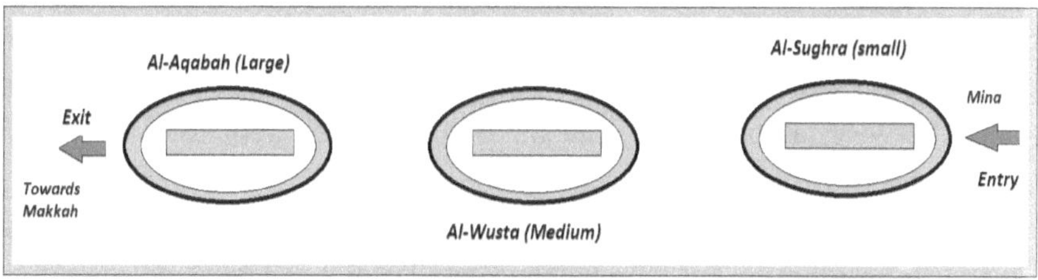

Photo: Nomenclature of Jamarat

Considering the large number of pilgrims each year, todays Jamarats are in the form of walls instead of pillars (walls were constructed in 2004). Jamarat building is multi-storeyed that has bridges. Provisions have been made so that pilgrim from one road can proceed to a particular bridge at a time so as to avoid traffic jam.

Summary of First day of Hajj

- Enter the state of Irham after purification (one is already in Makkah). For Qiran, one is already with Irham.
- Two rakah prayer
- Intention
- Talbiya

- Proceed towards Mina
- Perform Zuhr, Asr, Maghrib, Isha. Do not combine prayers.
- Recite Talbiya continuously; sleep

9th Zul Hijjah (2nd day of Hajj)

The Day of Arafat falls on the second day of Hajj. At dawn on this day, pilgrims proceed from Mina to a nearby hillside and plain called Mount Arafat and the Plain of Arafat, which is located about 20 kilometres from Makkah, the final destination for the pilgrimage. Pilgrims stay here until sunset and spend their time with devotion for Allah's forgiveness, repents with tears, and seek Allah's mercy. Pilgrims are supposed to offer Fajr salat in Mina.

One has to check with the travel agent on the availability of food. The time at which these meals are served can also vary, so be prepared to eat at irregular times. In Arafat, there are no food shops. It is a good idea to take some biscuits, dates, fruits and water when one departs from Mina. Some of the tents in Arafat have some carpet which one can also sleep on. Otherwise, a straw mat with air pillow can be kept for sleeping in Arafat and Muzdalifah.

One must ensure that he/she remains within the specified boundaries of Arafat during the 9th Zul Hijjah. The boundaries for Arafat and direction of Qibla are indicated by large signposts.

Hadith: Yahya related to me from Malik from Nafi that Abdullah ibn Umar (ra) used to pray Zuhr, Asr, Maghrib, Isha and Fajr at Mina. Then in the morning, after the sun had risen, he would go to Arafat. [Muwatta Imam Malik]

Hadith: It was narrated by Abdullah ibn Abbas (ra): The Messenger of Allah (saws) offered the noon prayer on the 8th of Zul-Hijjah (in Mina) and dawn prayer (Fajr) on the 9th of Zul-Hijjah (Yawm al-Arafat) in Mina. [Abu Dawud]

Takbir al-Tashreeq

After the prayer, the Prophet (saws) ordered everyone to remain in their places and proclaimed the majesty of the Allah with the following words:

Allahu Akbar, Allahu Akbar, La ilaha illallah, wallahu Akbar, Allahu

Akbar wa lillahil Hamd. He uttered these words after each prayer until Asr of the last day of Tashreeq. [Al-Bayhaqi, Sunan al-Kubra]

[Note: Starting immediately after Fajr Salat on the 9th of Zul Hijjah, Hajj pilgrims have to audibly recite Takbir al-Tashreeq at least once after every Fard Salah, up to and including Asr Salah on the 13th of Zul Hijjah, a total of 23 Fard Salats.]

When the Prophet (saws) arrived at Namirah, an area just before Arafat located in Wadi Uranah, he (saws) stayed in a tent which had been erected for him. His wives remained in tents around him. When the sun came down from its meridian, he (saws) sent for his she-camel, al-Qaswa, and he (saws) rode into the interior of Uranah valley, a spacious expanse where his companions were able to gather around him. He (saws) arrived at the bottom of the valley and, seated on his camel, addressed thousands of companions with a powerful speech, now known as Khutbatul Wida.

Last Khutbah of the Prophet saws (Khutbatul Wida)

Prophet Muhammad (saws) delivered his last sermon (Khutbah) on the 9th of Zul Hijjat, 10 years after Hijrat (migration from Makkah to Madinah) in the Uranah Valley of mount Arafat. This historical event also marked the Prophet's (saws) farewell pilgrimage to Makkah – it was the first and last Hajj performed by the Prophet (saws). The Prophet's (saws) words were clear and concise, touching upon the basic religious and ethical ideals of Islam with some of the most important rights Allah Almighty has over humanity, and humanity has over each other.

It was during this period that this verse was revealed:

"...Today I have perfected for you your religion, and completed My blessing upon you, and approved for you Islam as religion" (Surah Al-Maidah, Ch 5:3; interpretation of meaning)

After praising, and thanking Allah he (saws) said:

"**O People,** lend me an attentive ear, for I know not whether after this year, I shall ever be amongst you again. Therefore, listen to what I am saying to you very carefully and take these words to those who could not be present here today.

O people, just as you regard this month, this day, this city as Sacred, so regard the life and property of every Muslim as a sacred trust. Return the goods entrusted to you to their rightful owners. Hurt no one so that no one may hurt you. Remember that you will indeed meet your Lord, and that He will indeed reckon your deeds. Allah has forbidden you to take usury (interest), therefore all interest obligation shall henceforth be waived. Your capital, however, is yours to keep. You will neither inflict nor suffer any inequity. Allah has Judged that there shall be no interest and that all the interest due to Abbas ibn Abd Al-Muttalib (ra) shall henceforth be waived…

Beware of Satan, for the safety of your religion. He has lost all hope that he will ever be able to lead you astray in big things, so beware of following him in small things.

O people, it is true that you have certain rights with regard to your women, but they also have rights over you. Remember that you have taken them as your wives only under Allah's trust and with His permission. If they abide by your right then to them belongs the right to be fed and clothed in kindness. Do treat your women well and be kind to them for they are your partners and committed helpers. And it is your right that they do not make friends with any one of whom you do not approve, as well as never to be unchaste.

O people, listen to me in earnest, worship Allah, say your five daily prayers (Salah), fast during the month of Ramadan, and give your wealth in Zakat. Perform Hajj if you can afford to.

All mankind is from Adam and Eve, an Arab has no superiority over a non-Arab nor a non-Arab has any superiority over an Arab; also a white has no superiority over black nor a black has any superiority over white except by piety (taqwa) and good action. Learn that every Muslim is a brother to every Muslim and that the Muslims constitute one brotherhood. Nothing shall be legitimate to a Muslim which belongs to a fellow Muslim unless it was given freely and willingly. Do not, therefore, do injustice to yourselves.

Remember, one day you will appear before Allah and answer your deeds. So beware, do not stray from the path of righteousness after I am gone.

O people, no prophet or apostle will come after me and no new faith will be born.

Reason well, therefore, O people, and understand words which I convey to you. I leave behind me two things, the Quran and my example, the Sunnah and if you follow these you will never go astray.

All those who listen to me shall pass on my words to others and those to others again; and may the last ones understand my words better than those who listen to me directly. Be my witness, O Allah, that I have conveyed your message to your people". [Bukhari, Hadiths 1623, 1626, 6361; Muslim Hadith 98; Tirmizi Hadiths 1628, 2046, 2085; Musnad Imam Ahmed Hadith 19774.]

Hadith: Ibn Umar (ra) said the Apostle of Allah (saws) proceeded from Mina when he offered the dawn prayer on Yaum Al Arafat (9th of Zul Hijjah) in the morning till he (saws) came to Arafat and he (saws) descended at Namirah. This is the place where the imam (prayer leader at Arafah) takes his place. When the time of the noon prayer (Zuhr) came, the Apostle of Allah (saws) proceeded earlier and combined the noon (Zuhr) and afternoon (Asr) prayers. He (saws) then addressed the people (i.e., recited the Khutba) and proceeded. He stationed at a place of wuquf in Arafat. [Abu Dawud]

To proceed at noon on the Day of Arafat

Narrated Abdullah ibn Umar (ra): When al-Hajjaj killed Ibn Zubayr, he sent a message to Ibn Umar (ra) asking him: At which moment the Messenger of Allah (saws) used to proceed (to Arafat) this day? He replied: When it happens so, we shall proceed. When Ibn Umar (ra) intended to proceed, the people said: The sun did not decline. He (Ibn Umar ra) asked: Did it decline? They replied: It did not decline. When they said that the sun had declined, he proceeded. [Abu Dawud]

Talbiya and Takbir while proceeding from Mina to Arafat

Narrated Muhammad bin Abu Bakr Al-Thaqafi: I asked Anas bin Malik (ra) while we were proceeding from Mina to Arafat, "What do you use to do on this day when you were with Allah's Messenger (saws)?" Anas (ra) said, "Some of us used to recite Talbiya and nobody objected to that, and others used to recite Takbir and nobody objected to that." [Bukhari]

Virtue of day of Arafat

Narrated Abdur-Rahman bin Yamar (ra) that the Messenger of Allah (saws) said: "The Hajj is Arafat, the Hajj is Arafat, the Hajj is Arafat. The days of Mina are three: But whoever hastens to leave in two days, there is no sin on him, and whoever stays on, there is no sin on him (Ch

2:203). And whoever sees (attends) the Arafat before the rising of Fajr, then he has performed the Hajj." [Sunan Ibn Majah]

Aishah (ra) said that the Messenger of Allah (saws) said: There is no day on which Allah ransoms more slaves from the Fire than the Day of Arafat. He draws closer and closer, then He boasts about them before the angels and says: "What do these people want?" [Muslim, Sunan Ibn Majah]

Mount Arafat is where the beloved Prophet Muhammad (saws) delivered the last sermon to the Muslims who accompanied him for Hajj towards the end of his life.

The Prophet (saws) said: "The best invocation on the day of Arafat, and the best of all the invocations I ever offered or other holy Prophets before me ever offered is: *"Laa ilaaha ill-Allahu, waḥdahu laa shareeka lah, lahul-mulku wa lahul-ḥamdu, wa huwa 'alaa kulli shayin qadee*r (There is no god but Allah: He is Unique; He hath no partner, the whole universe is for Him and for Him is the praise, and He hath power over all things)." [Tirmizi]

The Prophet (saws) said, "Apart from the day of the Battle of Badr, there is no day on which the Shaitan is seen to be more humiliated, more rejected, more depressed and angrier, than on the day of Arafat, and indeed all this is only because of beholding the abundance of descending mercy (on the day) and Allah's forgiveness of the great sins of the servants." [Mishkat]

Abu Qatadah narrated, who said that a man asked Prophet (saws), "O Messenger of Allah (saws), what do you think of fasting on the day of Arafat?" To which the beloved Prophet Muhammad (saws) replied: "It expiates for the sins of the previous year and of the coming year." [Muslim]

Note: Fasting on the day of Arafat is considered mustahab (desirable) for those who are not participating in Hajj. For pilgrims, it isn't a Sunnah because Prophet Muhammad (saws) didnt fast on this day during the Farewell Pilgrimage. The people of knowledge consider it recommended to fast on the Day of Arafat, except for those at Arafat. [Tirmizi]

On 9th Zul Hijja, Allah SWT perfected the religion of Islam. Mount Arafat was the place where the following verses were revealed: *"Today I have perfected for you your religion and completed upon you My blessing, and I have chosen for you Islam as (your) religion."* (Ch 5:3)

Umar (ra) later clarified this by stating, "We surely know that day and the place where it was revealed upon the Prophet (saws). He was standing at Arafat on a Friday." [Bukhari]

To offer the two Salat together at Arafat (Zuhr and Asr)

Ibn Shihab said: Salim said, "In the year when Al-Hajjaj bin Yusuf attacked Ibn Az-Zubair, the former asked Abdullah (Ibn Umar (ra)) what to do during the stay on the Day of Arafat (9th of Zul-Hijjah). I said to him, "If you want to follow the Sunnah, you should offer the Salat just after midday on the Day of the Arafat. Abdullah bin Umar (ra) said, He (Salim) has spoken the truth. They (the Companions of the Prophet (saws)) used to offer the Zuhr and Asr prayer together according to the Sunnah, I asked Salim, "Did Allah's Messenger (saws) do that?" Salim said, "And in doing that do you (people) follow anything else except his (saws) Sunnah?" [Bukhari]

Malik said, "What we are all agreed upon here (in Madina) is that the imam does not recite the Quran out loud in Zuhr on the day of Arafat, and that he gives a khutba to the people on that day, and that the prayer on the day of Arafat is really a Zuhr prayer, and even if it coincides with a Jumua it is still a Zuhr prayer, but one which has been shortened because of travelling." [Muwatta Imam Malik]

Malik said that the imam of the pilgrims should not pray the Jumua prayer if the day of Arafat, the day of sacrifice or one of the three days after the day of sacrifice, was a Friday. [Muwatta Imam Malik]

The staying at Arafat (wuquf)

Narrated Muhammad bin Jubair bin Mutim: My father said, "(Before Islam) I was looking for my camel." The same narration is told by a different sub-narrator. Jubair bin Mutim said, "My camel was lost and I went out in search of it on the day of Arafat, and I saw the Prophet (saws) standing in Arafat. I said to myself: By Allah he is from the Hums (literally: strictly religious, Quraish were called so, as they used to say, We are the people of Allah we shall not go out of the sanctuary). What has brought him here?" [Bukhari]

Jabir Ibn Abdullah (ra) narrates: He (saws) mounted al-Qaswa (camel of the Prophet (saws)) and came to the place of standing, making his she-camel turn its back to the rocks and, before facing the Qibla. He remained standing until sunset when the yellow light had somewhat gone and the disc of the sun had disappeared. [Abu Dawud]

Jabir (ra) said then the Prophet (saws) said "I sacrificed here and the whole of Mina is the place of sacrifice". He (saws) stationed at Arafat and said "I stationed here and the whole of Arafat is the place of station (place for wuquf)". He (saws) stationed at Muzadalifah and said "I stationed here and the whole of Muzadalifah is the place of station." [Abu Dawud]

Narrated that Yazid ibn Shayban: We were standing in Arafah in a place far from the mawqif [where the Prophet (saws) stood]. Ibn Mirba al-Ansari came to us and said: I am from the messenger of the Messenger of Allah (saws), who says to you: "Stay where you are (for it is also the place of standing), for you are standing in the area where your father Ibrahim stood." [Abu Dawud and Tirmizi]

The Prophet (saws) informed them that wuquf on the 9th Zul Hijjah can be carried out anywhere within the confines of Arafat. He (saws) said: "I have stood here and all of Arafat is a place of standing." [Muslim]

Khutbah at Arafat

Yahya related to me from Malik from Nafi and Abdullah ibn Dinar from Abdullah ibn Umar that Umar ibn al-Khattab (ra) gave a Khutba to the people at Arafat and taught them the conduct of the Hajj, and one of the things he said to them in his speech was, "When you get to Mina and have stoned the Jamarat then whatever is haram for someone doing the Hajj becomes halal, except women and scent. No-one should touch women or scent until he has done tawaf of the House." [Muwatta Imam Malik]

Dua of the Prophet (saws)

The Prophet (saws), during the latter part of the day of Arafat, supplicated abundantly for the forgiveness of the Ummah. Allah informed the Prophet (saws): "I have accepted your supplication but I will not forgive the oppressors." The Prophet (saws) pleaded, "O my Lord, You have the ability to give the oppressed greater reward for their suffering at the hands of the oppressor, so forgive the oppressor." However, that part of the supplication was not accepted that evening but was accepted after the Prophet (saws) repeated the supplication at Muzdalifah. [Sunan Ibn Majah]

Raising the hands in supplication at Arfat

It was narrated that Usamah bin Zaid (ra) said: "I was a companion rider with the Prophet (saws) at Arafat. He (saws) raised his hands in supplication, so his she-camel began leaning and he dropped her halter, so he (saws) took the halter with one of his hands while he (saws) was raising the other hand." [Sunan Ibn Majah]

One who misses the day of Arafat

Sufyan bin Bukair bin Ata said: I heard Abdur-Rahman bin Yamur Dyili say: I saw the Messenger of Allah (saws) when he was standing at Arafat, and some people from Najd came to him and said: "O Messenger of Allah (saws), what is Hajj?" He said: "Hajj is Arafat. Whoever comes before Fajr prayer on the night of Jam (Muzdalifa), he has completed his Hajj. The days at Mina are three. But whosoever hastens to leave in two days, there is no sin on him and whosoever stays on, there is no sin on him." [Ch 2:203] Then he seated a man behind him on his mount and he started calling out these words. [Sunan Ibn Majah]

It was narrated from Urwah bin Mudarris At-Tai (ra) that he performed Hajj during the time of the Messenger of Allah (saws), and he did not catch up with the people until they were at Jam (Muzdalifah). He said: I came to the Prophet (saws) and said: "O Messenger of Allah (saws), I have made my camel lean (because of the long journey) and I have worn myself out. By Allah, there is no sand hill on which I did not stand. Have I performed Hajj?" The Prophet (saws) said: "Whoever attended the prayer (i.e., Fajr at Muzdalifah) with us and departed from Arafat, by night or day, may remove the dirt and has completed his Hajj." [Sunan Ibn Majah]

Narrated Abdur Rahman Yamar ad-Dayli (ra): I came to the Holy Prophet (saws) when he was in Arafat. Some people or a group of people came from Najd. They commanded someone (to ask the Prophet saws about Hajj). So, he called the Messenger of Allah (saws), saying: How is the Hajj done? He (saws) ordered a man (to reply). He shouted loudly: "The Hajj, the Hajj is on the day of Arafah. If anyone comes over there before the dawn prayer on the night of Muzdalifah, his Hajj will be complete. The period of halting at Mina is three days. Then whoever hastens (his departure) by two days, it is no sin for him, and whoever delays it there is no sin for him." The narrator said: He (saws) then put a man behind him on the camel. He began to proclaim this loudly.

Abu Dawud said: This tradition has been narrated by Mahran from Sufyan in a similar way. This version adds: The Hajj, the Hajj, twice. The version narrated by Yaya b. Said al-Qattan has the words: The Hajj only once. [Abu Dawud]

Summary of the day of Arafat

- Perform Fajr prayer in Mina
- Say Takbir Tashreeq: Allahu Akbar, Allahu Akbar, La Ilaha Ilallahu Wallahu Akbar, Allahu Akbar, Wa Lillahil Hamd
- Proceed to Masjid Namira if possible; listen to the Khutba; pray Zuhr and Asr
- Perform wuquf at Arafat till sunset; spend whole day with repentance with tears and supplication; the best supplication is to recite *Laa ilaaha ill-Allahu, waḥdahu laa shareeka lah, lahul-mulku wa lahul-ḥamdu, wa huwa 'alaa kulli shayin qadee*r
- Do not perform Maghrib prayer at Arafat
- Depart for Muzdalifa after sunset

Muzdalifah

People should be calm and patient on proceeding (from Arafat)

It was narrated from Usamah bin Zaid (ra) that he was asked: "How did the Messenger of Allah (saws) travel when he departed from Arafat?" He said: "He (saws) moved at a quick pace, and when he reached an open space he would make his camel run." [Sunan Ibn Majah]

Narrated Ibn Abbas (ra): I proceeded along with the Prophet (saws) on the day of Arafat (9th Zul-Hijja). The Prophet (saws) heard a great hue and cry and the beating of camels behind him. So he (saws) beckoned to the people with his lash, "O people! Be quiet. Hastening is not a sign of righteousness." [Bukhari]

Narrated Usama bin Zaid (ra): I rode behind Allah's Messenger (saws) from Arafat and when Allah's Messenger (saws) reached the mountain pass on the left side which is before Al-Muzdalifa he made his camel kneel and then urinated, and then I poured water for his ablution. He performed light ablution and then I said to him: (Is it the time for) the prayer, O Allah's Messenger (saws)!" He (saws) replied, "The (place of) prayer is ahead of you (i.e. at Al- Muzdalifa)." So Allah's Messenger (saws) rode till he reached Al-Muzdalifa and then he (saws) offered the prayer (there). Then in the morning (10th Zul-Hijja), Al-Faql (bin Abbas) rode behind Allah's Messenger (saws). Kuraib, (a sub-narrator) said that Abdullah bin Abbas (ra) narrated from Al-Fadl, "Allah's Messenger (saws) kept on reciting Talbiya (during the journey) till he reached the Jamrat." (Jamrat-Al-Aqaba) [Bukhari]

The offering of two Salat together at Al-Muzdalifa

Narrated Usama bin Zaid (ra): Allah's Messenger (saws) proceeded from Arafat and dismounted at the mountainous pass and then urinated and performed a light ablution. I said to him, "(Shall we offer) the prayer?" He (saws) replied, "The prayer is ahead of you (i.e. at Al-Muzdalifa)." When he (saws) came to Muzdalifa, he (saws) performed a perfect ablution. Then Iqamat for the prayer was pronounced and he offered the Maghrib prayer and then every person made his camel kneel at his place; and then Iqamat for the prayer was pronounced and he offered the (Isha) prayer and he did not offer any prayer in between them (i.e. Maghrib and Isha prayers). [Bukhari]

Narrated Ibn Umar (ra): The Prophet (saws) offered the Maghrib and Isha prayers together at Jam (i.e. Muzdalifa) with a separate Iqamat for each of them and did not offer any optional prayer in between them or after each of them. [Bukhari]

Ibn Masud (ra) said: "I never saw the Apostle of Allah (saws) observe a prayer out of its proper time except (two prayers) at Al-Muzdalifah. He combined the sunset and night prayers at Al- Muzdalifah and he offered the dawn prayer that day before its proper time. [Abu Dawud]

Summary of the night of Muzdalifah

- Leave Arafat after sunset
- Pray Maghrib and Isha with one Azan and two Iqamats
- Stay whole night in Muzdalifa
- Pray Fajr salat early
- Leave Muzdalifa before sunrise

- On the way, cross the valley of Muhassir fast
- Continue Talbiya
- Reach Mina

3RD Day of Hajj (10th Zul Hijjah)

To depart from Muzdalifa before sunrise

Narrated Amr bin Maimun: I saw Umar (ra) offering the Fajr (morning) prayer at Jam; then he got up and said, "The pagans did not use to depart (from Jam) till the sun had risen, and they used to say: Let the sun shine on Sabir (a mountain). But the Prophet (saws) contradicted them and departed from Jam before sunrise." [Bukhari, Sunan Ibn Majah]

Jabir (ra) said: The Messenger of Allah (saws) departed during the Farewell Pilgrimage in a peaceful manner, and he urged them to be peaceful. He told them to throw small pebbles. He hastened through Muhassir Valley, and said: "Let my nation learn its rites (of Hajj), for I do not know, perhaps I will not meet them again after this year." [Sunan Ibn Majah]

[Note: Wadi Muhassar is an area about six hundred meters wide and two kilometres in length. It is proclaimed to be the location where Abraha's grand army of his men and elephants was destroyed as they proceeded towards Makkah with the aim to destroy the Kaba and is mentioned in Surah Fil (*Alam tara kaifa*). It is a Sunnah for pilgrims to walk fast this area of punishment. This valley is between Muzdalifah and Mina]

Throwing on stones after sunrise

The Prophet (saws) stoned the jamaraat with seven pebbles (each). The stone should be thrown one by one separately and not all seven at a time. Minimum number of stones to be collected for all days is seventy.

It was narrated that Ibn Abbas (ra) said: We youngsters from the clan of Abdul-Muttalib came to the Messenger of Allah (saws), from Muzdalifah, on donkeys of ours. He (saws) started striking our thighs and saying: "O my sons, do not stone the Pillar until the sun rises." [Sunan Ibn Majah]

Weak, children and women may perform Jamarat Aqaba before sunrise

It was narrated from Aishah (ra) that Sawdah bint Zamah (ra) was a slow- moving woman, so she asked the Messenger of Allah (saws) for permission to depart from Muzdalifah ahead of the people, and he (saws) gave her permission. [Sunan Ibn Majah]

Narrated Salim: Abdullah bin Umar (ra) used to send the weak among his family early to Mina. So they used to depart from Al-Mashar Al-Haram (that is Al-Muzdalifa) at night (when the moon had set) and invoke Allah as much as they could, and then they would return (to Mina) before the Imam had started from Al- Muzdalifa to Mina. So some of them would reach Mina at the time of the Fajr prayer and some of them would come later. When they reached Mina, they would throw pebbles on the Jamrat (Jamrat-Al- Aqaba). Ibn Umar (ra) used to say, "Allah's Messenger (saws) gave the permission to them (weak people) to do so." [Bukhari]

Narrated Abdullah: (the slave of Asma (ra)) During the night of Jam, Asma (ra) got down at Al-Muzdalifa and stood up for (offering) the prayer and offered the prayer for some time and then asked, "O my son! Has the moon set?" I replied in the negative and she again prayed for another period and then asked, "Has the moon set?" I replied, "Yes." So she said that we should set out (for Mina), and we departed and went on till she threw pebbles at the Jamrat (Jamrat-Al-Aqaba) and then she returned to her dwelling place and offered the morning prayer. I asked her, "O you! I think we have come (to Mina) early in the night." She replied, "O my son! Allah's Messenger (saws) gave permission to the women to do so." [Bukhari]

Size of pebbles

It was narrated that Ibn Abbas (ra) said: On the morning of Aqabah, when he (saws) was atop his she-camel, the Messenger of Allah (saws) said: "Pick up some pebbles for me." So I picked up seven pebbles for him, suitable for Khazf. He (saws) began to toss them in his hand, saying: "Throw something like these." Then he (saws) said: "O people, beware of exaggeration in religious matters for those who came before you were doomed because of exaggeration in religious matters." [Sunan Ibn Majah]

Pelting stones on Aqaba

It was narrated that Abdur-Rahman bin Yazid said: "When Abdullah bin Masud (ra) stoned Aqabah Pillar, he went to the bottom of the valley and turned to face the Kaba, with the Pillar on his right-hand side. Then he threw seven pebbles, saying the Takbir with each one. Then he said: From here, by the One besides Whom there is none worthy of worship, did the one throw, to whom Surat Al-Baqarah was revealed." [Bukhari]

To say 'Allahu Akbar' on throwing every pebble

Narrated Al-Amash: I heard Al-Hajjaj saying on the pulpit, "The Surah in which Al-Baqara (the cow) is mentioned and the Surah in which the family of Imran is mentioned and the Surah in which the women (An-Nisa) is mentioned." I mentioned this to Ibrahim, and he said, Abdur-Rahman bin Yazid told me: I was with Ibn Masud (ra), when he did the Rami of the Jamrat-ul-Aqaba. He went down the middle of the valley, and when he came near the tree (which was near the Jamrat) he stood opposite to it and threw seven small pebbles and said Allahu-Akbar on throwing every pebble. Then he said: "By Him, except Whom none has the right to be worshipped, here (at this place) stood the one on whom Surat-al-Baqarah was revealed (i.e. Allah's Messenger saws)." [Bukhari]

When a person has stoned Jamrat al-Aqabah he should not stay there

It was narrated that Ibn Umar (ra) stoned Aqabah Pillar, but he did not stay there, and he mentioned that the Prophet (saws) had done likewise. [Sunan Ibn Majah]

When the pilgrim should stop reciting the Talbiyah

Narrated Ubaidullah bin Abdullah: Ibn Abbas (ra) said, "Usama bin Zaid (ra) rode behind the Prophet (saws) from Arafat to Al-Muzdalifa; and then from Al-Muzdalifa to Mina, Al-Fadl rode behind him." He added, "Both of them (Usama and Al-Fadl) said: The Prophet (saws) was constantly reciting Talbiya till he (saws) did Rami of the Jamarat-Al-Aqaba." [Bukhari]

What becomes permissible for a man when he stoned Aqabah pillar

It was narrated that Ibn Abbas (ra) said: "When you have stoned the Pillar, everything becomes permissible to you except your wives." A man said to him: "O Ibn Abbas, and perfume?" He said: "I saw the Messenger of Allah (saws) perfume his head with musk. Is that perfume or not?" [Sunan Ibn Majah]

Narrated Abdur-Rahman bin Al-Qasim: I heard my father who was the best man of his age, saying: I heard Aisha (ra) saying, "I perfumed Allah's Apostle (saws) with my own hands before finishing his Ihram while yet he has not performed Tawaf-al- Ifada." She spread her hands (while saying so.) [Bukhari]

Stoning the pillars on the days of Tashreeq

It was narrated that Jabir (ra) said: "I saw the Messenger of Allah (saws) stoning Aqabah Pillar at forenoon (i.e. on 10th Zul Hijjah), but after that day, he would do it after the sun had passed its zenith." [Sunan Ibn Majah]

The Khutbah on the day of sacrifice at Mina (3rd day)

Narrated Rafi ibn Amr al-Muzani (ra): I saw the Messenger of Allah (saws) addressing the people at Mina (on the day of sacrifice) when the sun rose high (i.e. in the forenoon) on a white mule, and Ali (ra) was interpreting on his behalf; some people were standing and some sitting. [Abu Dawud]

Narrated Abu Bakra (ra): The Prophet (saws) delivered to us a sermon on the Day of Nahr. He (saws) said, "Do you know what is the day today?" We said, "Allah and His Apostle (saws) know better." He (saws) remained silent till we thought that he might give that day another name. He (saws) said, "Isnt it the Day of Nahr?" We said, "It is." He (saws) further asked, "Which month is this?" We said, "Allah and His Apostle (saws) know better." He (saws) remained silent till we thought that he might give it another name. He (saws) then said, "Isnt it the month of Zul-Hijja?" We replied: "Yes! It is." He (saws) further asked, "What town is this?" We replied, "Allah and His Apostle (saws) know it better." He (saws) remained silent till we thought that he might give it another name. He (saws) then said, "Isnt it the forbidden (Sacred) town (of

Makkah)?" We said, "Yes. It is." He (saws) said, "No doubt, your blood and your properties are sacred to one another like the sanctity of this day of yours, in this month of yours, in this town of yours, till the day you meet your Lord. No doubt! Havent I conveyed Allah's message to you? They said, "Yes." He (saws) said, "O Allah! Be witness. So it is incumbent upon those who are present to convey it (this information) to those who are absent because the informed one might comprehend it (what I have said) better than the present audience, who will convey it to him. Beware! Do not renegade (as) disbelievers after me by striking the necks (cutting the throats) of one another." [Bukhari]

It was narrated from Sulaiman bin Amr bin Ahwas that his father said: I heard the Prophet (saws) say, during the Farewell Pilgrimage: "O people! Which day is the most sacred? three times. They said: The day of the greatest Hajj. He (saws) said: Your blood and your wealth and your honour are sacred to one another, as sacred as this day of yours, in this land of yours. No sinner commits a sin but it is against himself. No father is to be punished for the sins of his child, and no child is to be punished for the sins of his father. Satan has despaired of ever being worshipping in this land of yours, but he will be obeyed in some matters which you regard as insignificant, and he will be content with that. All the blood feuds of the Ignorance days are abolished, and the first of them that I abolish is the blood feud of Harith bin Abdul-Muttalib, who was nursed among Banu Laith and killed by Hudhail. All the usuries (interests) of the Ignorance days are abolished, but you will have your capital. Do not wrong others and you will not be wronged. O my nation, have I conveyed (the message)? (He (saws) asked this) three times. They said: Yes. He (saws) said: O Allah, bear witness! three times." [Sunan Ibn Majah]

Visiting the House (Kaba)

Narrated Aisha (ra): We performed Hajj with the Prophet (saws) and performed Tawaf-al-ifada on the Day of Nahr (slaughtering). Safiya (ra) got her menses and the Prophets (saws) desired from her what a husband desires from his wife. I said to him, "O Allah's Messenger (saws)! She is having her menses." He (saws) said, "Is she going to detain us?" We informed him that she had performed Tawaf-al-Ifada on the Day of Nahr. He (saws) said, "(Then you can) depart." [Bukhari]

Narrated Aisha (ra): The Companions of the Messenger of Allah (saws) who accompanied him did not go around the Kaba till they threw pebbles at the Jamrah (pillar at Mina). [Abu Dawud]

It was narrated from Abdullah bin Abbas (ra) that the Prophet (saws) did not walk quickly (Ramal) during the seven circuits of Tawaful-Ifadah (done on 10th day of Zul-Hijjah). [Sunan Ibn Majah]

It was narrated that Hanzalah said: "I saw tawus (Tawus here means a handsome boy) pass by the Corner. If he saw it crowded, he would pass by and he would not push his way in. And if he way it was free, he would kiss it three times, then he said: "I saw Ibn Abbas (ra) doing that." Ibn Abbas (ra) said: "I saw Umar bin Al-Khattab (ra) doing that, then he said: You are just a stone that can neither cause harm or bring benefit; were it not that I saw the Messenger of Allah (saws) kissing you I would not have kissed you." Then Umar (ra) said: "I saw the Messenger of Allah (saws) doing that." [Sunan Ibn Majah]

Tawaf is permissible at all times

It was narrated from Jubair bin Mutim (ra) that the Prophet (saws) said: "O Banu Abd Manaf, do not prevent anyone from circum-ambulating this House of praying at any time of the night or day he wishes." [Sunan Ibn Majah]

What to recite in the two rakahs of tawaf

It was narrated from Jabir bin Abdullah (ra) that when the Messenger of Allah (saws) came to Maqam Ibrahim he recited: "And take you the Maqam (place) of Ihrahim as a place of prayer." Then he (saws) prayed two Rakahs reciting the Opening of the Book (Al-Fatihah) said: "Kul ya aiyuhal kafirun" and "Kulhu allahu ahad." Then he went back to the Corner and touched it, then he went out to As-Safa. [Sunan Ibn Majah]

Prayer inside the Hijr

It was narrated that Aishah (ra) said: "I wanted to enter the House and pray therein, so the Messenger of Allah (saws) took me by the hand and took me into the Hijr and said: "If you want to enter the House, then pray here, for it is part of the House, but your people made it too small when they built it." [Sunan Ibn Majah]

Drinking from Zamzam

It was narrated that Muhammad bin Abdur-Rahman bin Abu Bakr said: I was sitting with Ibn Abbas (ra), and a man came to him and he said: "Where have you come from?" He said: "From Zamzam." He said: "Did you drink from it as you should?" He said: "How is that?" He said: "When you drink from it, turn to face the Qiblah and mention the name of Allah, drink three draughts and drink your fill of it. When you have finished, then praise Allah." The Messenger of Allah (saws) said: "The sign (that differentiates) between us and the hypocrites is that they do not drink their fill from Zamzam." [Sunan Ibn Majah]

It was narrated that Jabir bin Abdullah (ra) said: I heard the Messenger of Allah (saws) say: "The water of Zamzam is for whatever it is drunk for." [Sunan Ibn Majah]

It was narrated from Ibn Abbas (ra) that the Messenger of Allah (saws) drank from the water of Zamzam while standing. [Sunan Ibn Majah]

Hajj is not complete without Sai between Safa and marwah

It was narrated that Amr bin Umar (ra) said: The Messenger of Allah (saws) came and circum-ambulated the House seven times, then he prayed two Rakahs behind the Maqam and performed Sai between As-Safa and Al-Marwah, and he said: "Indeed in the Messenger of Allah (saws) you have a good example to follow." [Sunan Ibn Majah]

Hisham b. Urwa narrated on the authority of his father who reported: I said to Aisha (ra): I do not see any harm to me if I do not circum-ambulate between al-Safa and al-Marwa. She said: On what ground do you say so? (I said:) Since Allah, the Exalted and Majestic, says: "Verily al-Safa and al-Marwa are among the Signs of Allah." It (your assertion) were (correct), it would have been said like this: "There is no harm for him, that he should not circum-ambulate between them." It (this verse) has been revealed about the people of Ansar. Whenever they pronounced the Talbiya, they pronounced it in the name of al-Manat during the Days of Ignorance; so they (thought) that it was not permissible for them (for the Muslims) to circum-ambulate between and al-Marwa. When they (the Muslims) came with Allah's Apostle (saws) for Hajj, they mentioned it to him. So Allah, the Exalted and Majestic, revealed this verse. By my life, Allah will not complete the Hajj of one who has not circum-ambulated between al-Safa and al-Marwa. [Muslim]

Where to stand on Safa

It was narrated from Jabir (ra) that when the Messenger of Allah (saws) stood on top of As-Safa, he (saws) recited the Takbir three times and said: "La ilaha illallahu, Wahdahu la sharika lah, lahul-mulku wa lahul-hamdu, yuhyi wa yumitu, wa huwaala kulli shayin qadir (There is none worthy of worship except Allah alone with no partner or associate, His is the dominion and to Him be praise, He gives life and death, and He has power over all things)." He did three times, and supplicated, and did the same a top Al-Marwah. [Sunan Ibn Majah]

Jabir (ra) said: Messenger of Allah (saws) went out to As-Safa and said, "We will start with that with which Allah started. Then he recited: Verifly, as-Safa and Al-Marwah (two Mountains in Makkah) are of the symbols of Allah." [Sunan Ibn Majah]

It was narrated from Jabir bin Abdullah (ra) that when the Messenger of Allah (saws) came down from As-Safa, he would walk until he reached the bottom of the valley, then he would hasten until he came out of it. [Sunan Ibn Majah]

The place where one should stand on al-Marwah

It was narrated from Jabir bin Abdullah (ra) that the Messenger of Allah (saws) came to Al-Marwah and climbed up until he (saws) could see the House, then he (saws) said: "La ilaha illallah, Wahdahu la sharika lah, lahul-mulku wa lahul-hamdu, yuhyi wa yumitu, wa huwaala kulli shayin qadir (There is none worthy of worship except Allah alone with no partner or associate, His is the dominion and to Him be praise, He gives life and death, and He has power over all things)." He (saws) said that three times, then he (saws) remembered Allah, and glorified and praised Him, then he (saws) supplicated there for as long as Allah willed. And he (saws) did that until he had finished Sai. [Sunan Ibn Majah]

Shaving head after Hajj and its virtue

Narrated Ibn Umar (ra): Allah's Messenger (saws) (got) his head shaved after performing his Hajj. [Bukhari]

Narrated Ibn Abbas (ra): When the Prophet (saws) came to Makkah, he ordered his Companions to perform Tawaf round the Kaba and between Safa and Marwa, to finish their Ihram and get their hair shaved off or cut short. [Bukhari]

Narrated Abdullah bin Umar (ra): Allah's Messenger (saws) said, "O Allah! Be merciful to those who have their head shaved." The people said, "O Allah's Messenger (saws)! And (invoke Allah for) those who get their hair cut short." The Prophet (saws) said, "O Allah! Be merciful to those who have their head shaved." The people said, "O Allah's Messenger (saws)! And those who get their hair cut short." The Prophet (saws) said (the third time), "And to those who get their hair cut short." Nafi said that the Prophet (saws) had said once or twice, "O Allah! Be merciful to those who get their head shaved," and on the fourth time he added, "And to those who have their hair cut short." [Bukhari]

Sacrificing of Animals

Narrated Ibn Juraij: Ata said, "I heard Jabir bin Abdullah (ra) saying: We never ate the meat of the Budn for more than three days of Mina. Later, the Prophet (saws) gave us permission by saying: "Eat and take (meat) with you. So we ate (some) and took (some) with us." I asked Ata, "Did Jabir (ra) say (that they went on eating the meat) till they reached Madina?" Ata replied, "No." [Bukhari]

One who shaved his head before or after slaughtering his sacrifice

It was narrated from Abdullah bin Amr (ra) that the Prophet (saws) was asked about a man who slaughtered his sacrifice before shaving his head, or who shaved his head before slaughtering his sacrifice, and he said: "There is no harm in that." [Sunan Ibn Majah]

Narrated Ibn Abbas (ra): The Prophet (saws) was asked about a person who had his head shaved before slaughtering (his Hadi) (or other similar ceremonies of Hajj). He (saws) replied, "There is no harm, there is no harm." [Bukhari]

One who performs tawaf before Rami at Jamarat

Narrated Ibn Abbas (ra): A man said to the Prophet (saws), "I performed the Tawaf-al-Ifada before the Rami (throwing pebbles at the Jamarat)." The Prophet (saws) replied, "There is no harm." The man said, "I had my head shaved before slaughtering." The Prophet (saws) replied, "There is no harm." He said, "I have slaughtered the Hadi before the Rami." The Prophet (saws) replied, "There is no harm." [Bukhari]

Narrated Ibn Abbas (ra): The Prophet (saws) was asked about the slaughtering, shaving (of the head), and the doing of Rami before or after the due times. He said, "There is no harm in that." [Bukhari]

Summary of Nahr day (3rd day)

- Perfrom Fajr prayer in Muzdalifah and proceed to Jamarat before sunrise.
- Continue Talbiya.
- Reaching Jamarat, throw seven stones one by one at Jamarat ul-Aqaba (serial number 3 from entry).
- Recite 'Allahu Akbar' for each stone. Stop Talbiya.
- Women, children and weak can throw stones on Aqaba during night before sunrise and come back to Muzdaifah.
- After stoning, dont stay there and proceed to Makkah.
- Perfrom tawaf seven times as described in Umrah section. Offer two rakats salat near Makam Ibrahim. Drink Zamzam. Proceed to Safa.
- On Safa, say *Allahu Akbar* three times. Recite three times *La ilaha illallah, Wahdahu la sharika lah, lahul-mulku wa lahul-hamdu, yuhyi wa yumitu, wa huwaala kulli shayin qadir*. Pray to the Almighty.
- Go to Marwah. Run in between green lights. On Marwah, recite three times *La ilaha illallah, Wahdahu la sharika lah, lahul-mulku wa lahul-hamdu, yuhyi wa yumitu, wa huwaala kulli shayin qadir*. Supplicate.
- Complete sai.
- Sacrifice the Animal
- Shave the head/cut hair short
- Put off Irham
- Back to Mina and spend the night there.
- Or else, after Jamarat, go to hotel or tent. Shave your head after sacrifice. Take bath, put off Irham cloth. Take rest in hotel/tent and have your food. Proceed for Tawaf and Sai with usual cloth (This can be done during night also). Come back to Mina tent. Don't stay in hotel during night.

- Or, from Muzdalifa go to tent. Take rest and then do other rituals as per your convenience.

11th and 12th Zul Hijjah in Mina

Stay overnight in Mina during the nights of the days of At-Tashreeq

Ibn Umar (ra) reported that al-Abbas b. Abd al-Muttalib (ra) sought permission from Allah's Messenger (saws) to spend in Makkah the nights (which he was required to spend) at Mina on account of his office of supplier of water, and he (the Holy Prophet saws) granted him permission. [Muslim]

To do the Rami of the Jimar on 11th and 12th of Zul-Hijjah

On the 11th and 12th of Zul-Hijja, throwing of stones should be done on all three Jamart one by one serially.

Hadith: Narrated Wabra: I asked Ibn Umar (ra), "When should I do the Rami of the Jimar?" He replied, "When your leader does that." I asked him again the same question. He replied, "We used to wait till the sun declined and then we would do the Rami (i.e. on the 11th and 12th of Zul-Hijja)." [Bukhari]

Hadith: Narrated Salim bin Abdullah: Abdullah bin Umar (ra) used to do Rami of the Jamrat ul-Sughra with seven small pebbles and used to recite Takbir on throwing each stone. He, then, would proceed further till he reached the level ground, where he would stay for a long time, facing the Qibla to invoke (Allah) while raising his hands. Then he would do Rami of the Jamrat-ul-Wusta similarly and would go to the left towards the level ground, where he would stand for a long time facing the Qibla to invoke (Allah) while raising his hands. Then he would do Rami of the Jamrat-ul-Aqaba from the middle of the valley, but he would not stay by it. Ibn Umar (ra) used to say, "I saw Allah's Messenger (saws) doing like that." [Bukhari]

Summary of activities on 11th Zul Hijjah

- Wait till sun passes the zenith.
- Proceed to Jamarat.

- Throw seven stones on al-Sughra one by one. Each time say Allahu Akbar.
- Throw seven stones on al-Wusta one by one. Each time say Allahu Akbar.
- Throw seven stones on al-Aqaba one by one. Each time say Allahu Akbar.
- Come back to the tent in Mina. Stay there overnight.

Summary of activities on 12th Zul Hijjah

- Wait till sun passes the zenith.
- Proceed to Jamarat.
- Throw seven stones on al-Sughra one by one. Each time say Allahu Akbar.
- Throw seven stones on al-Wusta one by one. Each time say Allahu Akbar.
- Throw seven stones on al-Aqaba one by one. Each time say Allahu Akbar.
- Proceed to Makkah.

Hajj of one person performed by another person

Hajj on behalf of a deceased person to perform Hajj

It was narrated from Ibn Abbas (ra) that a woman vowed to perform Hajj but she died. Her brother came to the Prophet (saws) and asked him about that, he (saws) said: "Do you think that if your sister owed a debt you would pay it off?" He said: "Yes." He (saws) said: "Then fulfil the right of Allah, for He is more deserving that His rights should be fulfilled." [Sunan Ibn Majah]

Ibn Abbas (ra) said: The wife of bin Salamah Al-Juhani ordered that the question be put to the Messenger of Allah (saws) about her mother who had died and had not performed Hajj; would it be good enough if she were to perform Hajj on behalf of her mother? He (saws) said: "Yes. If her mother owed a debt and she paid it off, would that not be good enough? Let her perform Hajj on behalf of her mother." [Sunan Ibn Majah]

It was narrated from Ibn Abbas (ra) that a woman asked the Prophet (saws) about her father who had died and he did not perform Hajj. He (saws) said: "Perform Hajj on behalf of your father." [Sunan Ibn Majah]

Hajj of a woman on behalf of a living man

It was narrated from Abdullah bin Abbas (ra): Al-Fadl bin Abbas (ra) was riding behind the Messenger of Allah (saws) when a woman from Khatham came and asked him a question. Al-Fadl started looking at her and she at him, and the Messenger of Allah (saws) turned Al-Fadls face to the other side. She said: "O Messenger of Allah (saws)! The command of Allah has come for His slaves to perform Hajj, but my father is an old man and cannot sit firmly in the saddle; should I perform Hajj on his behalf?" He (saws) said: "Yes." That happened during the Farwell Pilgrimage. [Sunan Ibn Majah]

The description of the Prophet's (saws) Hajj

Jafar bin Muhammad reported on the authority of his father: We entered upon Jabir bin Abd Allah (ra). When we reached him, he asked about the people (who had come to visit him). When my turn came I said, "I am Muhammad bin Ali bin Hussain. He patted my head with his hand and undid my upper then lower buttons. He then placed his hand between my nipples and in those days, I was a young boy." He then said, "Welcome to you my nephew, ask what you like." I questioned him he was blind. The time of prayer came and he stood wrapped in a mantle. Whenever he placed it on his shoulders its ends fell due to its shortness. He led us in prayer while his mantle was placed on a rack by his side. I said, "Tell me about the Hajj of the Apostle of Allah (saws)." He signed with his hand and folded his fingers indicating nine. He then said Apostle of Allah (saws) remained nine years (at Madinah) during which he did not perform Hajj, then made a public announcement in the tenth year to the effect that the Apostle of Allah (saws) was about to (go to) perform Hajj. A large number of people came to Madinah everyone desiring to follow him and act like him. The Apostle of Allah (saws) went out and we too went out with him till we reached Dhu Al Hulaifah. Asma daughter of Umais gave birth to Muhammad bin Abi Bakr (ra). She sent message to Apostle of Allah (saws) asking him, What should I do? He replied, "Take a bath, bandage your private parts with a cloth and put on ihram." The Apostle of Allah (saws) then prayed (in the masjid) and mounted Al Qaswa and his she Camel stood erect with him on its back. Jabir said, "I saw (a large number of) people on mounts and on foot in front of him and a similar number on his right side and a similar number on his left side and a similar number behind him. The Apostle of Allah (saws) was among us, the Quran was being revealed to him and he knew its interpretation. Whatever he did, we did it. The Apostle of Allah (saws) then raised his voice declaring Allah's unity and saying "Labbaik (I am at thy service), O Allah, labbaik, labbaik, Thou hast no partner praise and grace are Thine and the Dominion. Thou hast no partner. The people too raised their voices in talbiyah which they used to utter. But the Apostle of Allah (saws) did not forbid them anything. The Apostle of Allah (saws) continued his talbiyah. Jabir said "We did not express our intention of performing anything but Hajj, being unaware of Umrah (at that season), but when we came with him to the House (the Kaba), he touched the corner (and made seven circuits) walking quickly with pride in three of them and walking ordinarily in four. Then going forward to the station of Ibrahim he recited "And take the station of Ibrahim as a place of prayer." (While praying two rakahs) he kept the station between him and the House. The narrator said My father said that Ibn Nufail and Uthman said I do not know that he (Jabir) narrated it from anyone except the Prophet (saws). The narrator Sulaiman said I do not know but he (Jabir) said "The Apostle of Allah (saws) used to recite in the two rakahs "Say, He is Allah, one" and "Say O infidels". He then returned to the House (the Kaba) and touched the corner after which he went out by the gate to Al Safa. When he reached near Al Safa he recited "Al Safa and Al Marwah are among the indications of Allah" and he added "We begin with what Allah began with". He then began with Al Safa and mounting it till he could see the House (the Kaba) he declared the greatness of Allah and proclaimed his Unity. He then said "there is no god but Allah alone, Who alone has fulfilled His promise, helped His servant and routed the confederates. He then made supplication in the course of that saying such words three times. He then descended and walked towards Al Marwah and when his feet came down into the bottom of the valley, he ran, and when he began to ascend he walked till he reached Al Marwah. He did at al Marwah as he had done at Al Safa and when he came to Al Marwah for the last time, he said "If I had known before what I have come to know afterwards regarding this matter of mine, I would not have brought sacrificial animals but made it an Umrah, so if any of you has no sacrificial animals, he may take off ihram and treat it as an Umrah. All the people then took off ihram and clipped their hair except the Prophet (saws) and those who had brought sacrificial animals. Suraqah (bin Malik) bin Jusham then got up and asked Apostle of Allah (saws)does this apply to the present year or does it apply for ever? The Apostle of Allah (saws) interwined his fingers and said "The Umarh has been incorporated in Hajj. Adding No, but forever and ever. Ali came from Yemen with the sacrificial animals of the Apostle of Allah (saws) and found Fathima among one of those who had taken off their ihram. She said put on coloured clothes and stained her eyes with collyrium. Ali disliked (this action of her) and asked Who commanded you for this? She said "My father". Jabir said Ali said at Iraq I went to Apostle of Allah (saws) to complain against Fathima for what she had done and to ask the opinion of Apostle of Allah (saws) about which she mentioned to me. I informed him that I disliked her action and that thereupon she said to me "My father commanded me to do this." He said "She spoke the truth, she spoke the truth." What did you say when you put on ihram for Hajj? I said O Allah, I put on ihram for the same purpose for which Apostle of Allah (saws) has put it on. He said I have sacrificial animals with me, so do not take off ihram. He (Jabir) said "The total of those sacrificial animals brought by Ali from Yemen and of those brought by the Prophet (saws) from Madinah was one hundred." Then all the people except the Prophet (saws) and those who had with them the sacrificial animals took off ihram and clipped their hair. When the 8th of Zul Hijjah (Yaum Al Tarwiyah) came, they went towards Mina having pit on ihram for Hajj and the Apostle of Allah (saws) rode and prayed at Mina the noon, afternoon, sunset, night and dawn prayers. After that he waited a little till the sun rose and gave orders for a tent of hair to be set up at Namirah. The Apostle of Allah (saws) then sent out and the Quraish did not doubt that he would halt at Al Mash ar Al Haram at Al Muzdalifah, as the Quraish used to do in the pre- Islamic period but he passed on till he came to Arafah and found that the tent had been setup at Namirah. There he dismounted and when the sun had passed the meridian he ordered Al Qaswa to be brought and when it was saddled for him, he went down to the bottom of the valley and addressed the people saying "Your lives and your property must be respected by one another like the sacredness of this day of yours in the month of yours in this town of yours. Lo! Everything pertaining to the pre-Islamic period has been put under my feet and claims for blood vengeance belonging to the pre-Islamic period have been abolished. The first of those murdered among us whose blood vengeance I permit is the blood vengeance of ours (according to the version of the narrator Uthman, the blood vengeance of the son of Rabiah and according to the version of the narrator Sulaiman the blood vengeance of the son of Rabiah bin Al Harith bin Abd Al Muttalib). Some (scholars) said "he was suckled among Banu Sad (i.e., he was brought up among Bani Sad) and then killed by Hudhail. The usury of the pre-Islamic period is abolished and the first of usury I abolish is our usury, the usury of Abbas bin Abd Al Muttalib for it is all abolished. Fear Allah regarding women for you have got them under Allah's security and have the right to intercourse with them by Allah's word. It is a duty from you on them not to allow anyone whom you dislike to lie on your beds but if they do beat them, but not severely. You are responsible for providing them with food and clothing in a fitting manner. I have left among you something by which if you hold to it you will never again go astray, that is Allah's Book. You will be asked about me, so what will you say? They replied "We testify that you have conveyed and fulfilled the message and given counsel. Then raising his forefinger towards the sky and pointing it at the people, he said "O Allah! Be witness, O Allah! Be witness, O Allah! Be witness! Bilal then uttered the call to prayer and the iqamah and he prayed the noon prayer, he then uttered the iqamah and he prayed the afternoon prayer, engaging in no prayer between the two. He then mounted (his she Camel) al Qaswa and came to the place of standing, making his she Camel Al Qaswa turn its back to the rocks and having the path taken by those who went on foot in front of him and he faced the Qiblah. He remained standing till sunset when the yellow light had somewhat gone and the disc of the sun had disappeared. He took Usamah up behind him and picked the reins of Al Qaswa severely so much so that its head was touching the front part of the saddle. Pointing with is right hand he was saying "Calmness, O People! Calmness, O people. Whenever he came over a mound (of sand) he let loose its reins a little so that it could ascend. He then came to Al Muzdalifah where he combined the sunset and night prayers, with one adhan and two iqamahs. The narrator Uthamn said: He did not offer supererogatory prayers between them. The narrators are then agreed upon the version: He then lay down till dawn and prayed the dawn prayer when the morning light was clear. The narrator Sulaiman said with one adhan and one iqamah. The narrators are then agreed upon the version. He then mounted Al Qaswa and came to Al Mashar Al Haram and ascended it. The narrators Uthaman and Sulaiman said: He faced the qiblah praised Allah, declared His greatness, His uniqueness. Uthamn added in his version and His Unity and kept standing till the day was very clear. The Apostle of Allah (saws) then went quickly before the sun rose, taking Al Fadl bin Abbas behind him. He was a man having beautiful hair, white and handsome colour. When the Apostle of Allah (saws) went quickly, the women in the howdas also began to pass him quickly. Al Fadl began to look at them. The Apostle of Allah (saws) placed his hand on the face of Al Fadl, but Al fadl turned his face towards the other side. The Apostle of Allah (saws) also turned away his hand to the other side. Al Fadl also turned his face to the other side looking at them till he came to (the Valley of) Muhassir. He urged the Camel a little and following a middle road which comes out at the greatest jamrah, he came to the jamrah which is beside the tree and he threw seven small pebbles at this (jamrah) saying "Allah is most great" each time he threw a pebble like bean seeds. He threw them from the bottom of the valley. The Apostle of Allah (saws) then went to the place of the sacrifice and sacrificed sixty-three Camels with his own hand. He then commanded Ali who sacrificed the remainder and he shared him and his sacrificial animals. After that he ordered that a piece of flesh from each Camel should be put in a pot and when it was cooked the two of them ate some of it and drank some of its broth. The narrator Sulaiman said that he mounted afterwards the Apostle of Allah (saws) went quickly to the House (the Kaba) and prayed the noon prayer at Makkah. He came to Banu Abd Al Muttalib who were supplying water at Zamzam and said: Draw water, Banu Abd Al Muttalib. Were it not that people would take from you the right to draw water, I would draw it along with you. So they handed him a bucket and he drank from it. [Sunan Ibn Majah, Abu Dawud]

The farewell tawaf

Narrated Ibn Abbas (ra): The people were ordered to perform the Tawaf of the Kaba (Tawaf-al-Wada) as the last thing, before leaving (Makkah), except the menstruating women who were excused. [Bukhari]

It was narrated that Ibn Abbas (ra) said: "The people were going in all directions, and the Messenger of Allah (saws) said: No one should depart until the last thing he does is (Tawaf around) the House." [Sunan Ibn Majah, Abu Dawud]

It was narrated that Aishah (ra) said: The Messenger of Allah (saws) mentioned Safiyyah (ra) and we said: She has got her menses. He (saws) said: Aqra Halqa! I think that she has detained us. I said: O Messenger of Allah (saws), she performed Tawaful-Ifadah on the Day of Sacrifice. He said: No then, tell her to depart. [Sunan Ibn Majah]

Madinah Munwara

Madinah was known as Yathrib before Islam. It existed for over 1,500 years before the Holy Prophet (saws) migrated from Makkah. The year of this migration (Hijrah), marks the start of the Hijri Islamic calendar.

Haram (sanctuary) of Al-Madinah

Narrated Anas (ra): The Prophet (saws) said, "Madinah is a sanctuary from that place to that. Its trees should not be cut and no heresy should be innovated nor any sin should be committed in it, and whoever innovates in it a heresy or commits sins (bad deeds), then he will incur the curse of Allah, the angels, and all the people." [Bukhari]

Abdullah b. Zaid b. Asim (ra) reported Allah's Messenger (saws) as saying: Verily Ibrahim (as) declared Makkah sacred and supplicated (for blessings to be showered) upon its inhabitants, and I declare Madinah to be sacred as Ibrahim (as) had declared Makkah to be sacred. I have supplicated (Allah for His blessings to be showered) in its sa and its mudd (two standards of weight and measurement) twice as did Ibrahim (as) for the inhabitants of Makkah. [Muslim]

Superiority of Al-Madinah. It expels (evil) persons

Narrated Abu Huraira (ra): Allah's Messenger (saws) said, "I was ordered to migrate to a town which will swallow (conquer) other towns and is called Yathrib and that is Madina, and it turns out (bad) persons as a furnace removes the impurities of iron." [Bukhari]

The one who avoids living in Al-Madinah

Narrated Ibn Umar (ra) that a freed a slave girl of his came to him, and said: "Times have become hard on me and I want to go to Al-Iraq." He said: "Why not to Ash-Sham the land of the resurrection? Have patience you foolish lady; I heard the Messenger of Allah (saws) say: Whoever endures its hardships and difficulties (Al-Madinah) then I will be a witness, or an intercessor for him on the Day of Judgement." [He said:] There are narrations on this topic from Abu Saeed, Sufyan bin Abi Zuhair, and Subaiah Al-Aslamiyyah. [Tirmizi]

Iman (Belief) returns and goes back to Al-Madina

Narrated Abu Huraira (ra): Allah's Messenger (saws) said, "Verily, Belief returns and goes back to Madina as a snake returns and goes back to its hole (when in danger)." [Bukhari]

Sin of that person who harms the people of Al-Madina

Narrated Sad (ra): I heard the Prophet (saws) saying, "None plots against the people of Madina but that he will be dissolved (destroyed) like the salt is dissolved in water." [Bukhari]

Ad-Dajjal will not be able to enter Al-Madina

Narrated Anas bin Malik (ra): The Prophet (saws) said, "There will be no town which Ad-Dajjal will not enter except Makkah and Madina, and there will be no entrance (road) (of both Makkah and Madina) but the angels will be standing in rows guarding it against him, and then Madina will shake with its inhabitants thrice (i.e. three earthquakes will take place) and Allah will expel all the non-believers and the hypocrites from it." [Bukhari]

Narrated Abu Said Al-Khudri (ra): Allah's Messenger (saws) told us a long narrative about Ad-Dajjal, and among the many things he mentioned, was his saying, "Ad-Dajjal will come and it will be forbidden for him to pass through the entrances of Madina. He will land in some of the salty barren areas (outside) Madina; on that day the best man or one of the best men will come up to him and say, I testify that you are the same Dajjal whose description was given to us by Allah's Messenger (saws). Ad-Dajjal will say to the people, If I kill this man and bring him back to life again, will you doubt my claim? They will say, No. Then Ad-Dajjal will kill that man and bring him back to life. That man will say, Now I know your reality better than before. Ad-Dajjal will say, I want to kill him but I cannot. [Bukhari]

Love for Madina

Narrated Anas (ra): Whenever the Prophet (saws) returned from a journey and observed the walls of Madina, he would make his Mount go fast, and if he was on an animal (i.e. a horse), he would make it gallop because of his love for Madina. [Bukhari]

Narrated Zaid bin Aslam from his father: Umar (ra) said, "O Allah! Grant me martyrdom in Your cause, and let my death be in the city of Your Apostle (saws)." [Bukhari]

People will abandon Al-Madinah

Salid b. Musayyib heard Abu Huraira (ra) say that Allah's Messenger (saws) said about Madina: "Its inhabitants will abandon it, whereas it is good for them and it will become the haunt of beasts and birds." (Imam Muslim said that Abu Safwan, one of the narrators whose name was Abdullah b. Abd al-Malik, was an orphan and Ibn Juraij took him under his care for ten years.) [Muslim]

Abu Huraira (ra) heard Allah's Messenger (saws) say: "They (the residents of Madina) will abandon Madina whereas it is good for them and it will be haunted by beasts and birds, and two shepherds will come out from Muzainah intending (to go) towards Madina and tending their herd, and will find nothing but wilderness there until when they will reach the mountain path of Wada, they will fall down on their faces. [Muslim]

Masajid in Madinah

During the Hijrat of the Prophet (saws), when he (saws) was approaching towards Madina, people tried to get hold of the camel Al-Qaswa. The Prophet (saws) said, "Let her go her way, for she is under the command of Allah SWT." Al-Qaswa kept walking until it stopped and knelt down in a large courtyard owned by two orphans, Suhayl (ra) and Sahil (ra). When the two boys learned that Prophet Muhammad (saws) wanted to build a mosque on their land, they offered the land as a gift without a second thought. Prophet (saws) disentombed the graves, cleared the bushes, and started constructing Masjid al-Nabawi.

Hadith: Anas bin Malik (ra) narrates, "The location where the Prophets Mosque (saws) was built belonged to Banu Najjar. In it, there were date-palm trees and graves of the idolaters. The Prophet (saws) said to them: Name its price. They said: We will never take any money for it. The Prophet built (saws) it, and they were assisting him, and the Prophet (saws) was saying: The real life is the life of the Hereafter, so forgive the Ansar and the Muhajirah. Before the mosque was built, the Prophet (saws) would perform prayer wherever he was when the time for prayer came." [Sunan Ibn Majah]

Photo: The Prophet's (saws) Minbar and Holy Grave (the biggest hole)

Originally Masjid Nabawi was an open-air building. After an expansion during the reign of several rulers, Masjid Nabawi includes the final resting place of the Prophet Muhammad (saws) and Abu Bakr (ra) and

Umar (ra). The most notable feature of the Masjid is the green dome, originally Aishas (ra) House where the tomb of Muhammad (saws) is located. Visitors can have a look of the Prophets (saws) Minbar.

The construction of the Masjid of the Prophet (saws)

Anas b. Malik (ra) reported: The Messenger of Allah (saws) came to Madina and stayed in the upper part of Madina for fourteen nights with a tribe called Banu Amr b Auf. He then sent for the chiefs of Banu al-Najir, and they came with swords around their necks. He (the narrator) said: I perceive as if I am seeing the Messenger of Allah (saws) on his ride with Abu Bakr (ra) behind him and the chiefs of Banu al-Najjar around him till he alighted in the courtyard of Abu Ayyub. He (the narrator) said: The Messenger of Allah (saws) said prayer when the time came for prayer, and he prayed in the fold of goats and sheep. He (saws) then ordered mosque to be built and sent for the chiefs of Banu al-Najjar, and they came (to him). He (saws) said to them: O Banu al-Najjar, sell these lands of yours to me. They said: No, by Allah. We would not demand their price, but (reward) from the Lord. Anas (ra) said: There (in these lands) were trees and graves of the polytheists, and ruins. The Messenger of Allah (saws) ordered that the trees should be cut, and the graves should be dug out, and the ruins should be levelled. The trees (were thus) placed in rows towards the qibla and the stones were set on both sides of the door, and (while building the mosque) they (the Companions) sang verses along with the Messenger of Allah (saws): O Allah: there is no good but the good of the next world, so help the Ansar and the Muhajirin. [Muslim]

The superiority of offering Salat in Makkah and Al-Madina

Narrated Abu Huraira (ra): The Prophet (saws) said, "Do not set out on a journey except for three Mosques i.e. Al-Masjid-Al-Haram, the Mosque of Allah's Messenger (saws), and the Mosque of Al-Aqsa, (Mosque of Jerusalem)." [Bukhari]

Narrated Qazaa Maula: (freed slave of) Ziyad: I heard Abu Said Al-Khudri (ra) narrating four things from the Prophet (saws) and I appreciated them very much. He said, conveying the words of the Prophet (saws):

1. "A woman should not go on a two-day journey except with her husband or a Dhi-Mahram.
2. No fasting is permissible on two days: Id-ul-Fitr and Id-ul-Adha.
3. No prayer after two prayers, i.e. after the Fajr prayer till the sunrises and after the Asr prayer till the sun sets.
4. Do not prepare yourself for a journey except to three Mosques, i.e. Al-Masjid-Al-Haram, the Mosque of Aqsa (Jerusalem) and my Mosque." [Bukhari]

Riyadil Jannah

Narrated Abdullah bin Zaid Al-Mazini (ra): Allah's Messenger (saws) said, "Between my house and the pulpit there is a garden of the gardens of Paradise (riyadil Jannah)." [Muslim, Bukhari]

Narrated Abu Huraira (ra): The Prophet (saws) said, "Between my house and my pulpit there is a garden of the gardens of Paradise, and my pulpit is on my fountain tank (i.e. Al-Kauthar)." [Muslim, Bukhari]

The Prophet's (saws) Masjid and Masjid Al-Haram

Abu Hurairah (ra) narrated that: Allah's Messenger (saws) said: "Salat in this Masjid of mine is better than a thousand Salat in another, except for Masjid Al-Haram." [Tirmizi]

Abu Zarr (ra) reported: I said: Messenger of Allah (saws), which mosque was set up first on the earth? He (saws) said: Al-Masjid al-Haram (the sacred). I (again) said: Then which next? He (saws) said: It was the Masjid Aqsa. I (again) said: How long the space of time (between their setting up)? He (the Holy Prophet saws) said: It was forty years. And whenever the time comes for prayer, pray there, for that is a mosque; and in the hadith transmitted by Abu Kamil (the words are): "Whenever time comes for prayer, pray, for that is a mosque (for you)." [Muslim]

Regarding the Grave of the Holy Prophet (saws)

Ata b. Yasar (ra) reported Allah's Messenger (saws) as saying, "O God, do not let my grave become an idol which is worshipped. Gods anger is severe against people who take the graves of their prophets as mosques." [Mishkat]

Ibn Juraij said: My father told me that the Companions of the Prophet (saws) did not know where to bury the Prophet (saws) until Abu Bakr (ra) said: I heard the Messenger of Allah (saws) say: "A Prophet is not to be buried except where he died." So, they removed his bed and dug a grave for him beneath. [Musnad Ahmad]

Narrated Urwa (ra): When the wall fell on them (i.e. graves) during the caliphate of Al-Walid bin Abdul Malik, the people started repairing it, and a foot appeared to them. The people got scared and thought that it was the foot of the Prophet (saws). No one could be found who could tell them about it till I (Urwa) said to them, "By Allah, this is not the foot of the Prophet (saws) but it is the foot of Umar." [Bukhari]

Aisha (ra) narrated that she made a will to Abdullah bin Zubair, "Do not bury me with them (the Prophet (saws) and his two companions) but bury me with my companions (wives of the Prophet saws) in Al-Baqi as I would not like to be looked upon as better than I really am (by being buried near the Prophet saws)." [Bukhari]

Narrated Amr bin Maimun Al-Audi: I saw Umar bin Al-Khattab (ra) (when he was stabbed) saying, "O Abdullah bin Umar (his son)! Go to the mother of the believers Aisha and say, Umar bin Al-Khattab sends his greetings to you, and request her to allow me to be buried with my companions." (So, Ibn Umar conveyed the message to Aisha.) She said, "I had the idea of having this place for myself but today I prefer him (Umar) to myself (and allow him to be buried there)." When Abdullah bin Umar returned, Umar asked him, "What (news) do you have?" He replied, "O chief of the believers! She has allowed you (to be buried there)." On that Umar said, "Nothing was more important to me than to be buried in that (sacred) place. So, when I expire, carry me there and pay my greetings to her (Aisha ra) and say, Umar bin Al-Khattab asks permission; and if she gives permission, then bury me (there) and if she does not, then take me to the graveyard of the Muslims. I do not think any person has more right for the caliphate than those with whom Allah's Messenger (saws) was always pleased till his death. And whoever is chosen by the people after me will be the caliph, and you people must listen to him and obey him," and then he mentioned the name of Uthman, Ali, Talha, Az-Zubair, Abdur-Rahman bin Auf and Sad bin Abi Waqqas. By this time a young man from Ansar came and said, "O chief of the believers! Be happy with Allah's glad tidings. The grade which you have in Islam is known to you, then you became the caliph and you ruled with justice and then you have been awarded martyrdom after all this." Umar replied, "O son of my brother! Would that all that privileges will counterbalance (my short comings), so that I neither lose nor gain anything. I recommend my successor to be good to the early emigrants and realize their rights and to protect their honour and sacred things. And I also recommend him to be good to the Ansar who before them, had homes (in Madina) and had adopted the Faith. He should accept the good of the righteous among them and should excuse their wrongdoers. I recommend him to abide by the rules and regulations concerning the Dhimmis (protectees) of Allah and His Apostle (saws), to fulfil their contracts completely and fight for them and not to tax (overburden) them beyond their capabilities." [Bukhari]

Sending blessings on the Prophet saws (Salawat, صلوات)

Salawat means to praise and honour the holy prophet Mohammad (saws) with great love and compassion. Literal meaning of Salawat is Prayers, and *Salah* is a singular form of *Salawat*.

Salah that is recited in prayer is considered the most authentic and prominent. It is the best form of salutation that was taught by the Prophet Muhammad (saws) in his Hadith Sahih al-Bukhari. Reciting salah is one of the greatest acts of worship in Islam. It is the best way to express our love towards our beloved Prophet Muhammad (saws). The significance of salawat is greatly highlighted in Hadiths.

Hadith: Anas (ra) narrated: The Prophet (saws) said "None of you will have faith till he loves me more than his father, his children, and all mankind." [Bukhari]

Hadith: The Prophet (saws) said: "Before whomsoever my mention is made, he should recite salat upon me." [Sunan an-Nasai]

Hadith: Narrated Abu Hurayrah (ra): The Prophet (saws) said: If any one of you greets me, Allah returns my soul to me and I respond to the greeting. [Abu Dawud, Musnad Ahmad]

Hadith: Narrated Abu Hurayrah (ra): The Prophet (saws) said: Do not make your houses graves, and do not make my grave a place of festivity. But invoke blessings on me, for your blessings reach me wherever you may be. [Abu Dawud]

Hadith: Abu Hurairah (ra) reported that the Messenger (saws) of Allah said: "May his nose soil with dust in whose presence mention is made of me and he does not supplicate for me." [Tirmizi]

Hadith: Prophet (saws) said: "On the Day of Judgment the person closest to me will be the one who has sent the most Durood into me." [Tirmizi]

Hadith: The Messenger of Allah (saws) said, "A visitor came to me from my Lord Almighty and he said: Whoever among your nation blesses you, Allah will record for him ten good deeds, He will erase ten bad deeds, He will raise him ten degrees, and the angel will respond with the same." [Musnad Aḥmad, Sunan an-Nasai]

Hadith: The Prophet (saws) said: Allah Almighty has appointed a group of angels who travel the world, and in my Ummah, whoever sends salutations to me, those salutations are presented to me by these angels." [Ibn Hibban]

Hadith: The Prophet (saws) said: When any one of you prays, let him begin by praising Allah, then let him send blessings upon the Prophet (saws), then let him ask for whatever he wants. [Tirmizi]

Hadith: Fadalah bin Ubayd (ra) reported: Allah's Messenger (saws) was sitting amongst us, there entered a person and he prayed as saying, "O Allah! Forgive me, have mercy upon me." Thereupon Allah's Messenger (saws) said, "O worshipper! You have made haste in praying. When you pray and sit (at the end) laud Allah of what He is worthy of and send blessings upon me and then supplicate Him." The narrator said: Then another man prayed after him and he lauded Allah and invoked blessings of Allah upon the Prophet (saws), and the Prophet (saws) said to him, "O worshipper! Make a supplication and it would be responded." [Tirmizi]

Hadith: Once Umar bin Khattab (ra) said to his nation: The supplication is stopped between the heaven and the earth and nothing of it ascends, till you invoke blessings on your Prophet (saws). [Tirmizi]

Hadith: It was narrated that Ubayy ibn Kab (ra) said: I said: O Messenger of Allah (saws), I send a great deal of blessings upon you, how much of my supplication should be sending Durood upon you? He (saws) said: "Whatever you wish." I said: One quarter? He said (saws): "Whatever you wish, and if you do more, that will be better for you." I said: One half? He (saws) said: "Whatever you wish and if you do more, that will be better for you." I said: Two thirds? He said (saws): "Whatever you wish and if you do more, that will be better for you." I said: I will make the entire of my supplication for you. He (saws) said: "Then your concerns will be taken care of and your sins will be forgiven." [Tirmizi]

Hadith: Kab Ibn Urjah (ra) relates that the Prophet (saws) said: Come near the minbar and we came near the minbar. When he (saws) reached the first step, he (saws) said, "Amen". When he (saws) ascended to the second step, he (saws) said, "Amen," and when he (saws) stepped onto the third step, he (saws) said, "Amen." They said, "Messenger of Allah (saws), we heard you say Amen three times." He (saws) said: When I went up the first step, Jibril, may Allah bless him and grant him peace, came to me and said: Wretched is the slave to whom Ramadan comes and when it passes from him is not forgiven. I said, Amen. Then he said: Wretched is the slave who has one or both of his parents alive and they do not let him enter the Garden. I said, Amen. Then he said: Wretched is a slave who does not bless you when you are mentioned in his presence, and I said: Amen." [Mustadrak Al-Hakim, Bayhaqi]

Hadith: Messenger of Allah (saws) said: "Of your best days is Friday. On it, Adam was created; and on it his (soul) was taken; and on it is the blowing (of the Trumpet); and on it is the Collapse. Therefore, increase in sending your Salat upon me, for your salat upon me are presented to me." They said: "O Messenger of Allah (saws)! And how will our Salat upon you be presented to you after you have perished?" He (saws) replied: "Indeed, Allah, the Mighty and Sublime, has prohibited the earth from (destroying) the bodies of the Prophets." [Abu Dawud, Ibn Hibban, Mustadrak Al-Hakim]

Hadith: Aws ibn Aws (ra) reported: The Messenger of Allah (saws) said, "Verily, the best of your days is Friday. Adam was created on it, on it he died, on it the trumpet will be blown, and on it the shout will be made. Thus, send blessings upon me often, for your blessings are presented to me." [Abu Dawud]

Masjid Quba

The Quba Masjid plays an important role in Islamic history and the Holy Quran mentions about it that the mosque was built on piety. It was the place where the Prophet (saws) and his companion Abu Bakr (ra) first stayed after migrating from Makkah to Madinah. It is believed that the first stone of the mosque was laid by the Prophet Muhammad (saws) himself when he came to Madinah.

Hadith: Abu Al-Abrad the freed slave of Banu Khatmah narrated that he heard Usaid bin Zuhair Al-Ansari (ra) and he was one of the Companions of the Prophet (saws) narrated that the Prophet (saws) said: "The Salat in Masjid Quba is like Umrah." [Tirmizi]

Hadith: Abdullah b. Umar (ra) reported that Allah's Messenger (saws) used to come to Quba, i. e. (he came) on every Saturday, and he used to come riding or on foot. Ibn Dinar (another narrator) said that Ibn Umar (ra) used to do like this. [Muslim]

Hadith: Ibn Umar (ra) reported that Allah's Messenger (saws) came to the mosque at Quba riding and on foot, and he observed two rakahs of (Nafl prayer) in it. [Muslim]

Masjid Qiblatain

Masjid Qiblatain is known as masjid of two Qiblas. Allah's Messenger (saws) received the Quranic revelation here to change the Qibla from Bait Al-Maqdis in Jerusalem (that lasted for 16 months) to the Holy Kabah in Makkah. Masjid al-Qiblatain is significant to Muslims as first congregational salat facing the Kabah was offered. The relevant Quranic verse is as follows (interpretation of meaning):

Verily, We have seen the turning of your (Muhammeds) face towards the Heaven. Surely, We shall turn you to a Qibla (prayer direction) that shall please you, so turn your face in the direction of Al-Masjid Al-Haram (at Makkah). And wherever you people are, turn your faces (in prayer) in that direction." [Ch 2:144]

After this revelation from the Almighty, Prophet Muhammad (saws) changed direction and faced the Kaba in the middle of the prayer, and so did the companions in congregation.

The Mount Uhud

The Mount Uhud is located on the North of Madinah. It is 7.5 Km long and about 1 Km high. It is the place where second most important battle between Muslim and non-believers of Makkah was fought. The Muslims lost the battle and the holy teeth of the Prophet (saws) were martyred. Mount Uhud contains the graves of 70 companions who were martyred including Hamza (ra).

The Archers Hill is a small mountain in front of Mount Uhud. The hill is also known as Jabal al-Rumah and Jabal Ainain. In the battle of Uhud, 50 archers that were posted on the Archers Hill. During the battle, the archers left their post thinking the battle was over and went to collect the spoils of war. At the same time, the Makkan army, led by Khalid ibn al-Walid, attacked the Muslims, which resulted in a great loss of life and injuries to the Prophet (saws).

Cave of Uhud is the place where Prophet (saws) and his companions took shelter when the lost the battle. Narrated Anas (ra): that the Messenger of Allah (saws), Abu Bakr, Umar, and Uthman climbed Uhud (mountain) and it shook them, so the Prophet of Allah (saws) said: "Be firm O Uhud! For there is none upon you except a Prophet, a Siddiq, and two martyrs." [Tirmizi]

Hadith: Abu Humaid (ra) reported: We went out along with Allah's Messenger (saws) in the expedition of Tabuk, and Abu Humaid further related: We proceeded until we reached the valley of Qura; and Allah's Messenger (saws) said: I am going forth, so he among you who wants to move fast with me may do so; and he who likes to go slowly may do so. We proceeded until Madina was within our sight, and he said: This is Tabah (another name of Madina); this is Uhud, the mountain which loves us and we love it. [Muslim]

Hadith: Narrated Jabir bin Abdullah (ra): Allah's Messenger (saws) shrouded every two martyrs of Uhud in one piece of cloth and then he would ask, "Which of them knew more Quran?" When one of them was pointed out he would put him first in the grave. He said, "I am a witness on these." Then he ordered them to be buried with blood on their bodies. Neither did he offer their funeral prayer nor did he get them washed. (Jabir bin Abdullah added): Allah's Messenger (saws) used to ask about the martyrs of Uhud as to which of them knew more of the Quran." And when one of them was pointed out as having more of it he would put him first in the grave and then his companions. (Jabir added): My father and my uncle were shrouded in one sheet. [Bukhari]

Hadith: Narrated Uqba bin Amir (ra): Allah's Messenger (saws) offered the funeral prayers of the martyrs of Uhud eight years after (their death), as if bidding farewell to the living and the dead, then he ascended the pulpit and said, "I am your predecessor before you, and I am a witness on you, and your promised place to meet me will be Al- Haud (i.e. the Tank) (on the Day of Resurrection), and I am (now) looking at it from this place of mine. I am not afraid that you will worship others besides Allah, but I am afraid that worldly life will tempt you and cause you to compete with each other for it." That was the last look which I cast on Allah's Messenger (saws). [Bukhari]

Jannatul Baqi

Jannatul Baqi, also known as Baqi al-Gharqad is the main graveyard in Madinah, located to the southeast of the Prophet's (saws) Masjid. It contains the graves of many members of the Prophet's (saws) family, companions of the Prophet (saws), Tabiin, scholars and righteous people.

Hadith: Abdullah ibn Umar (ra) narrates that the Prophet (saws) said: Whoever is able to die in Madinah should do so, for surely, I will intercede for the one who dies in Madinah. [Sunan Ibn Majah, Tirmizi]

Hadith: Muhammad b. Qais said (to the people): Should I not narrate to you (a Hadith of the Holy Prophet saws) on my authority and on the authority of my mother? We thought that he meant the mother who had given him birth. He (Muhammad b. Qais) then reported that it was Aisha (ra) who had narrated this: Should I not narrate to you about myself and about the Messenger of Allah (may peace be upon him)? We said: Yes. She said: When it was my turn for Allah's Messenger (may peace be upon him) to spend the night with me, he turned his side, put on his mantle and took off his shoes and placed them near his feet, and spread the corner of his shawl on his bed and then lay down till he thought that I had gone to sleep. He took hold of his mantle slowly and put on the shoes slowly, and opened the door and went out and then closed it lightly. I covered my head, put on my veil and tightened my waist wrapper, and then went out following his steps till he reached Baqi. He stood there and he stood for a long time. He then lifted his hands three times, and then returned and I also returned. He hastened his steps and I also hastened my steps. He ran and I too ran. He came (to the house) and I also came (to the house). I, however, preceded him and I entered (the house), and as I lay down in the bed, he (the Holy Prophet saws) entered the (house), and said: Why is it, O Aisha, that you are out of breath? I said: There is nothing. He said: Tell me or the Subtle and the Aware would inform me. I said: Messenger of Allah (saws), may my father and mother be ransom for you, and then I told him (the whole story). He said: Was it the darkness (of your shadow) that I saw in front of me? I said: Yes. He struck me on the chest which caused me pain, and then said: Did you think that Allah and His Apostle (saws) would deal unjustly with you? She said: Whatsoever the people conceal, Allah will know it. He said: Jibril came to me when you saw me. He called me and he concealed it from you. I responded to his call, but I too concealed it from you (for he did not come to you), as you were not fully dressed. I thought that you had gone to sleep, and I did not like to awaken you, fearing that you may be frightened. He (Jibril) said: Your Lord has commanded you to go to the inhabitants of Baqi (to those lying in the graves) and beg pardon for them. I said: Messenger of Allah (saws), how should I pray for them (How should I beg forgiveness for them)? He said: Say, Peace be upon the inhabitants of this city (graveyard) from among the Believers and the Muslims, and may Allah have mercy on those who have gone ahead of us, and those who come later on, and we shall, God willing, join you. [Muslim]